MY1 ? ?9

COLORADO MOUNTAIN COLLEGE   SP
BD166.   Frank. S. L.

W9-DFI-139
1 03 0000150411

DISCARDED

BD   Frank
166   Real and
F

Reality and Man

REALITY AND MAN

An Essay in the Metaphysics of Human Nature

by
S. L. FRANK

translated from the Russian
by
NATALIE DUDDINGTON

with a Foreword
by
Georges Florovsky
Professor Emeritus,
Harvard University

TAPLINGER PUBLISHING COMPANY
New York

First Published in the United States, 1966
TAPLINGER PUBLISHING CO., INC.
29 East Tenth Street
New York, New York 10003

Copyright © 1965 by Tatiana Frank

All rights reserved. No portion of this book may
be reproduced in any form without the written per-
mission of the publisher, except by a reviewer who
may wish to quote brief passages in connection with
a review for a newspaper or magazine.

Library of Congress Catalogue Card Number:
66-12950

PRINTED IN THE UNITED STATES

Contents

*

v

CONTENTS

Foreword

Philosophers do not normally expect to be followed by sheer obedience. Nor do they seek a blind adherence to their systems. Since times of Socrates the craft of philosophers has been commonly conceived as *maieutics,* a kind of intellectual and spiritual midwifery. The philosopher's aim is actually to awaken the others, to alert them to problems, and then to assist them, by guidance and advice, in their own search for solutions. In brief, philosophy is an invitation to pilgrimage. Philosophical arguments and conceptions must be pondered and critically assessed. Criticism means discernment. The original meaning of the word *crisis* in Greek was precisely that: discernment, discrimination, judgment, decision. And every one has to decide for himself, to make his own decision. The study of philosophical ideas is engagement, an intimate participation in the philosopher's quest. And only this manner of study can be profitable and instructive. Philosophical convictions cannot be simply imposed. Moreover, agreement is not the only way in which one may express his appreciation or respect for the philosopher's work. Disagreement is also not seldom a respectful tribute.

Simon Frank was an expert master of this philosophical maieutics, an excellent guide and companion in philosophical search. He was himself, by nature and by temperament, a seeker. All his writings are, in a certain sense, personal documents, a diary of his own philosophical life. There is a strong element of personal witness in his meditations—"meditation" is his own favorite word. The moving force of his own search was his ardent "thirst for reality." It was much more than just an intellectual adventure. Frank was desperately concerned with the problem of human existence, with the dignity and predicament of Man. The ultimate goal of his philosophical inquiry may be properly described as Justification of Man. The problem he wanted to solve was an existential problem. In his later years Frank professed to be a religious philosopher. Indeed, for him this expression was rather a pleonasm. He never regarded "faith" and "reason," religion and philosophy, as separate and mutually independent spheres. He never indulged in conventional apologetics which is concerned with "reconciliation." On the contrary, he considered religion and philosophy as aspects and components, and also as stages, of the same indivisible spiritual endeavour. The metaphysical analysis leads to the discovery of the ultimate Ground of all being and existence, "the Unfathomable," to use his own term. But only faith is able to discern the true character of this Divine Ground. The philosophical search itself culminates in the Encounter, the personal encounter with the Living God. Only in this encounter is philosophical quest completed and vindicated. Thus, "faith" and "reason" ultimately converge upon each other. The "unbelieving" philosophy is for Frank at least an incomplete and narrow philosophy. It misses the true dimension of Reality. It remains, as it were, always on the surface. It does not dig deeply enough to reach the *last* foundations or the *first* principles. It cannot cope adequately with the problem of Man, in its very depth and in its drastic complexity. It reduces Man's existence to what is not essential for him. To realize, or even to preserve, his essential "humanity," Man has to detect the deeper dimension of his existence, to rediscover, as it were, his ultimate root in eternity,—that is, to find himself in the presence of God. Except in communion with the Living God, Man cannot be truly and fully human, cannot be himself. This conviction was the very heart of Frank's philosophy. Man and God are intrinsically correlated. Man is rooted in the Divine abyss of the Being. On the other hand, any philosophy which disregards or ignores the mystery of the Divine is bound also "to dehumanize" Man. In the last resort, it is inevitably a philosophy of death and despair. The truth of this grave indictment can

FOREWORD

be convincingly illustrated by the conclusions and contentions of the contemporary atheistic Existentialism. At this
point Frank had an important message to deliver, in the
present situation of confusion, vacillation, and trouble. It
was a timely message, at once a warning and a call, and also
an encouragement.

Frank himself was a committed Christian. He joined the
Church in his mature age. He came to the Christian truth by
the way of intensive philosophical meditation which led him
finally to the encounter with the Gospel. His major guides on
the road were Plotinus and Nicolas of Cusa, especially the
latter—"my only philosophical teacher," he used to say. Frank
regarded himself as a Platonist, a "Christian Platonist" indeed,
standing in a long and venerable tradition. Platonism was for
him a kind of *philosophia perennis,* a normative model, and
also a method, of philosophical thinking. Creative originality
of Frank cannot be contested or minimized. And yet, in fact,
his philosophy was but a new variation on the old "Platonic"
theme. Now, it has been so often contended that Platonism
and Christianity were actually incompatible and mutually exclusive. Accordingly, in this case "Christian Platonism" should
be regarded as an illegitimate blend. The charge is quite
serious and in no case can be simply ignored. But the ultimate
problem is much larger. Is "Christian Philosophy" possible at
all, or is it also an illegitimate and contradictory task or
project? Was Frank's religious philosophy a "Christian philosophy," that is, a *distinctively* "Christian" philosophy? The
question is pertinent and legitimate, since Frank himself emphatically insisted on the ultimate convergence of faith and
metaphysics. As a matter of fact, the problem of "Christian
Philosophy" is one of the burning issues of the contemporary
philosophical thought. It is only in the perspective of the on-
going discussion of this basic problem that Frank's own contribution can be properly evaluated or assessed. The problem
itself is of immense complexity and cannot be dealt with just
in passing. But it must be at least noted. It has been vigor-
ously debated in the recent decades, especially in France, and
many prominent scholars and thinkers took part in the de-
bate. The controversy was inconclusive, but by no means
sterile. No agreement has been reached, but controversial

issues were sharpened and clarified. The disagreement of the learned does not disavow the problem itself—it is still there and has not lost its urgency and sting. Precisely because the issue proved to be so utterly disruptive, it should not be hastily shelved. The crux of the problem can be accurately focussed. Is there anything *specific* in the Christian *faith,* or in Christian *experience,* which should be taken into account by the philosopher in his own search and investigation, *within his own and proper area of study?* Was "the condition" of the philosopher changed at all by the arrival of Christianity? Has Christianity any particular metaphysical "implications" or, to use the wording of Maurice Blondel, *des exigences philosophiques?* Now, of course, all these questions may be answered in the negative and the problem itself may be dismissed. And actually negative answers were frequently given, for divers reasons, even by the professing Christians. It would suffice to quote in this connection the startling statement of Père Mandonnet, the renowned historian of the Western Medieval philosophy and the founder of the *Société Thomiste:* "Indeed, Christianity has changed the world, but it did not change philosophy: *Certes le Christianisme a transformé le monde, mais il n'a pas transformé la philosophie."* Indeed, as an avowed Thomist, Père Mandonnet had to plead for the complete autonomy of the philosophical field. But Frank obviously would not have accepted his paradoxical claim. For Frank *the condition* of the philosopher has been radically changed by the Gospel. New vistas have been disclosed which the philosopher has no excuse to ignore. It is doubtful, however, whether Frank was prepared to admit that *the content* of philosophy has been changed also. Was he ready to face "the Christian Challenge to Philosophy," to use the phrase of a recent English author, to the full extent? Moreover, was he fully aware of the true dimension of this "challenge?" Was he not rather inclined to adjust the Christian message to the "exigencies" of the old Platonic *philosophia perennis?* Of course, he was not the first to do so. It is a delicate question, indeed. But it is a valid question and, actually, it has been already asked, if rather in disguise. One must be cautious and precise at this point. The question is not about the "challenge" of Christian *theology*—and consequently there is no implicit intention to curtail the philosopher's freedom or to make philosophy once more again an *ancilla theologiae*—but about the challenge of the Christian *Event* and of the Christian *experience*, or of the Christian *faith*.

Frank had an invincible prejudice against the "traditional" theology, and his distrust was only growing with years. His phrasing was becoming increasingly bitter, biting, and nervous. He tended to dismiss "theology" altogether, as a superfluous and useless accretion, or even as a "sinful chat" and "intellectual fun." Indeed, "theology" was for him a kind of abstract rationalism which was, by its very nature, incommensurable with the ultimate and "metalogical" Mystery of God, ineffable and unfathomable. Frank's insistence on the priority of experience, in prayer and contemplation, was certainly legitimate and sound. Only it was also a commonplace of "traditional" theology itself. "Doctrines" are always but approximations, in relation to the fulness of spiritual vision. Yet, they have their own indispensable function in the totality of religious life, and this function is not just "symbolic" or "pragmatic," as Frank suggests. And it is hardly reasonable to reduce the whole of religious experience to the *silentium mysticum*. Moreover, in this case philosophy also becomes superfluous and must be discarded as "intellectual fun." The *apophatic* pathos of Frank's philosophy is excessive. He tends to suppress any "word" about God. In addition, Frank uses the term "theology" in a wide and extended sense. It covers "the whole luxury of old dogmatic teachings and controversies," that is, actually all dogmata and doctrines. But the real reason of Frank's radical opposition to the "traditional" theology is much deeper than just a mistrust of reason. His real disagreement is not with the method, but with the content itself. And he was fully aware of that. In fact, he had a "theology" of his own, and it differed substantially from the "traditional." His reading of the New Testament was highly selective. The crucial message of the Gospel consisted, in his interpretation, in the final revelation of the Kingdom of God, that is of the "eternal structure of reality," in the disclosure of "eternal perspectives" and of "eternal foundations." Frank himself underlined the close similarity of this interpretation of the Gospel with the Platonic vision of the ideal Heavenly

World. The message of the Gospel was just a message about
the "Divino-human" nature of Man, a reminder of the "eternal Fatherland" of Man. It was not an oral message, it was
disclosed in the life of Jesus. However, Frank was rather em-
barrassed by that excessive attention which has been given
by the "traditional" theology to the Person of Christ. It could
only obscure the Message. Indeed, he opposed categorically
the interpretation of the Gospel in the terms of Redemption
or Salvation. At least, it was useless: "do we really need any
such doctrines," he asked. Indeed, the Cross, strangely
enough, did not belong to the core of the Gospel, as Frank
read it. The core of the Gospel is in the new assurance that
Man actually does not belong to "this world," and that there
is another "better" world. In fact, it is still the old Platonic
pattern. Only now it has been, as it were, authenticated by the
Gospel of Jesus Christ. And Frank does not urge "to flee"
from this present world, as both Plato and Plotinus did of
old. He calls and summons for struggle, for the resolute struggle with the forces of evil and destruction, of hatred, cruelty,
and despair, which now so conspicuously dominate the his-
toric scene. Yet, he does not believe that victory is possible
within "this world," on that level of existence, even for God
himself. Frank deals with this theme in his exciting book,
Light in the Darkness (1949), which, unfortunately, has not
yet been translated in any Western language. It is, perhaps,
one of his best and strongest books, and his moral pathos
reaches here its climax. But it is a thoroughly pessimistic
book. Frank had no hope for history. It was for him a tragedy
without any immanent catharsis. There is actually no growth
in history. Frank was looking to the end of history, to the
last events. His "eschatology," however, was but loosely related to the actual course of history. It was rather an abroga-
tion of history, a kind of escape, than a consummation. Time
itself was for Frank a realm of disruption and disintegration.

The overarching metaphysical conception of Frank was
that of "All-embracing Unity." It was, in fact, rather a vision
than a conception. The Being is a Unity, in which everything
is correlated and tied together. To quote his own words, "in
the being everything is correlative or rather interwoven and
melted together." It is a fulness of Life which cannot be

grasped in any logical definitions, since definitions inevitably separate. At this point Frank is close to the famous aphorism of Bergson: *La vie deborde la raison*. The Being is continuous, without any splits, and for the same reason always, as it were, "indefinite" and infinite. It is always in movement and in flux. It is an "Ocean of Being," as Plotinus said. It has no limits. Everything is possible within it and Frank warns emphatically against the use of the word "impossible." Now, it is obviously, first of all, a vision of the Living Cosmos, a "Chain of Being" in which all links cannot be isolated and cannot be really distinguished or separated from each other. And still, for Frank, it is not yet the Ultimate Reality. It is rooted in a deeper Ground, which should be identified as "Holiness" and "Divinity." Thus we come to a certain duality, or a "dyad,"—the Cosmos and God. But Frank applies even to this distinction his general method of continuity. God and Cosmos are also continuously correlated. Their "duality" is actually within a higher Unity, or even Oneness. That higher Unity has no definite name. It is at that point that Frank's conception has been challenged by Nicholas O. Lossky, in his penetrating review of the first book of Frank, *The Object of Knowledge* (1915). It was a valid criticism. It seems that in Frank's conception God is essentially but a foundation of the Cosmos. Indeed, Frank is suspicious of the concept of Transcendence because it would endanger the continuity of Being. On the other hand, Lossky strongly contended that God stands, as it were, "outside" the Cosmos and should not be included in the "all-embracing Unity." In fact, Frank was never clear on the ultimate "relation" between God and Cosmos. He was convinced that his idea of indefinite "potentiality" of the Being, as of the Might, could serve as a foundation of freedom. Indeed, there is nothing "impossible" and the range of "possibilities" is infinite. Yet, all "possibilities" are implied and contained in the "all-embracing Unity," so that actually there is no room for any "novelty." Strictly speaking, it is difficult to see, how, within the overarching scheme of Frank, any ultimate event, including the solution of casual predicaments, is possible. There is no room for any "contingency" in the Being. The Universe of Frank is in continuous motion, like an Ocean, but it does not move anywhere. It is ultimately an unbreakable chain.

It would be out of place to attempt in this short preface even a cursory survey of Frank's philosophical system, or rather of his "vision." The purpose of these few pages was only to call the attention of the prospective reader of this particular book of Frank to the problems involved and to remind of the wider context in which these problems should be visualized. Valid questions and objections may be raised at various points of Frank's conception. One may have difficulty in accepting his contentions. But the reader must be aware of the actual situation: Frank's failures and shortcomings, if there are any, are not his own. They are implied in that Platonic *philosophia perennis* which limited his philosophical horizon. On the other hand, Platonism is a noble option. This must be admitted and recognized even by those who are, for valid reasons, unable to accept it. In the present age, when "retreats from Christianity" and various attempts at the "reconstruction of belief" are so strangely and strikingly intermingled with each other, the valiant attempt of Frank to demonstrate that "faith" and "search," that is, a free intellectual research, can and must be wedded together is of timely significance. His arguments must be pondered. They are stimulating. But, as always, they must be assessed in a wider perspective. "Faith," without any further qualification, is a vague and ambiguous term. The "Christian Challenge to Philosophy" must be faced and met. It seems that it cannot be met adequately within the limits of the alleged *philosophia perennis*. But one should come to this conviction by the way of critical examination, and not by the way of prejudice. Frank's philosophy, as, indeed, any creative philosophical system, is itself a problem, a challenge, a question. And it must be studied in this spirit, that is, as a philosophical *hypothesis*.

The Western reader may be tempted to read Frank as a Russian writer and look in his books for specifically Russian contribution. Of course, Frank was a Russian thinker and stood in Russian cultural tradition. But, as philosopher, he was wrestling with universal and common problems. It may be even said that he was rooted in Western tradition more than any of his Russian contemporaries and companions. Moreover, "Russian Philosophy" itself must be regarded not

FOREWORD

so much in the perspective of the peculiar cultural history of Russia as in the perspective of that common philosophical quest which originated in Ancient Greece and was carried on in Christian Europe. Only in this context can it be properly appreciated.

Princeton University.   Georges Florovsky.
June 15, 1966

Preface

*

The present book is an attempt to give a more mature and thorough formulation of the philosophical system which I have been thinking out for the last forty years. The early version of it is expounded in my book *The Object of Knowledge*, 1915 (in Russian; translated into French as *La connaissance et l'être*, 1937). During those long years my views have of course undergone a certain development, but the intuition of reality as an all-embracing unity has remained unchanged and determines my entire outlook.

The first two chapters are concerned with the idea of reality as the ultimate ground of being, distinct from the world of fact; the third chapter is intended to elucidate and justify the idea of God as the primary source of reality and the principle of absolute holiness. These three chapters provide a general philosophical introduction to the problem of man. Thus the book as a whole is an essay in the metaphysics of human nature or in philosophical anthropology (the first sketch of it is given in my book *The Human Soul*, 1917). My main object is to affirm the indissoluble connection between the idea of God and the idea of man, i.e. to justify the conception of 'Godmanhood' in which I find the central meaning of the Christian faith. Accordingly, the purpose of the book is to overcome the fatal dissension between faith in God and faith in man which is so characteristic of the spiritual life of modern Europe and is the main source of its troubled and tragic character.

My thesis is on the whole similar to Vladimir Solovyov's main contention based on religious and philosophical intuition. I must confess—to my shame—that the similarity became clear to me only when my own theory had finally taken shape; Solovyov's influence

PREFACE

upon me had evidently been unconscious, but I willingly and gratefully acknowledge myself to be his disciple in this respect. Consciously my philosophical thought has been determined by Platonism and in particular by its two greatest representatives— Plotinus and Nicolas of Cusa. I also owe a great deal to mystical literature.

The fundamental idea of 'God-manhood' as I understand it involves the combination of a sober awareness of the empirical world's imperfection, and therefore of man's tragic position in it, with a metaphysical apprehension of reality as a harmonious all-embracing unity having its primary basis in absolute Spirit and absolute Holiness. Acknowledging the element of truth contained in the acute sense of the tragedy of human existence, prevalent at the present day, I endeavour to show that it is compatible with a religious attitude which gives meaning to life.

I foresee that my book will not satisfy either one or the other of the two mutually opposed spiritual camps. Philosophers and unbelieving thinkers will consider it an illegitimate confusion between independent rational thought and traditional religious faith; theologians and unreflecting believers will regard as illegitimate the very attempt to give a free philosophical interpretation to questions, the only answer to which they find in the authority of the Revelation and traditional church doctrine. It is characteristic of both these camps, and indeed of the whole spiritual atmosphere of our day, to be prejudiced against and reject philosophical thought based upon religious and metaphysical experience. In answer I content myself with saying that I am following the classical tradition of philosophy. It is an unquestionable fact that in every period of the flowering of spiritual culture philosophy was both independent and religious, and it was in that form that it was fruitful and needed by all thinking people. This was the case at the time of Athenian enlightenment in the fifth–fourth centuries B.C., at the highest peak of mediaeval culture in the thirteenth century, during the Renaissance, at the epoch of tempestuous development of scientific thought in the seventeenth century, and of German idealism at the end of the eighteenth and beginning of the nineteenth centuries. And, on the contrary, a contemptuous and negative attitude to the very idea of philosophically interpreting the mysteries of existence is a sign of degeneration of spiritual culture. But be that as it may, those who in the words of Hegel 'are doomed to be philosophers', however modest they may

PREFACE

be, will not be disturbed by criticism based upon a lack of understanding, or a rejection of the true nature of philosophy.

'Docta ignorantia' which is the source of all my ideas inevitably
implies that every philosophical system, including of course my own,
as an attempt rationally to express the super-rational essence of
reality, must be understood as only an approximate, schematic,
or at best merely relatively true reflection of the real truth. This
'real truth' remains our guiding star, and for that very reason is
unattainable. As an Arabian proverb puts it, 'God knows best'.

S. L. FRANK

London, September 1949

CHAPTER I

Reality and the World of Fact

*

1. The World of Fact and Ideal Being

All human knowledge, beginning with the everyday knowledge upon which our practical life is based, and ending with the highest achievements and the most far-reaching discoveries of science and philosophy, is an answer to the question what is the nature of reality? what truly is? Distinction is often drawn between mere description, and causal explanation of the contents of reality, but it is obvious that in the last resort the two coincide: the discovery of the causes of events is the discovery of those contents of reality which 'produce' the events in question, or from which the events 'follow'. However great in other respects may be the difference between the lofty task of *rerum cognoscere causas* and the most primitive, immediate perception of that which lies before us, in both cases our cognitive activity is concerned with discovering the nature of reality and answering the question as to what truly is.

We have perpetually to ask and to answer that question in order both to enrich and to correct our knowledge. All human knowledge is inevitably limited; it embraces only an infinitesimal portion of reality, and beyond it lies—to use Newton's expression—the boundless ocean of the unknown. On the other hand, all human knowledge is subject to error, because percepts may be deceptive, and concepts may be combined in an arbitrary, objectively unjustifiable fashion; hence we are faced with the continual and endless task of revising our knowledge, rejecting false ideas and judgments and replacing them by others which may rightly be said to express true insight into reality. Thus, all of us, whether we are aware of it or not, are engaged throughout life in solving the question as to what truly *is*.

B   I

It is continually set before us both by the practical need of finding our bearings in the surrounding world and by the disinterested love of knowledge which, as Aristotle pointed out, is inherent in every human being and is present both in the simple curiosity of a child and in the thinker's and the scientist's quest for truth.

But what, exactly, is meant by the phrase 'that which truly is'? In the first instance it is generally taken to mean all that we come across in our surroundings, all that is present in the world as we contemplate it, and is, as it were, forced upon us from without as an undeniable fact—in contradistinction to 'opinions', 'imaginings', 'suppositions', which have their source in our own selves. We regard that definite presence, independent of us, as empirically-given, and call our encounter with it 'experience'. The totality of everything that really is constitutes, then, the 'empirical reality' which, roughly speaking, is the same as 'the world'. We distinguish the subjective element in our consciousness—the capricious and unstable play of our presentations, thoughts and images, different in every individual mind—from the objective, which is 'given' as the same for all and must inevitably be recognized as present. That objective element in its totality forms the 'empirical reality'—the world common to us all, which we must take into account as something that 'actually is'.

Closer inspection shows that the empirical reality (or 'the world') is wider than it at first sight appears. It is not confined to the totality of all that is external to us, that surrounds us in space and is given to us concretely or sensuously. In other words it is not confined to what we call 'material being'. Unprejudiced observation easily detects the erroneousness of the view called 'materialism' which often gains possession of human minds and consists in identifying the empirically-given reality with material being, i.e. with existence in space. That which is not sensuously given as a part of the spatial picture of the world, that which we can neither see nor hear nor touch and which we call 'mental' is given no less directly and objectively than events of the material world. It confronts us as a certain reality independent of us, just as a stone or a wall does; it often acts upon us of itself, and invades us as a power the objective nature of which we cannot fail to recognize. Only recently Hitler's cruelty, insane love of power and *mania grandiosa* have been for mankind an empirical reality no less objective and far more powerful and menacing than a hurricane or an earthquake. But the same is

2

true of the small things of everyday life: it is sometimes far more difficult to get over a person's caprice or obstinacy, hostility or dislike, than to overcome material obstacles; on the other hand, conscientiousness, goodwill and a serene state of mind of the people around us often proves to be of greater help than all material goods. Both material and mental events, inextricably interwoven with one another, at any rate in certain realms of being, together and with equal right, enter into the composition of the 'empirical' world—of that which confronts our mental gaze and is in that sense external.

It might seem at first sight that, at any rate, our own mental life as an 'inner', 'subjective' sphere is something that differs from and transcends the 'external' objective world. We shall see later that this surmise contains a faint glimpse of a certain very important truth. But at the present stage it must be said that, in so far as our own mental life is an object of knowledge and observation, it too forms part of the world of fact. That becomes obvious as soon as we cease to ascribe to the phrase 'external to us' the narrow and artificial meaning of remoteness in space, but take it in its essential meaning of 'independent of us', i.e. independent of our acts of cognition directed upon it. From this general point of view our own mental life is clearly an objective empirical reality like everything else; psychology, the basic method of which is introspection, is an empirical science no less than other branches of knowledge. In this respect there is no difference whatever between my own mental life and that of others. Both are of the nature of actual fact, sometimes unaffected by our will, and in any case independent of our cognitive gaze. True, *my* mental life is 'given' and 'confronts me' in a somewhat different and more intimate way, it is closer to 'me' as a knowing subject; it is not, however, identical with the knowing subject, but is given me in experience and recognized by me as a part of the empirical world. In cognizing my own mental life, I must—just as in the case of external objects—distinguish that which is actually present in it from what I merely imagine or believe to be present; and I may also discover in it something new and hitherto unknown to me. This alone is sufficient to show that it is a component part of what I call 'the world of fact', i.e. of what is given me in experience as something which truly is and is discriminated by me.[1]

[1] It follows from this that the very distinction between the 'subjective' and the 'objective' elements of experience is not a real distinction between separate

3

REALITY AND THE WORLD OF FACT

The world of fact thus proves to consist of what is sensuously given as part of external experience in the narrow sense, i.e. of 'material' events in space, and of what is given just as concretely, but non-sensuously, i.e. of events directly apprehended by me and called 'mental'. But is this an exhaustive description of the contents of reality?

Before answering this question we must consider what is the essential characteristic of 'the real' as opposed to the 'apparent', 'the imaginary', 'the supposed'. It consists not in 'the real' being sensuously or even concretely given, but merely in its being something that stands over against me, as an object upon which I direct my mental gaze, which I discriminate, recognize and register as actually present. This alone distinguishes that which truly is from the apparent, the supposed, the imaginary. The totality of all that truly is would be more correctly defined as the *objective* rather than as the 'empirical' reality. What exactly is the difference between those two definitions?

Long ago philosophical thinkers reached the conviction and in-controvertibly proved that the objective world contains not only empirically given material, but something else as well, namely, that which constitutes its 'form'. It is an 'ideal' element, revealed to the purely intellectual contemplation. Kant has shown that space is not a part of the concrete material of our external sensous experience, but is present as it were over and above that material; he has shown too that time, apart from which we have no experience whatever, is itself also not given in experience, is not its 'matter', but its condition, the form in which experience is given. And finally he has shown that a whole series of general elements and relations which we include in the world's content—such as cause, quality, relation, thing (or 'substance') etc.—are not 'given' in experience in the same manner as its sensous and concrete material is given, but are present in it

realms of being, but only a *distinctio rationis* depending upon the point of view from which we consider the correlation. The events of my inner life—my moods, dreams, fancies etc., as they actually occur in me and exist for me alone—are contrasted by me as something 'subjective' with the objective reality which is 'universally binding'. But those same events as objects of thought and observation—not merely for another, say, for a psychoanalyst, but for myself as well—are an objective reality with which I must reckon as with any other objective fact. From this point of view it is not those facts that are 'subjective', but the wrong interpretation of them: their inclusion in a sphere of reality to which they do not really belong would be 'subjective' in the sense of being mistaken and illusory. More will be said of this later.

4

in a different way, constituting its 'forms'. To the list of these formal elements must be added the purely *logical* relations.

Relations of identity, difference, logical subordination, ground and consequence seem at first glance to belong not to the objects themselves, but to our thought about them; in the so-called formal logic they are usually treated as 'laws of thought'. Unprejudiced contemplation of the objective world shows, however, that they too form part of it and are 'real'.

Recognition of the ideal elements of being, first discovered by Plato, was expressed in modern philosophy most clearly by Kant, but it is essentially independent of Kant's artificial and debatable theory of knowledge. It will be remembered that for Kant the presence in experience of those ideal elements—which he regards as forms of human consciousness—vitiates the objective reality of the world of fact. He takes that world to be, so to speak, a picture which we ourselves create by imposing upon the sensuous material the forms inherent in our own consciousness. Though that picture is universally-binding, it is not the true reality, but only an objectified complex of our presentations—a stable illusion common to all human beings.

There is no need to enter here upon a critical examination of Kant's theory. The truth which it contains in a distorted form and in conjunction with wrong preconceptions and assumptions will become apparent to us later. As already said, simple unprejudiced description of the contents of experience makes it perfectly clear that ideal elements form part of the world of fact no less than does its sensuous, concretely given material. In view of this, it is more fitting to speak of that which truly is as 'the objective' rather than the 'empirical' world, for in the latter term emphasis is generally laid upon the 'material' aspect of being, i.e. upon sense-data.

This substitution of one term for another does not change anything in our interpretation of 'that which truly is'. Its general scheme or picture is still the same familiar world in which we live, which confronts us with the intrinsically compelling necessity of actual fact. Ideal forms appear in it as belonging to the very stuff of which it is made, as its qualities or relations. Thus, extension in space is, as it were, merely a property of material phenomena, and time—a form in which world-processes take place; and the same thing applies to all other ideal elements. We contrast them as mere forms or attributes, with matter as the true substratum of being,

5

constituting as it were the fundamental, substantial basis of all that is. Just as a golden ring is different from a golden vase or a golden snuff-box, and yet all three are only species of articles made of gold and are valued primarily as such, so ideal forms and relations seem to be merely complementary, as it were secondary, to 'the things themselves', i.e. to the concretely given contents of being. Twice two is four, the diameter divides a circle into two equal halves, there is identity and difference, unity and multiplicity, permanence and change, and so on—all those relations confront us as properties of the objective world, in no way differing in this respect from empirical facts such as 'iron is heavier than wood, water is a liquid, and a stone is a hard body'. The totality of all that truly is—'the objective reality'—still remains a world-system, an interconnected multiplicity of certain 'things' or concrete entities possessing a number of different qualities, 'empirical' or ideal, and standing in various relations to one another. This general picture expresses the point of view of 'common sense'—the sober mental attitude determined by practical needs.

'The world' thus conceived may be wider or narrower. Thus, in so far as we regard the substantival substratum of cosmic being as inevitably given in a concrete or sensuous form, the world coincides with what we call 'nature': all that truly is forms part of its all-embracing unity. Such a view is called 'naturalism'. We may, however, think of the objective reality as transcending the 'natural' world and including the realm of the unseen—such entities as God, angels, incorporeal spirits or souls and so on. However great in other respects the difference between such 'supernaturalism' and 'naturalism' may be, their conception of reality is of the same logical type. Both conceive of the world as a totality or system of concretely existing things or entities with their qualities and relations. The classical instance of this interpretation of reality is the philosophy of Aristotle (and the system of St. Thomas Aquinas, based upon it). It is precisely this type of thought that Kant designated by the name of 'dogmatic metaphysics'. According to it, all that is fits into a certain general picture of cosmic being, i.e. of the all-embracing unity of concrete objective reality. The 'heavenly' or 'superheavenly' world of metaphysics—including both Aristotle's 'first mover' and the Creator in the Christian metaphysics of the Tomistic type— forms part of one single universe. That can be seen from the fact that God occupies a definite place in it, concretely depicted in

6

Dante's metaphysical poem, and this general scheme is not affected by any further refinements and subtleties of metaphysical thought. As already said, the picture of the world as an all-inclusive, objective, systematic unity may be wider or narrower, simpler or more complex, but that alters nothing in the general conception of reality as a completed, intellectually comprehensible all-embracing system of objectively and concretely existing things or entities with their multifarious qualities and relations.

However self-evident the truth of such a view may appear, the very fact that in spite of the different forms it may take it stands for a definite type of philosophical thought, alongside of other and quite different types, shows that its presuppositions are not so indisputable as they seem. According to it the 'objective' world is primary, further unanalysable and therefore all-embracing: beyond the system of self-contained concrete things or entities forcing themselves upon our mental gaze there is supposed to be nothing but the sphere of 'subjective', arbitrary and mistaken presentations or opinions. The world of fact and 'true being' are taken to be identical.

But is this really the case? In the history of human thought this theory has been opposed by another which, from the name of its founder, may be called Platonism. The main difference between them lies in the first instance, in their interpretation of the 'ideal' elements of being. They must accordingly be considered more closely.

However natural it may seem to regard the ideal elements as merely certain properties or relations forming part of the world of fact, there is something in that view which is open to doubt. To begin with, we are accustomed to think—and have sufficient grounds for doing so—that all existence is in time and has the common characteristic of coming into being, lasting, changing and disappearing. Its ideal forms, however, have quite a different character: they are non-temporal or super-temporal. Numerical and geometrical relations, the general principle of functional dependence or of causal connection between events, the relations of identity and difference, logical subordination and co-subordination and so on—not merely remain unchanged or last forever and can neither arise nor disappear, but are clearly apprehended as being *outside* time, on quite a different plane of reality or in a different dimension of it than all the concretely existing world-entities. Since non-temporal relations include relations of identity and difference, which hold of *all* contents of being,

7

all those contents have a non-temporal aspect. If I concentrate attention on any content as such, regardless of its forming part of the temporal stream of events—for instance, if I think of the 'red colour', I clearly see that redness as such is eternal; it is 'something', or, to put it differently, it in some sense *is* quite independently of the fact that in concrete things it may fade or be replaced by another colour; and if there were not a single red thing left in the world, that which we conceive as 'redness' would not have changed, but would have preserved its meaning. But that implies that ideal elements have two aspects: on the one hand they form part of the world of fact and are merely the formal side of it, and on the other, they *subsist* without any reference to their existence in the world of fact. Taken in this aspect, ideal elements are not a part of 'the world'; they are as it were an eternal supercosmic reservoir of patterns, from which the contents of the concrete, temporal, empirical existence are drawn. This discovery of Plato's is so self-evident that no objections or doubts can affect it. If it shocks the so-called 'common sense' it is solely because the mental horizon of 'common sense' is deliberately limited: 'being' means for it, from the very first, only that which happens in time and is localized in time and space, i.e. the concrete contents of experience; everything beyond it is merely a subjective invention.[1] But to identify concrete existence in space and time with the wider and more general conception of 'objective' or true being is an unwarranted assumption.

All criticism of the Platonic vision of the 'world of Ideas' is based upon a misunderstanding. As a modern Russian Platonist N. O. Lossky has pointed out, the assertion that 'horse in general' *is* a reality is taken to mean that such a horse is grazing in some particular meadow, and the obvious absurdity of this is supposed to be a convincing argument against Platonism. But such a method of disproof does not logically differ from the materialistic fallacy. When a man's mental horizon is limited to the perception of material things, it is not hard to prove that only matter truly is—simply because 'that which truly is' has been beforehand taken to mean 'that

[1] It may seem at first sight that exception is made for at least one reality—God, as an eternal and omnipresent Being. Without going into a detailed discussion of this complex question it is sufficient to point out here that owing to the general logical presuppositions of this type of thought the eternity of God is actually thought of as endless duration in time, and that in spite of God's activity being omnipresent, He is thought of as somehow localised in space ('in heaven').

which exists after the manner of a material thing', and everything else therefore appears to be a mere 'subjective invention'. But obstinate repetition of an arbitrary assumption is not proof. Ideal being is a different kind of reality than the concretely existing things localized in space and time and has the form of super-spatial and super-temporal unity, but that by no means gives us a right to deny that it truly is.

The discovery of the supertemporal ideal aspect or sphere of being does not in the least conflict with the realistic contention that ideal elements form part of the 'empirical' or objective reality as qualities or relations of concretely existing things. For, as already pointed out, those ideal elements have two aspects or, as it were, two kinds of being: supertemporal in essence they are present in the temporal world, finding in it so to speak their concrete embodiment. Hence Aristotle's polemics against Plato and the age-long dispute between empirical realists or 'men of common sense' and the 'idealists' is pointless. The two positions are reconcilable and compatible: to use scholastic terms, *universalia* are simultaneously *in rebus* and *ante res*. But once this is recognized, we come to see that the so-called 'objective world', even in the widest sense of the term, does not exhaust the whole of being. All existence, all that forms part of the actual world, must be included within a wider conception of *reality* which contains supertemporal ideal being as well.

The same thing may be brought out in another way. 'Objective existence' does not exhaust the whole of being, either in so far as it is *existence*, i.e. being in time, or in so far as it is *objective*, i.e. is the totality of objects standing over against our thought. In a certain sense, of course, ideal contents are as objective as the empirical; they are just as binding for us as the latter. But objects of thought or of intellectual contemplation are related to thought in a different way than the objects of sensuous or concretely-visual experience are. While standing over against the knowing subject as something given, and in that sense external to him as 'objects' of thought, they are not external to thought itself, but seem to be within it, included in it. A house, a table, a stone or even such mental events as toothache, hunger or thirst are something totally different from the thought directed upon them. But, for instance, mathematical and logical relations and all abstract general ideas, while being objects of thought, are somehow within thought itself and belong to the very nature of it. This finds clear expression in the fact that we can be aware of them 'with our eyes shut', plunged as it were into the inner world of thought. Their very designation as 'ideal' suggests their dual, so to speak, border-land character. 'Idea' in the Platonic sense means a certain objective reality; 'idea' as commonly used means a product or phase of our own thought. This is the source of the temptation to regard ideal contents as purely subjective creations of our thought and to deny their objective significance as constituent elements of true being. It lies, too, at the root of Kant's mistaken attempt to treat the ideal elements as 'forms' of our own consciousness, which we impose upon reality, thus distorting it or replacing it by a subjective picture. This obviously erroneous theory is based upon a profound intuition of a certain truth, wrongly understood and bound up with false assumptions. The sphere of 'thought' or 'spirit' to which the 'world of ideas' or super-temporal ideal being belongs is not a psychological process of human thinking with all that is inevitably 'subjective' in it: it is the universal element of thought or ideality as such, free from all subjectivity—something which we may approximately describe as universal reason. The relation of our actual human thought to that universal ideal element is different from our relation to 'objects' which confront us from outside only. We ourselves live in that element and belong to it, at any rate in part.

It will be remembered that Plato, starting with the conception of Ideas as self-subsistent eternal patterns or prototypes objectively abiding in the 'supercelestial sphere', was faced later on with a number of difficulties with regard to the relation of Ideas to one another and especially to the world. As can be seen from his later dialogues he recognized the problems this involved, but he did not solve them. The neoplatonists were therefore essentially right in modifying his doctrine and proclaiming Ideas to be contents of the universal reason, as it were eternal thoughts or designs of God. This does not in the least take away from their 'objectivity' in the general sense of true being, but merely shows that they are not external or alien to thought, not something it stumbles against, but something so to speak transparent for thought and akin to it.

For the purposes of the present argument there is no need to go into a detailed discussion of this complex problem. The only point of importance to us is this: being, or that which truly is, is not limited either to existence, i.e. to a system of temporal things and processes, or to 'the world of objects' in the sense of contents forced upon our thought from without and confronting it as irreducible facts independent of, and alien to it (and in that sense 'external'). True being has a deeper level which is more intimately connected with our consciousness; on that level we not merely 'have' it as something external, but have it in such wise that we ourselves somehow inwardly belong to it.

The same conclusion may be reached in another and more general way, independently of the problem as to the reality of the ideal elements of knowledge. Something in our mind involuntarily protests against the attempt to include everything within a system of *objects of thought* even when interpreted in the widest possible sense. It is not hard to see what calls forth this protest. We feel that we then lose the immediacy of our perception of reality, that a mirrored reflection is substituted for reality itself; the living bond with reality which forms the very core of our existence is replaced by an artificial, dispassionate, formal relation which we call 'objective knowledge'. True, there is no denying that the conception of reality as an object of thought directed upon it—an object of cold, passionless intellectual contemplation—is potentially universal: one may stand in such a relation to all that is, just as, in principle, one may see anything in the world reflected in a mirror. But from the fact that a mirror can reflect everything visible, it does not in the least follow that we are doomed to see everything only as a mirrored reflection. In the same way the fact that the attitude of 'objective knowledge' may apply to anything empirically accessible to us by no means implies that it is the only possible attitude.

The point is that in addition to sensuous and intellectual contemplation we have another and primary kind of knowledge which may be called living knowledge. In it the known does not confront us from without as something different from ourselves, but is somehow merged with our very life. Our thought springs from the depths of a self-revealing reality, and is carried on within it. That which we experience as our *life* reveals itself to us—to our thought, which is inseparably present in that life. The full meaning of this remark will be made clear later; at present it is sufficient to say that by comparison with this primary kind of knowledge, the point of view of objective knowledge involves an artificial narrowing, so to speak, an emasculation of consciousness. *Primum vivere, deinde philosophari.* Thought in its objectivized form is only a superstructure on this foundation of living knowledge.

2. *The Reality of the Subject*

We have seen that ideal elements are a species of being which transcends existence in space and time. The same kind of being is to be found at the opposite pole of the cognitive field, through the consideration of 'living knowledge' as distinct from knowledge of objects. People unfamiliar with the idea of living knowledge will ask in surprise 'but what more can there be for us to know except the totality of the objects of knowledge?' A simple and self-evident answer to this question at once suggests itself: beyond the confines of the world of objects there is at any rate *the actual mental gaze directed upon it*. That mental gaze implies the mysterious and not easily definable reality of its source or bearer and is given us in a different way than all the objects of knowledge.

A characteristic instance of mental blindness which fails to observe this irrefutably obvious fact is to be found in Hume's famous denial of the reality of the self. 'When I enter most intimately into what I call *myself*, I always stumble on some particular perception or other, of heat or cold, light or shade, pain or pleasure. I . . . never can observe anything but the perception.'[1] In the present connection it is irrelevant to point out that Hume's assertion about our mental life consisting solely of perceptions has been finally disproved by closer psychological analysis. The real point of importance is this: the assertion that 'I cannot find in myself any I'—for this is what Hume's words amount to—is self-contradictory. If there were no 'I' at all, there would be no one to seek it. It is perfectly natural that I cannot find 'myself' among objects, for I am the seeker—not an object, but a subject. I cannot meet my own self for the simple reason that my self is that which *meets* everything else. Thus an absent-minded man will sometimes look in the room for the spectacles which he is wearing: he does not see them because he is looking *through* them.

It will be remembered that in modern philosophy the credit of discovering the reality which transcends the world of objects belongs to Descartes: he expressed it in his formula *cogito ergo sum*. For Descartes himself that idea signified primarily and almost exclusively the discovery of a perfectly secure basis for absolutely certain knowledge: I may doubt whether any content of objective knowledge actually exists or is only an idea in my mind, but I cannot doubt the reality of my own thought; it is a self-contradiction to doubt the

---

[1] David Hume, *Treatise on Human Nature*, vol. I, part IV, section 6.

reality of the doubt itself, and therefore of my doubting thought. Descartes himself, however, did not fully grasp the full significance of his discovery. Having found this starting point of knowledge he goes on to build a metaphysic of the objective type: he transforms the thinking self into a substance, which, alongside of other kinds of substances forms part of the world's structure. But the use which Descartes made of his discovery does not prevent us recognizing that he discovered a special kind of reality, different in principle from the world of objects—a reality which we generally fail to notice simply because it is too close to us and coincides with him who seeks it. Speaking approximately and in familiar terms it may be said that the 'I' which is conscious of itself in the very act of thinking is a reality in which subject and object coincide. In its primary nature, however, it is a reality in which there is neither object nor thought directed upon it: it is given us not as standing over against our cognizing thought, but as an actual self-revealing and self-evident reality. In other words this reality is revealed to us in the form of *living knowledge*.

It will be remembered that the same discovery was made twelve centuries before Descartes by St. Augustine; but for him, in contradistinction to Descartes, it was a true revelation which revolutionized his life as well as his philosophy. It is premature to speak here of how it helped Augustine to find God through insight into the peculiar nature of the Divine reality; it is sufficient to note the general widening of Augustine's philosophical horizon in consequence of it. There is no doubt that his discovery of the self-evidence of the thinking ego revealed to him a new dimension of being, unnoticeable from our usual point of view—namely, the primary reality which lies beyond the confines both of infinite space and even of the human soul understood as a special component part of the world. This is hinted at in Plato's philosophy and more clearly indicated in Plotinus's mystical speculation which directly influenced St. Augustine; but it was to Augustine that the self-evidence of the super-cosmic, trans-objective reality was for the first time made apparent in all its significance. This reality is not a dumb, passive conglomeration of facts confronting our thought and revealing itself to it from without, but is self-subsistent, immediate life revealing itself to itself; and as the primary essence of our own being, it is seen by us to be the primary essence of reality as such. In other words, it is a reality which transcends the supposedly all-embracing system of objective existence and lies at the basis of it. It does not confront us from without, but is given to us from within as the ground in which we are rooted and out of which we grow.

Another man of genius, nearer to us in time, who made the same discovery afresh, thereby giving rise to quite a new type of philosophical thought ('the German Idealism') was Kant. Starting, like Descartes, with the problem of trustworthiness of knowledge Kant demonstrated the reality of the world of objects. The unsophisticated consciousness takes this world to be an absolute, self-contained and all-embracing reality, but Kant saw that it was only the correlate (or, in his interpretation, the 'product') of the cognizing thought itself, and therefore had only a limited and relative significance. The questionable details of Kant's system are not relevant in this connection; what is important is his argument that complete and all-embracing insight into reality cannot be gained through theorizing about the structure of the world of objects (or, as Kant calls it, through 'dogmatic metaphysics'). The truly all-embracing whole is not the world of objects, which is merely a correlate of theoretical reason, but the realm of 'consciousness' which transcends it. In moral life—in the striving of the will towards absolute duty, and in the religious attitude based upon this—that consciousness transcends the theoretical knowledge of the world of objects and, quite independently of it, following its own paths and guided by other criteria of truth, discovers the true, transcendental reality ('thing in itself'). Further development of this line of thought (in Fichte and Hegel) finds this reality beyond the objective sphere in the deeper and more primary principle of 'spirit'. This conclusion naturally follows from the discovery that not the object confronting our thought, but the subject in his immediate givenness to himself is the revelation of the true nature of reality. There is a great deal that is vague, debatable, and untrue in the philosophical systems founded by Kant and his successors upon this primary intuition, but permanent value attaches to the general result of the change in consciousness—in Plato's language, of 'the soul turning its gaze' from outside inwards—in virtue of which reality is revealed to us not as a world of objects external to us, but as that which lives and acts in the depths of self-consciousness.

The generally prevalent so-called 'realistic' attitude is, however, so firmly established that it often persists in spite of being clearly shown to be limited and indeed untenable. The erroneous idea that all that is, all that in any sense deserves to be termed real, must in the last resort form part of the world of objects, is easy to defend because, as already pointed out, we really can include in the objective world everything that is, by looking upon it from a particular angle. Hence nothing is simpler than to adopt the point of view from which the inner, primary reality revealing itself to itself, discovered under different forms by St. Augustine, Descartes and Kant, will appear to us as a part of the objective world. We may regard it as merely the sphere of our own mental life—as the subjective little world which every man bears within himself and which obviously, together with its bearer, belongs to the realm of existence as a somewhat peculiar and on the whole unimportant element in it, an 'epiphenomenon'. These unstable and in a sense illusory little worlds of mental life, characteristic of certain organisms, form part of the objective world of organic and inorganic matter. From this standpoint all that appeared profound, mysterious and transcendental in the depths of self-consciousness evaporates at once, for consciousness itself proves to be a part—and an insignificant part—of that same world of objects. This explains the historical paradox of the sudden downfall of the great systems of German idealism, and the ease with which Kant's philosophy was interpreted in the positivist sense as the discovery of subjectivity, i.e. of all human ideas being psychologically conditioned, and Hegel's grand metaphysical theory suddenly developed into Feuerbach's anthropological materialism. Indeed every religious or philosophical intuition, every manifestation of the invisible primary reality in the depths of the spirit may, for an external observer, assume the semblance of a subjective interplay of ideas in the human mind which is itself only an infinitesimally small part of the universe.

However easy and natural such a standpoint may seem, those who have had the living experience of the immediate inner self-revelation of reality will at once perceive that it is both artificial and untenable. To begin with, there obviously remains the simple fact, already referred to, that even if all that is be included within the framework of objective existence, exception must be made at any rate for the cognitive gaze directed upon it. Furthermore, the objective world, with which from this point of view we are solely concerned, is not the actual reality in its living concreteness and substantival depth, but only a mental *picture* of it, somewhat like a mirrored reflection. Such a reflection reproduces exactly the material contents of the world and yet remains illusory, for it has none of the tangible massiveness that forms the very essence of reality as true self-subsistent being. Thus in the best *nature morte* the colour, shape and size of fruit may be the same as in nature, but the tangibility, taste, fragrance, juiciness—all that we have in the experience of eating it—are absent or, at best, indirectly suggested. In the same way the mental picture of 'being' is one thing, and the immediately experienced reality apprehended from within is quite another, though the external contents of both may be identical. Whenever the self-revelation of reality in the inner experience is viewed from without as 'a mental event', the 'picture' is substituted for the real thing: the dimension of depth, the indescribable element of genuineness and significance vanishes at once. It is one thing to experience from within the joys, the sufferings and the deepest revelations of love, and quite another psychologically to study and observe from without 'the mental process of being in love'; were it not so, Faust, rich in learning and wisdom, would not have complained that though he had gained objective knowledge of all things, he had missed life itself, for he had never tasted and therefore never known its inmost mysterious essence.

While distinguishing the act of experiencing from the knowledge of it, i.e. from the thought directed upon it, we must not forget that such knowledge may take two entirely different forms. Thus a lover may not only enjoy his love, suffer from it, and experience all the emotions connected therewith, but may also think about it and try to understand what is happening to him. But such intellectual analysis of one's own experience from within is utterly different from dispassionate observation of somebody else being in love, or from a scientifically-psychological analysis of the process. Or, to take another example, it is one thing to know social and political life from within, to take part in it, to have a living experience of it and enter into it emotionally, and quite another to study it as a naturalist studies the life of an ant-heap. In the first case the living experience in all its vitality, concreteness and fulness directly reveals itself to the thought which apprehends it from within; such thought discovers a dimension of reality, inaccessible to the second type of thought which apprehends from without, as it were, only the external picture or the outer layer of the reality before it.

We must not be confused by the general consideration that all thought and knowledge consist in the subject's cognitive activity being directed upon an object. This is true in a general sense, but the object and the cognitive act directed upon it may be given us in two totally different ways. It is essential to distinguish between the object remote from us, confronting us from without (not in a spatial, but in a purely epistemological sense) and the object abiding within our mental life and revealing itself from within. Just as ideal objects are a reality dwelling in the sphere of thought itself and having the same type of being as it, so the objects of which we are speaking now belong to the sphere of the inner *life*: both the knowing subject and the known object, though theoretically distinguishable, abide in the same realm of being. The German philosopher Dilthey, who devoted himself to problems of spiritual life, distinguished between these two types of knowing by using two different terms, *begreifen* and *verstehen*. It is precisely because living knowledge reveals to us the depths of reality inaccessible to objectival knowledge that we cannot hope to apprehend reality completely and as a whole while remaining within the confines of 'objective existence' and constructing 'systems of ontology'.

It is to the credit of modern existentialism, in spite of all its defects and limitations as a general philosophical theory, that its founder Kierkegaard was the first (unless we count Pascal) to insist that *Existenz*, man's concrete and immediate being-for-himself is deeper, more primary and quite other than his mental life as the domain of objective psychological inquiry; it is a reality completely overlooked by philosophers who strive to understand the whole of being through an objective contemplation of it. That primary, immediate being-for-self is a reality in and through which man transcends the world of objective fact and discovers quite a new dimension of being; in that dimension he finds the ultimate depths of reality and has them directly in his own self.

Thus it becomes manifest that reality in its living concreteness is wider and deeper than 'the world of objective fact'. A philosophy adequate to the task of obtaining true knowledge of reality is therefore always based upon the living inner experience, in some sense akin to the experience that is called 'mystical'.

3. *Reality as spiritual life*

But what, precisely, does that experience signify? In other words, what reality is revealed to us in it? To answer that question in full would mean to anticipate the outcome of all the arguments that follow. At present it is only possible to indicate, so to speak, the general outline of that reality.

We have already seen that the reality in question is that of the subject himself. It should be noted in the first instance that this 'subject' is far from being merely 'the knower' or the bearer of 'pure thought'. In that capacity he is simply a point, devoid of any content—the point from which the cognitive gaze issues. It may appear at first sight that everything else forms part of what that gaze detects, i.e. of the objective world—in other words that in Descartes' formula the whole content of *sum* is exhausted by *cogito*, or, to use Kant's terms, that the subject is merely a content-less and purely formal bearer of 'consciousness in general'. In truth, however, this is not the case. The 'subject' is after all a certain concrete entity; that which I call my 'self' has a rich and complex content: it is the fulness of a living reality which I do not observe from without, but have directly in me as my own inner life. The power of looking outwards, of being the mental gaze directed upon objects is one of the functions of my inner life, but by no means the whole of it. The 'subject' as the formal bearer and source of the mental gaze is so to speak located *within* the subject as the bearer of the directly self-revealing life, but the two do not coincide: the subject in the second sense may be compared to a sphere rather than to a point.

That sphere includes, in the first instance, all that I experience and that appears to external, objective observation as my 'mental life', in so far as it is bound up with the indescribable depths, the absolute, primary, self-given reality which I call my 'self'. My sensuous, bodily sensations (e.g. physical pain or hunger) and images that appear before me (e.g. in dreams) are not as such felt to be a part of my inner life; they are merely given to me and invade me, so to speak, from without; they come from the periphery and not from the depths of my self. Sometimes the same character attaches to feelings and desires that are actually indistinguishable from sensations: sudden irritation, a sense of pleasure, a desire to take or do something 'get hold of me' and possess me; they do not arise out of my own depths, and are not experienced as rooted in them. But when experiences and emotions are felt, as it were, to live in me and to arise from within, from the depths of my 'self', they are for me the contents of that unique, self-revealing and self-conscious reality which I call my 'self'.

In other words, some of my experiences—those of the peripheral type—naturally transform themselves into an 'objective' picture given to me and observed by me as something different from myself. Experiences of this kind are easily expressible in words—and that is the way in which we objectify them and describe to others. Thus, for instance, I describe to a doctor my bodily sensations, and in doing so I clearly distinguish them from that which forms the intimate content of my inner life and which I can only tell—and even then with great difficulty—to a close friend or to a priest at confession. It is this intimate content that I experience as the manifestation of my real self. That inner reality is often called 'spiritual' as distinct from 'mental'. My spiritual life is directly accessible to me alone, for it is the content of my 'self'; it cannot be observed from without. As will be shown later, another person can only come to know it through quite a special act of knowing that has nothing in common with the cold observation of me as an 'object', or an element of the external reality. On the basis of such specific experience my spiritual life can in a derivative way become, like all else, an object of thought.

It must not be imagined that the distinction between the spiritual and the mental life is an objective, clearly definable distinction between two separate layers of the inner life, different in their material content. The difference lies not so much in the objective content of experience as in its character. One and the same fact may be a purely superficial 'mental event' or a deeply intimate and essential content of my inmost 'spiritual' life, according to how it is experienced. Thus, being in love may be merely a peripheral event in my mental life, sometimes, indeed, an almost physical sensation or feeling which I calmly and easily recognize as happening to me, or it may deeply penetrate into my hidden 'self' and, indeed, arise and take place in it, forming part of my 'spiritual life'. Spiritual life in general lies beyond the confines of the 'world of objects' and belongs to the inner, self-revealing, given-to-itself reality which is inaccessible to external observation; hence, its distinction from 'mental' life is not a distinction between two 'objects', accessible to general knowledge, but is only recognizable from within by the subject himself. It is the distinction between the super-cosmic essence of the subject's *Existenz*, his inner reality, and the superficial layer which covers as it were the kernel of his 'self' and, though belonging to him, does not form part of his inner being.

In short, 'spiritual life' is only another name for life experienced as actual self-revealing reality in contradistinction to the world of objects whether physical or mental. It is remarkable that there are a number of people—at the present day they are probably the majority—to whom it never occurs, at any rate in the usual course of things, that the true basis of their being is to be found in that deeper level, manifesting itself as 'spiritual life'. They have self-consciousness, of course, since in the human being it is inseparable from consciousness, i.e. they are aware of their experiences. But since their whole attention is directed outwards, upon the perception of external facts, their experiences are for them a kind of unsubstantial and unessential shadow that quietly and almost imperceptibly accompanies the outer course of their life; and in so far as they attend to those experiences and try to account for them, they regard them too as it were from outside, i.e. as events forming part of the world of objects. They may know their mental life as a complex of events and processes, but they have no true self-consciousness in the specific and significant sense of the term, i.e. their self as a unique primary *reality*, incomparable to anything else, eludes their attention. For those who know that reality, the awareness of it always comes as a sudden discovery—or, rather, a revelation, in connection with some particularly deep and stirring experience. It then suddenly appears that my habitual 'I' is not simply an indifferent, colourless and almost unnoticeable companion of my external life, but has concrete fulness and substantial depth in virtue of which it is a bearer of a certain self-subsistent, mysterious and absolutely unique transcendent reality, hidden from the eyes of the world. The classical instance of such a revelation is to be found in St. Augustine's *Confessions*.

The usual type of mind bent upon the perception of the objective world, and as it were hypnotized by its specific characteristics, will be sure to protest against this. For the sake of clarity the protest must be considered, even at the risk of repeating what has already been said. Positivists, as well as metaphysicians concerned with the objective world of existence, will say that this vaunted transcendent reality revealed in the depths of the self can be reduced to the simple and well-known fact that every human being not only forms part of the objective world common to all, but also has his own special little world of subjectivity. That little world consists simply of all kinds of illusions, fancies, dreams, visions and subjective feelings, and is the vague, shifting and purely personal sphere in which everyone is shut in and which, in contradistinction to objective being, is devoid of any universal significance. By insisting upon the primary nature and the unique value of that underlying reality we simply encourage man, to his detriment, to sink into the personal subjective sphere and cut himself off from the sober and firm common basis of human existence as an integral part of the world of objective fact.

There are two arguments in this contention, both of them erroneous. One is easily answered by an additional explanation of what has been pointed out above. The other requires fuller discussion which may lead us further.

While adhering for the present to the general statement that the primary reality is the reality of the subject's inner life, we must do away once for all with the obvious though highly prevalent ambiguity in the ordinary usage of the words 'subjectivity' or 'subjective being'. They are generally taken to mean at the same time and without sufficient demarcation 'the illusory', 'the fictitious', 'the apparent', as well as 'everything that belongs to the subject's realm of being'. But those two meanings are totally different, and it would be wiser to designate them by two different words—e.g., 'subjective' and 'subject's'. When a mental fact, such as a presentation, is wrongly taken to be a sign or testimony of some fact in the external objective world, we call it subjective in the sense of illusory. It is never the fact itself that is illusory, or mistaken—that would be simply meaningless. It is only the interpretation of a fact that may be mistaken—i.e. the judgment passed upon it. Ringing in one's ears may be mistaken for the ringing of the front door bell; a dream may be confused with an event in the external, coherent and stable reality equally perceived by all; when we observe our error, we call the fact that gave rise to it 'merely subjective'. That does not prevent it, however, from being as real as the external reality to which it is wrongly referred. The ringing in one's ears is different from a ring at the door, but in itself it is fully and indisputably real; if it is continual it is an illness that requires medical treatment. A dream is not a part of the external reality, but it is a real event in human life, sometimes more important than certain external events in it; it is not for nothing that psycho-analysts investigate dreams. This implies that, as already pointed out, 'the subjective' in the sense of belonging to the subject's inner life, in so far as it is made an object of observation and knowledge, itself forms part of the 'objective world' and there can be no question of calling it illusory or apparent and ascribing to it a kind of pseudo-being.[1]

This has a close bearing upon our 'mental life'. Although its contents are experienced and recognized as taking place 'in me'— in every separate individual—and therefore differing from the external material world common to us all, they somehow naturally and of themselves form part of the objective sphere and have the same kind of reality. The case is different, as we have seen already, with the peculiar reality of man's inmost self-consciousness, revealed in the 'spiritual life'. It is qualitatively or, more exactly, categorically distinct from all objective existence and yet it is not less, but rather more, real than it. It is therefore utterly inappropriate to designate that primary, most certain and self-evident reality as subjective, implying by that term a contemptuous rejection of it as fictitious, illusory or unessential. Such an attitude merely confirms the fact, already pointed out, that we easily fail to observe the reality with which we coincide or in which we abide, simply because our attention is wholly taken up with things that confront us from without. The reality of the subject himself is not 'subjective'; though not forming part of the world of objects, it is an actual and in a sense self-subsistent, stable and primary reality. That reality is far more weighty and significant than the world of objects. I can to a certain extent 'shut my eyes' to the world of objects, draw away from it, detach myself and lose touch with it, but I can never and in no way escape from the inner reality of my own 'self': it is the very essence of my being and it remains in me even when I do not notice it. It is precisely in this sense that both religion and philosophy have always taught that a man's 'soul' or life is of more importance and value to him than all the riches and kingdoms of the world. Everything external and objective has significance for me only in so far as it is related to this basic and immediate being of my own self. The external world is a comparatively unimportant accompaniment of our true being which reveals itself in the primary, unmediated reality of personal inner life.

[1] It will be pointed out later that there are other reasons for calling our mental experiences subjective. But then that term must be understood in a very different sense from the one that has just been criticized.

REALITY AND THE WORLD OF FACT

4. Reality as the Basis of my Being

Let us now consider the second implication of the positivists' argument quoted above. There can be no doubt of the genuineness and importance of the reality revealed to us in the inner life, but it may be asked whether that reality is a self-contained sphere, separate and distinct for every individual. In that case, to be absorbed in it would mean to detach oneself from the universal reality of our common world and as it were to desert the general life, hiding in the solitary depths of purely individual being as one does in dreams. All that has hitherto been said about reality as 'the sphere of inner life' seems to support this view.

The idea that the inner reality is self-enclosed and individually isolated has its psychological source in the naive conception, due to a kind of unconscious materialism, that the 'soul' is situated somewhere inside the body; through the sense organs it comes into contact with the external material reality, but from within it is enclosed in the impenetrable sheath of the body and is therefore something like a small self-contained sphere, separate for every human being.

The crudeness of the mythology presupposed by this popular idea will become apparent if we recall the old and indisputable truth established by Descartes that 'the soul' is not extended, i.e. no spatial determinations are directly applicable to it. The statement that 'the soul' is within the body really implies only two things: first, our organic sensations and the general sense of physical well-being or discomfort to which they give rise are localized within the body; secondly, our outer perceptions, determined by the action of the external environment upon our body, depend upon the body's position in space: we see, hear and touch different objects according to where our body happens to be. In other respects, however, my mental life is independent of my body and is everywhere and no-where: I can recall the past, can dream about the future, can mentally visit places far distant from my body; I have a number of other mental contents of which it is altogether impossible to say 'where' they are. To speak in a general sense of my self or my inner life being localized within my body, or to apply any spatial determinations to it, is as absurd and meaningless as to say, e.g. that truth is situated within a triangle or that goodness dwells at such and such a degree of longitude. Sober and dispassionate consideration of mental life compels us to admit that 'the soul', being in one respect somehow

23

connected with the individual body and therefore, through its mediation, indirectly localized, in another respect is by its very nature non-spatial or super-spatial. Accordingly, there are no grounds whatever for concluding that it is shut in within the body. And as to the inner primary reality which lies in an altogether different dimension of being than the world of objects, it would be a mere confusion of thought to place it somewhere in the material universe and conclude that it therefore is limited. When we apprehend that reality as it is in itself, i.e. apprehend it from within, it appears to us—in so far as pictorial images are symbolically and indirectly applicable to it—not as a small, self-contained sphere but rather as a peculiar kind of infinity, as something that recedes into immeasurable fathomless depths. Thus we could picture the inner reality of our self as a kind of subterraneous cavern: there is a small entrance to it from outside, from the external layer of 'objectivity', and inside it is a vast, complex and potentially infinite world. In the words of Heraclitus 'one cannot find the limits of the soul even after treading all its ways—so deep are its foundations.'

There are, however, more subtle ways of maintaining that man is shut in and isolated in his inner life; at the present day this is done, for instance, by Heidegger. Just as modern physicists in speaking of the curvature of space maintain that the world is finite though unlimited, so Heidegger, having discovered the boundless fulness of the peculiar reality present within man's inner being (his *Existenz*), affirms that, nevertheless, it is finite and self-contained. From his point of view, although 'the soul' is an immeasurable universe, it is a universe shut in within itself and abiding forever within its own boundaries; it is 'cast into the world' from outside—a world common to all—and in that sense coexists with all other 'souls', but from within it exists only in and for itself and remains as it were in life-long solitary confinement.

This conception, however, is essentially invalid. Psychologically it is due to a kind of spiritual blindness—a special disease of our time—that destroys the normal, healthy sense of life. In truth, it is precisely at this point that clear insight, undeceived by external appearances and popular theories, discovers the most essential and fundamental feature of the realm of being which, in contradistinction to the world of fact, I have called the primary reality. So far that reality has been identified with the subject's being, with 'my inner life'. But although 'my inner life' revealed to me from within is, so to speak, the nearest and most immediately given stratum of the primary reality, it is by no means the whole of it. That stratum is from its very nature unthinkable except in connection with something else that lies beyond it. In dealing with the world of fact we are used to fix upon separate objects, separate self-subsistent entities (physical or mental)—'substances' as traditional philosophy calls them. From the point of view of common sense this separateness is an irreducible primary characteristic of all self-sufficient, self-contained individual existence. But even a purely scientific analysis of the objective world compels us to modify this conception: the presence of temporal and spatial relations, causal ties, interaction, functional dependence, creative activity etc. implies that existence is inwardly interconnected and has a common background; we have to think of the multiplicity of separate elements as lying within a certain unity that embraces and pervades it. When the usual popular conception of the external world of objects is applied to a totally different realm of primary self-revealing being, closer inspection shows it to be utterly untenable. The point is that this primary reality is from its very nature perpetually transcending itself, going beyond its own limits. The whole significance of such transcendence and the variety of its forms will become apparent later. At present it is only important to note its general character, for it throws light on the range and significance of the reality in question.

The essential meaning of this transcendence is that I cannot have 'my own being' except as a part of being in general, which transcends mine. To be conscious of a limit and to transcend it means in this case one and the same thing. This correlation has already been noted by Descartes when he discovered the primary reality in the subject of thought. In and through being conscious of my self as finite, I know the infinite and have it in me. Descartes rightly pointed out that, although in language the term 'limited' or 'finite' comes first and has a positive meaning, while the 'unlimited' or 'infinite' is derivative and is formed through negation of the first, in truth the very reverse is the case. It is precisely the infinite as 'the fulness of all' that is primary and is positively given, while the conception of the finite is formed through the negation of that fulness. The finite is that which does not contain the fulness and is therefore only a part; the finite is that which has limits, and a limit is a line of demarcation between 'one' and 'the other', i.e. it means division within an all-embracing whole.

25

Colorado Mountain College
West Campus
Glenwood Springs, Colorado 81601

The same co-relation may be expressed in another way. In dealing with the world of fact we are accustomed to regard all negation and distinction implied by it not as a constituent part of the concrete objective content, but as merely a formal instrument of our thought. When we say that a horse is not a ruminating animal or that a whale is not a fish, it seems self-evident that those negative definitions do not concern the actual, positive content of the objects themselves: the 'not's are obviously not something to be seen in the real horse or whale. From the practical point of view this is perfectly true, but that is only because the objects are determined by a differentiation that has already been made; it is, so to speak, *behind* them, and that is the only reason why it is not *in* them: for, clearly, without distinction and differentiation we could have no idea of separate objects at all. On the other hand, the primary, self-revealing reality, not being an object of thought, *has everything within itself.* Its division into parts is its own immanent structure; but that means that it cannot reveal itself to us except as an all-embracing unity; each part of it manifests itself just as a part of the whole which includes it; hence, that which is external to it constitutes its being, no less than that which belongs to it. This correlation has been expressed by Plotinus who interpreted with the insight of genius the primary reality intuitively apprehended through the depths of the spirit: 'Here below (in the sensuous world) no one part could be begotten by any other, for each part has its own individual existence. On the contrary, in the intelligible world every part is born from the whole, and is simultaneously the whole and a part; wherever is a part, the whole reveals itself. . . . Every being contains within itself the entire intelligible world, and also beholds it entire in any particular being. All things there are located everywhere. Everything there is all, and all is each thing.'[1]

Nothing, it seems, could be more 'separate', more self-contained than my own being, that which I call my self. And in a sense this is unquestionably true: the being which I call 'mine' is constituted by having its own special *centre*, and any attempt to deny this (as for instance in the Indian philosophy) obviously contradicts a certain empirically given and therefore incontrovertible fact. And yet when I try to make clear what exactly I mean by my 'self' I can only do so by dividing it off from 'all other being'. That means, I cannot have

[1] Ennead. V 8, 4; III 2, 1 and many other passages. (Quoted from K. S. Guthrie's translation.)

my own being, be conscious of it as 'mine', unless I have—in a different sense, but in as *primary* a way—that 'other' being. I have my being as a part of universal being, i.e. in immediate connection with other being which is not mine. The primary reality given from within by no means coincides with 'my' being, my inner life: it is my life against the background of all-embracing being. Primary reality from its very nature is not limited or determinate in content; on the contrary, it is always given as something infinite and unlimited. It is only against the background of this infinite all-embracing being that my own being stands out as its inalienable part; it is not a self-contained sphere, but as it were a sprouting plant whose roots go deep into the general soil of reality. My inner being or 'soul' is not enclosed from within, not isolated from all else; in the 'inward' direction, the soul does not find any end or barrier that limits it. On the contrary, it expands, passing imperceptibly into that which is no longer itself and merging in it. Although it still remains conscious of the distinction between itself and that which lies beyond it and is other than it, the distinction becomes less clear and definite as the final depths are reached. Thus, (to anticipate for a moment) in mystical experience the soul is aware of God as of a reality into which it flows or which flows into it and lives in it, and at the same time is conscious that this indissoluble unity is a union of two—of itself and of God Who transcends it.

Let us try to express this elusive relation in yet another way. With reference to the world of objects the distinction between 'myself' and that which is external to me, given me from without, is reflected in language in the clear distinction between 'being' and 'having'. I *have* food, clothing, a dwelling place, relatives, friends and the whole of the external world in which I live, but I obviously *am* not that; my own being is made up of the totality of my experiences—of that which takes place in me and enters into the sphere of my 'self'. Now, this clear distinction, based upon the obvious difference between 'outside' and 'within', undergoes an essential transformation and loses its unambiguous and easily definable significance when applied to the primary reality revealed in the depths of the self. It is only to superficial observation that it appears wholly to coincide with my 'self' because I can have access to it through the depths of my personal spirit. Keener insight detects that here too the distinction between what I am and what I have is preserved, but it acquires a more subtle and as it were less obvious

27

meaning, for the spatial categories of 'outside' and 'within' must now be understood in a symbolical and not a literal sense. If, for lack of other terms, we keep the usual words 'to be' and 'to have', we shall have to say that in this case I *am that which I have*, or, in other words, that the verb 'to be' is used here in two senses. In the narrow sense I am 'myself' in contradistinction to that which I have and which lies beyond me; in a wider sense, I also—indirectly—am that which I *have*, i.e. I belong to the sphere of being which I have, for it is of the same nature as my own self. My own existence consists in my belonging to the common ground of all existence; this does not mean that I am dissolved or sunk in that ground, which is, on the contrary, the source of all that is positive in my own existence as an individual; yet, in virtue of my belonging to it, my individuality is not shut in or isolated, but shares in the universal life. While distinguishing 'myself' from what I 'have' (or from what 'has' me), I at the same time possess all that lies beyond me in such wise that it is in me or I am in it. This is precisely what is meant by saying that the basic immanent feature of my inner being is the element of transcendence—i.e. participation in being which lies beyond the confines of my 'self'.

5. Reality as all-embracing fulness and the basis of the world of fact

In order to grasp the primary and essential nature of transcendence, it is useful to note how deeply rooted it is in what I call my 'self'—in other words, to see to what extent my going beyond my 'self', and abiding within it are in the last resort identical.

It is usual to regard the self as something that is purely inward and immediately present in all its fulness in our experience, and to find in this its essential difference from the non-self which is transcendent and only indirectly accessible to us. That view underlies Descartes' idea expressed in the formula *cogito ergo sum* and, in general, of the conviction that the standpoint of subjective idealism is self-evident and that the truth of realism is hard to prove. But however paradoxical it may at first sight appear, the view in question is a mere illusion. That which we call the self—the subject's being-for-itself—is, strictly speaking, not purely immanent, i.e. is not actually present in experience in all its fulness. We mean by the self a time-embracing wholeness of personality—a bearer of reality which abides throughout the temporal span of our life including the past, the present and the future; the self is unthinkable except as a unity bridging over the stream of time that flows from the past through the present into the future. But in all that stream only the present moment is the truly immanent, actually present reality; the past and the future are not given—they are both absent and lie beyond experience. If we limit ourselves to the truly immanent, self-given reality, the present moment will be the only thing left us. 'Momentism' and not subjective idealism or even solipsism should be our creed. But this is obviously a *reductio ad absurdum* of this whole train of thought; the present moment is only an ideal line of demarcation between the past and the future and is unthinkable apart from its connection with both. The present moment, as a dividing line between that which is no longer and that which is not yet, could not itself *be*, if the past and the future were wholly excluded from our thought; it would then remain a mere negation and we should be reduced to the obvious absurdity of maintaining that 'nothing is'.

Hence it is clear that the alleged immanence of the self is constituted by the element of transcendence—of extending into the past and the future, of directly possessing that which lies beyond the confines of actual experience. In saying 'I am' I transcend the limits of actual, immediately present existence: I *am* only because I *have* something beyond the actual being of the moment; I cannot even say 'beyond *my* actual being' for unless I had something distinct from myself, I would not be myself and therefore could not call anything 'mine'.

But if that be so, if 'myself' and 'mine' are in the first instance constituted by the fact of transcendence, no priority attaches to the self as compared with the not-self; subjective idealism cannot substantiate its claim to be more self-evident than realism. Let us re-state our argument once more. The minimum of truly immanent being—that which we have at the present moment—cannot be defined as 'my idea' or 'my presentation' for, as just pointed out, the very meaning of 'myself' and 'mine' disappears if the past and the future are left out of account. That minimum would be quite different from the subject's being; it would be something neutral, and our truly immanent starting point would be not '*cogito ergo sum*' but '*aliquid (hic et nunc) est*'. That *aliquid* would be neither subjective nor objective, but perfectly neutral being in general without any specific determinations. But since a moment is thinkable only as the dividing line between the past and the future, i.e. as indissolubly connected with them, that past and future could not be 'mine' but would be past and future in general—the boundless, all-embracing fulness of time. Just as immediately as I have my own being in my past and future, I have also the all-embracing fulness of being in general. In both cases—in both dimensions of being—that which is absent from the immanent experience and lies beyond its confines proves to be directly possessed by me, as self-evidently as the 'immanent'. That was first pointed out by Parmenides: 'behold how securely the absent is present to the mind.'

The transcendence which constitutes the self or self-consciousness is from its very nature unlimited and knows no bounds. While constituting the being of my 'self' it also—in another dimension—binds it indissolubly to the 'not self'. To have self-consciousness, to be aware of oneself as 'I' means to be conscious of oneself as participating in the infinite, all-embracing being which transcends me. 'To be' means to form part of all-embracing being, to be rooted in it. 'I am' and 'something else is', *sum* and *est*, the being of the subject and the being of the object—are indissolubly interconnected, for both flow simultaneously from the primary reality of the pure *esse* or *ens*. That primary reality is not '*in* me' and not '*outside* me', or, rather, it is both together, both in me and outside me—because *I myself am in it*. It is the all-embracing and all-pervading unity of being in general, participation in which constitutes all particular entities both in the form *sum* (subjective being, being for oneself) and in the form *est* (objective being—for me).

This, by the way, provides the solution of the fundamental riddle of epistemology that has tormented human thought from the time of Descartes and Locke, or indeed from the time of the Greek Sceptics. The sting of it is not what it is generally supposed to be. Its usual formulation 'how do I know that my presentations reflect a reality external to me?' is based upon a preconceived idea of consciousness as a closed-in sphere and expresses perplexity as to how the human mind can get at things outside it. Once this false assumption is given up, and consciousness is seen to be somewhat like a light sending forth its rays on to what lies beyond it,[1] the riddle is disposed of: the knower has the content of knowledge not within him but before him, and that which he sees is not he himself, but a reality external to him.

[1] That position is established in Lossky's intuitivism and in the English critical realism of Hobhouse, Moore, Alexander and others.

Such a solution, however, presupposes the existence of an objective reality, which is not merely external to me, but independent of me: objectivity belongs to that which is there when I do not apprehend it, and when my consciousness is not directed upon it at all. But how do I know this? and how is such an idea possible? If 'to know' means to perceive, see, apprehend by means of consciousness directed upon an object—or, in other words, if 'to be' means to reveal itself to the cognizing mind, the idea presupposes an impossibility: in order to know that something is there when I do not perceive it, one ought to have some magic faculty of seeing without looking. Tolstoy tells how in his youth he was tortured by the doubt whether in man's absence or behind his back, things behave in the same way as they do in his presence; he wondered if they led a secret life of their own when they were not looked at, and he tried to catch them so to speak, in the act, by turning round suddenly; but obviously that was useless, for as soon as he looked they at once assumed their usual appearance. How do I know for instance that what is behind me goes on existing when I do not see it? Whence comes our certitude that objective reality is the coherent, regular, stable whole which we never see as such—for what we do actually see are only separate, disconnected parts of it, changing with every change in our field of vision? It would be easy to show—and Hume has shown it already—that by no indirect reasoning can we reach the idea of an objective reality independent of us, for all our inferences presuppose it and are based upon it. If the world of fact were primary, self-subsistent and irreducible to anything else and we had no other connection with it than the cognitive gaze directed upon it, the existence of a coherent world could not be proved or indeed entertained at all.

We have, however, another connection with it—not through the mediation of the cognitive process directed upon it from without, but directly and immediately, through co-belonging to the all-embracing and all-pervading oneness of the primary reality. Since from the very beginning I have my own inner being as part and parcel of the all-embracing general being, I know 'at first-hand' things which I am not perceiving and which lie beyond the spatial and temporal limits of perception. I do not know what exactly is there when I am not seeing it, but I know for certain that something is there unknown to me. I possess with absolute certitude that which is not given to me, not revealed to me in perceptual experience. The very possibility of the world of objects existing independently of me (i.e. of my cognitive gaze) is conditioned by our co-belonging to the all-embracing primary reality which interpenetrates my own being and constitutes its essence. I am connected with that objective world as it were by a subterranean stratum of the primary reality. It is only in virtue of this fundamental ontological bond that our derivative, cognitive relation to the world of external objects is possible.[1]

It is easy to see why primary reality exercises a unifying function which alone enables the knowing subject to come into touch with the object, or to know that the object apprehended exists independently of him. The reason is *the supertemporal oneness* of reality. If existence in time were the only form of being accessible to us, we could have no guarantee that anything existed when we were not perceiving it, or that it outlived the act of perception; and this implies that we could have no conception of objective existence. We have it only because we know that all temporal existence, both our own and external to us, has for its background the all-embracing supertemporal unity of being. In virtue of it the idea of emptiness or non-being in the absolute sense becomes impossible; beyond the confines of anything that our cognitive gaze may reach at any given moment there eternally *is* the fulness of positive being. Hence, if any particular content disappears, this can only mean that it has been replaced by some other positive content.

That which confronts us as the world of objects is itself subject to time, exists in time, consists of temporal processes. We contemplate it against the background of a supertemporal unity—apart from which, as already said, the very conception of objective existence would be impossible—but this supertemporal aspect is rooted in primary reality, which, so to speak, bestows it upon the world of objects. This is only another way of saying that beyond the confines of the temporal world there is ideal being which is supertemporal, is once for all, independently of whether it is found in the empirical world and, if so, of when and where it is found in it. As already pointed out, in ideal being thought and the content of thought coincide; in other words, ideal being is the real unity which connects the subject with the object.

Ideal being is not merely the self-subsistent being of abstract

[1] The argument briefly indicated here is expounded fully in my book *La connaissance et l'être* (Paris 1937, Fernand Aubier, Editions Montaigne).

non-temporal contents or a separate 'world of ideas': it is only thinkable as forming part of all-embracing consciousness or thought. Supertemporal oneness is not an abstraction or an impersonal and lifeless store-house of contents that enter the world of fact; it is the concrete fulness of living reality, the unity between the subject and the object of thought—the living source that gives rise both to our self and to all that confronts it as the 'not-self'. It is precisely in this aspect that reality forms an inseverable bond between my 'self' and the external world. As the unity between the subject and the object, the knower and the known—a unity that transcends them both—reality reveals to us the primary meaning of *being*. Reality is the primary general element which bestows being and objectivity upon every content included in and belonging to it. Objectivity (in the broad sense) means being rooted in reality. On the other hand, the self as the subject of knowledge is merely a particular manifestation of that aspect of the all-embracing reality in which it knows itself—a particular manifestation as it were of a universal 'all-seeing eye'.

The foregoing clearly shows the falsity of the idea that lies at the basis of all forms of individualism (e.g. of Heidegger's existentialism)—the idea, namely, that primary reality coincides with the closed-in and finite sphere of 'one's own' inner life or *Existenz*, peculiar to each individual. Equally false is the contention, based on a similar assumption, that reality must not be sought on the path of withdrawing into the depths of the self, since on that path we forsake the objective world common to and binding upon all, and hide in the shell of individual 'inner life'. The individualistic standpoint rivals in absurdity the contention that 'to stand on one's own feet' means to have in one's feet the ground upon which one stands. Just as 'standing on one's feet' means resting against the ground external to us, so 'having inner being' means finding, through it, support in the primary reality which transcends mere inner being as such and connects it from within with all that is. To be aware of oneself as a reality distinct from the external world of fact is to be aware of being inwardly and directly rooted in the all-embracing primary reality.

The inward path is not an escape from the common objective world into the closed-in sphere of subjectivity. The very reverse is the case. Only through penetrating into the primary reality do we find our true inner bond with the objective world. The path inwards, into oneself, leads not to a kind of dark enclosure, but on the contrary brings us out into the boundless expanse of universal being. One might compare it with going down into the Underground for the sake of reaching as directly and as quickly as possible the most distant parts of a huge city. The analogy breaks down because the only purpose of the Underground is to hasten and simplify our connection with the distant parts of the town surface, while penetration into primary reality, besides serving the utilitarian and derivative purpose of connecting us with the whole expanse of the objective world, has a prior, intrinsic and infinitely greater value for us: it reveals our connection with the transcendent basis of being. It thus infinitely widens our spiritual horizon and frees us from the illusion of being totally subject to the world of objects as to an omnipotent and overwhelming *fait accompli*. The inner bond with primary reality frees us from the power of this world and enables us to take a creative part in it.

What has been said gives a preliminary explanation of the essential duality of human existence, due to its connection both with the world of fact and with the primary reality.

Through his body and carnal life, and the external layer of his mind determined by its connection with the body, man in himself forms part—a subordinate and insignificant part—of the objective world. He is born in and from it, and dwells in it; he is partly formed by heredity, upbringing, environment and all the processes and events in that world, and is partly engaged in building it up and changing it. Through his depths—through the kernel or root of his being, and in that sense through his true essence—he belongs to the transcendent primary reality (in which, as we have seen, the 'objective world' too has its root and source). Man thus has a dual nature, and every theory of life which fails to take account of both aspects of his being is bound to be inadequate. But this duality is not merely coexistence, or opposition between two heterogeneous principles. It is based upon an essential unity and is interpenetrated by it. Man is not simply dual, but is a bi-unity. The two natures coexisting in him and opposed to one another are intimately interconnected and to a certain extent in harmony; this must be taken into account as much as the duality. Man's participation in the world of fact, directly determined by his 'carnal' psycho-physical nature, is at the same time rooted in his spiritual, transcendent life; hence, the part we play in the world is, or at any rate may be, under the control and guidance of the spirit and express our transcendental essence. The structure of our being is complex and antinomic, and all artificial simplication distorts it. To avoid this, we must now expound more fully the peculiar nature of primary reality as the innermost core of being.

CHAPTER II

Reality and the Knowledge of it

*

1. Knowledge of reality as concrete description and as docta ignorantia

The considerations put forward in the preceding chapter should have convinced the reader that in addition to the world of fact there is something which truly *is*—not less, but rather more truly than the world of fact—and which, in contradistinction to it, I call 'reality'. It immediately reveals itself to us in the first instance as our inner spiritual life; and at the same time it inevitably transcends the purely inner, personal world of the self, uniting it from within to that which lies beyond it and constitutes the all-embracing and all-pervading unity and basis of all that is.

But how are we to define more closely the meaning of 'reality'? And is it possible to define it as we define any other idea?

At first sight this seems to be an impossible and objectless task. All description and definition, all logical analysis presuppose a certain multiplicity and consist in breaking it up, in discriminating one part from another and discovering the relations between them. Something that is absolutely primary, simple, and at the same time all-embracing, may be experienced, but cannot possibly be described, expressed in words or defined; we may know *it*, but we cannot know anything *about it*—beyond the very fact that it is given us, is present, *is*. This appears to be the nature of that which has been designated by the term 'reality'. Just as we know perfectly well what we mean by our own existence—know it incomparably better and more intimately than anything else—and yet are unable to express it in words or to describe the content of it, so, having attained in our inner experience insight into 'reality' in its general, all-embracing sense, we know what this basis and background of our own being is, and yet are

36

unable to express or define this knowledge or to analyse its content. From the nature of the case it would appear to be a kind of mute, inexpressible knowledge. In so far as to understand, to fathom, means to express by means of notions, i.e. to establish differences and interconnections between things, to explain one thing by reference to its relation to something else—'reality' is essentially the same as 'the unfathomable'.[1] It is clear from what has just been said that 'the unfathomable' does not mean 'the unknown', the 'hidden', 'the unfamiliar'. On the contrary, it is perfectly manifest, and is only mysterious in so far as it is inexplicable, irreducible to anything else, and inaccessible to logical analysis. It is what Goethe called 'an open mystery' (*offenes Geheimnis*). The field of consciousness or experience is wider than that of thought; thought helps us to disentangle its multifarious contents, but does not extend to that ultimate datum which is both the primary basis and the general essence of all that we experience.

The position may be expressed in another way. We have *something* in view and discriminate something in it, or assert something about it; logically this is the distinction between the subject and the predicate of a judgment; it is precisely this duality between reality itself and the content of it that imparts to our knowledge the character of judgment, i.e. of an assertion of something about something else.[2] This seems to imply that it would be a logical contradiction to try and 'know' or 'understand' or 'explain' reality itself, the subject, in its categorial distinction from the predicate. For 'to know' and 'to understand' means to discriminate 'contents' inherent in reality, to discover the properties which it possesses or of which it is the bearer. An attempt to know in that sense reality as such, its actual essence, in contradistinction to the contents inherent in it, seems to be essentially mistaken, since it contains a *contradictio in adjecto*.

At first sight this argument appears perfectly convincing. But whatever truth there may be in it, such a negative attitude does not lead anywhere and indeed causes us to lose sight of the most essential aspect of the idea of reality, or else involves us in a hopeless contradiction.

As already pointed out (Chapter I, 4) reality in so far as it is an all-embracing unity contains every negation within it, for the simple reason that there can be nothing outside it. The element of negation

[1] See my book *The Unfathomable* (in Russian), Paris 1938.
[2] See my book *La connaissance et l'être*, Paris 1937, ch. 1.

merely expresses its inner discreteness. But if this be so, in distinguishing reality from all its rationally determinable contents and
opposing it to them as something purely irrational and therefore
undefinable, we actually apply to it the very category of logical
discrimination which is inapplicable to it. We thus fall into a peculiar
contradiction between the form and the content of our statement:
in asserting that reality is undefinable and unfathomable we sharply
and univocally distinguish it from all else, and thereby define it in
the same way as we define anything else. By logically distinguishing
the all-embracing unity from everything particular, i.e. by excluding
everything particular from it, we transform it, too, into something
particular and deprive it of its all-embracing character. We replace
the concrete all-embracing unity by an abstract unity exclusive of
multiplicity. To use St. Augustine's apt phrase we are thus entangled
in a hopeless and fatal 'struggle between words' (*pugna verborum*).

Augustine uses this expression with reference to the idea of God's
unfathomableness. In acknowledging God to be 'unfathomable' we
define Him, ascribe to Him a certain definite quality, i.e. diminish His fulness which transcends reason, and substitute for His
trans-rational reality a logically definite, though negative, concept.
It will be helpful in this connection to consider the main contentions
of the so called 'negative theology', taking it, of course, on its purely
logical side in so far as it is relevant to the subject under discussion;
at the present stage of our inquiry we have nothing to do with
theology as such, and have not yet dealt with the idea of God at all.

'Negative theology', dating back to the unknown Christian
mystic designated by the name of Dionysius the Areopagite,
teaches that we reach an understanding of God, or approach Him,
only through *denying* to Him all the qualities known to us from our
experience of the created world. And since all our ideas are derived
from that experience, we can have no positive definitions of the
nature of God. We do not know and cannot say what God is; we
only know what He is not. We only know that He is absolutely
heterogeneous to all that we know from our experience of created
being. We have no right to apply to God any spatial or sensuously
concrete ideas, or, indeed, even such spiritual and abstract categories
as 'mercy' or 'being' etc., for all these concepts as generally used
are burdened with implications applicable to earthly, created existence and are therefore inadequate to express God's transcendent
nature.

38

But what, exactly, is meant by saying that we only know what God is not, and do not know what He is? In our usual, logically-informed knowledge negation implies distinction (in addition to its didactically-psychological significance of rejecting false opinions). We cognize or define something by distinguishing it from something else. Affirmative and negative judgments are merely different logical forms, correlative aspects of knowledge as determination, i.e. as awareness of something definite. Hence it follows that negation in its ordinary logical sense of distinction is only possible with respect to separate, particular contents, for it implies selection between them. In that case, what can be the meaning of the negative theology's demand to deny *all* known or thinkable characteristics with regard to God? If negation be taken in its ordinary logical sense, it must be said that to deny to some object all possible and conceivable characteristics is to deprive it of all content: to deny *all*, simply means to assert nothing. On such an interpretation, negative theology would be tantamount to absolute agnosticism with regard to God – it would be simply reduced to the assertion that we cannot know anything whatever about Him.

Of course, in fact 'negative theology' has something utterly different in view. Its adherents are not dry pedants who 'define' the nature of God through the logical function of negation, and they are anything but agnostics. They have a special, inexpressible, *positive* vision of God, and in saying that God is different from all else, they only want to bring out the truth that their vision is inexpressible. If, however, we attempt to express its positive content in abstract logical form, we shall have to say that to deny with reference to God all positive characteristics simply means to deny them as particular and derivative determinations. God is neither *this* nor *that* because He is everything at once and is the primary source of all. But that means that the logical form in and through which we know everything particular, singular, derivative is, as such, inapplicable to God. 'Negative theology' is guided by the intuition that the nature of God as the first source and primary basis of being is super-logical and super-rational, and for that very reason eludes all logical determinations which have meaning only with reference to particular and derivative forms of being. All positive characteristics are denied in order to convey the *categorial* difference between God and all that we meet in earthly experience.

The most obvious and historically the most important result of this view is the apprehension of the Divine reality as absolutely transcendent and detached from all accessible 'earthly' reality. The mind is plunged into some completely new, unknown dimension of being and recedes into dark depths which lead infinitely far from the familiar 'earthly' world. There is no need to consider here the usual practical consequence of this religious attitude—the boundless and immeasurable spiritual detachment, somewhat reminiscent of the Hindu religion; it is only its general logical aspect that is of moment to us.

It is perfectly obvious that there is a certain amount of truth in refusing to apply to God the logical form in which we think of all other contents of being. But the precise meaning of such refusal must be made clear if we are to avoid a contradiction which has already been mentioned and may be formulated as follows. Negation as such conditions the logical form of knowledge (since negation is a means of determining one particular content in contra-distinction to all others). If we apply negation to the logical form itself we are involved in the contradiction of using that form in the very act of denying it.

In so far as we attempt to cognise the nature of God solely through its *negative* relation to all earthly experience and logical form, we inevitably subordinate it to that form and make it into something limited, exclusive and particular. For negation as such, whatever it may be applied to, is precisely the form of rational 'earthly' knowledge.

Accordingly, in order to apprehend the truly transcendent and absolutely unique nature of God, simple negation in its customary logical sense is useless: the categories of earthly existence must be overcome in a special, *super-logical* way. This can only be done by going beyond the law of contradiction, i.e. of the incompatibility of the affirmative and the negative judgments. Only thus can we really rise above everything particular, 'earthly' and subordinate; only by embracing and including it can we reach the sphere that lies above it.

The founder of negative theology understood this very well. The true import of his 'mystical theology' was not mere negation of earthly conceptions as applied to God, but a certain unity or combination of affirmation and negation, transcending the habitual logical forms of thought. Although no positive determinations in their usual sense are applicable to God, they are applicable to Him in a different, metaphorical sense. It cannot be said, for instance, that God is 'good' in the sense of possessing this quality as something that determines His nature, but at the same time it can and must be said that, being the source of goodness, He is 'surpassing good'; He cannot be called existent in the usual, 'created' sense of existence, but as the source of all existence He must be recognized as 'surpassingly' existent. 'It should not be thought that here negation contradicts affirmation, for the first cause, rising above all limitations, transcends all affirmations and all negations'.[1]

Let us apply now this consideration to the general problem of reality. In what exact sense must we pronounce it to be 'unfathomable' and what follows from this definition rightly understood?

Reality is unknowable in so far as we mean by knowledge immediate apprehension of the nature of an object knowable in a *conceptual* form. For reality is essentially different from any particular content apprehended through concepts; its nature lies precisely in its complete, self-contained and self-sufficient concreteness, as opposed to any abstract content in which the object of thought is determined as something particular by distinguishing it from all else and discriminating its relation to that 'else'. But in saying that reality is other than the content of a notion we must guard against taking the idea of otherness in its usual logical sense; or we would fall into the contradiction already mentioned and transform reality into a specific *notion*, i.e. into an abstract particular content (which is to be found wherever one thing is logically distinguished from another).

But how is it possible to have something in mind except as a definite particular content, i.e. as an abstract notion? The argument of the preceding chapter started with the admission that our experience is wider than our thought. This of course is indisputable, and in virtue of it we can come into touch with that which eludes the conceptual form. But must such experience remain dumb and inexpressible, and therefore unconscious and utterly inaccessible to thought? There is at least one actual testimony to the contrary—namely, art, and in particular poetry as the art of the word. Poetry is a mysterious way of expressing things that cannot be put in an abstract logical form. It expresses a certain concrete reality without breaking it up into a system of abstract notions, but taking it as it

[1] *Mystical Theology*, I, 2.

actually is, in all its concreteness. This is possible because the purpose of words is not limited to their function of designating concepts: words are also the means of spiritually mastering and imparting meaning to experience in its actual, super-logical nature. The existence of poetry shows that experience is not doomed to remain dumb and incomprehensible, but has a specific form of expression, i.e., of being 'understood' just in that aspect of it which transcends abstract thought.

This would seem to imply that to express reality in its concreteness, i.e. as distinct from concepts, must be the work of poetry alone and that philosophy, being purely intellectual, must give up the task as obviously beyond its powers. A closer consideration of the problem leads, however, to quite a different conclusion. If poetry is the highest and most perfect way of using the super-rational, immediately 'expressive' function of words, this means—as linguists have observed long ago—that all speech to a certain extent partakes, or can partake, of the nature of poetry, and that the difference between poetry and prose is not absolute, but relative. All that we call 'expressiveness' in speech is the poetical element in it. True, poetry in the narrow and specific sense of the term utilizes the expressive power of the purely irrational aspect of words—of the involuntary associations of ideas, images, emotions connected with the nuances of meaning and even with the actual auditory texture of words, so to speak, with their 'aura'. But poetry also includes another aspect of expressiveness, accessible to prose as well: thoughts and concepts expressed by words are in poetry so combined that their purely rational, abstract meaning is transcended and they convey concrete reality precisely in so far as it rises above concepts and differs from them in principle. This is the meaning of what may be called *description* of concrete reality[1] in contradistinction to the logical analysis of it. Accordingly, such description is possible for philosophy as well.

In addition to the general method of describing the super-logical

---

[1] This has been aptly expressed by one of the greatest literary artists of the nineteenth century—Leo Tolstoy: 'In all that I wrote I have been guided by the need to put together thoughts inwardly interconnected for the sake of self-expression, but every thought, separately expressed in words is terribly lowered when taken by itself, apart from the particular conjunction in which it is found. And the conjunction is made not by thought, but by something else, and to express the ground of that conjunction directly in words is impossible.' *Tolstoy's Letters*, coll. by P. Sergeyenko, vol. I, 1910, p. 118.

nature of reality by such a combination of words and ideas as gives a tacit, conceptually inexpressible knowledge of it, philosophy has its own special way of transcending the limitations and inadequacy of abstract knowledge. By directing our thought upon its logical form, i.e. by considering the form, extent and conditions of logical rational knowledge as a whole, we can learn its limitations. In doing so, we use the power of abstract logical knowledge as it were *against* it, i.e. against its tendency to impoverish and distort reality—we use it as an antidote against itself, on the homeopathic principle *similia similibus curantur*. Observing the limited nature of abstract knowledge we indirectly apprehend, by contrast with it, the unique character of that which lies outside its range—namely of reality itself. Thus—to take an example that goes to the root of the matter— in giving an abstract explanation of the principle of definition through logical distinction and contraposition, we transcend that principle in and through understanding its conditions—that is, we transcend the confines of abstract knowledge, and in doing so indirectly apprehend the concrete reality that lies beyond it. (This is the positive significance of applying the principle of negation to the logical form of knowledge itself). But the perceived contrast between reality and the sphere of rational knowledge will then no longer be a *logical* relation, i.e. will not be negation in the logical sense constitutive of the world of concepts only. The contrast will be super-logical. We will thus obtain indirect knowledge by means of *ignorance*, that is, by means of contrasting reality with the domain of the logically knowable. This is the form of knowledge described by Nicolas of Cusa, the main representative of this line of thought, as *docta ignorantia*—'wise ignorance'.

Thus concrete experience of reality is not doomed to remain 'dumb' and inexpressible. It is intellectually attained through 'description', i.e. a combination of concepts which, taken together, suggest what reality is; and it can be indirectly expressed through a form of thought which may be described as transcendental thinking. In it thought is directed upon itself and recognizes the general formal nature of the domain of particular, logically definable contents, and in doing so it transcends that domain and gains insight into the actual essence of reality which lies beyond it.

True philosophy, i.e. intellectual apprehension of the whole as such, is in the first instance rational knowledge, i.e. it finds expression in notions like all other knowledge. But in so far as it aims at describing reality and recognizes the limitations of the logical aspect of knowledge, it can transcend abstract thought and intuitively apprehend and express the super-rational. In contradistinction to all particular knowledge directed upon abstractly-differentiated particular elements of being, *philosophy is the rational transcendence of the limitations of rational thought.* It is intellectual life nurtured by the living intuition of super-rational reality and conscious of its directly inapprehensible nature.

This indirect knowledge, or knowledge through ignorance, is not confined to the mere general awareness of the super-rational nature of reality. By contrast with the multiplicity of elements that constitute the domain of rational knowledge, we can grasp and indirectly determine the multiplicity in the structure of reality itself; and the manifestations of that multiplicity can be elucidated by concrete intellectual description.

I pass now to consider in greater detail the nature of 'wise ignorance' or transcendental thought. The subject requires a special mental effort on our part, for we must go beyond the so-called 'common sense' and our habitual ways of thinking. This may be unacceptable both to lazy minds used to a routine determined by the practical needs of everyday life, and to un-introspective scientific thought, working with simple and clear abstract definitions and distinctions; but we must have the courage to say, at the risk of incurring ridicule, that philosophy, as distinct from positive knowledge, *only begins where 'common sense' ends.* Sound philosophy, i.e. philosophy adequate to its subject, must inevitably go beyond what is usually called 'sound sense'. Accordingly, our exposition will make demands on the reader's patience.

2. *Reality as the unity of opposites and a concrete unity of multiplicity*

Our starting point, suggested by the whole of the foregoing argument, is the general distinction between reality and every concrete particular content. The latter is, as we have seen, constituted by its negative relation to other contents. Every separate definite entity is a certain 'this', and the property of being 'this' is determined by being different from 'the other'; the general formal nature of every 'this' consists in its being 'this and not something else', and is unthinkable apart from this negative relation. In the language of formal logic determinateness is constituted by the law of contradiction.[1] Therefore, having established the difference in principle between reality and all logically determined contents, the first and most general assertion we can make about reality is that it is *not* anything determinable as 'this and not that'. Reality is not something (logically) determined, because it is an all-embracing, superlogical unity; everything that may be said to be 'other than' some particular logically determined content, or to lie beyond it, is within reality or is included in it; in this sense, reality as having everything within itself can only be defined as 'this and the other'. Obviously, however, we cannot rest content with such an assertion or regard it as an exhaustive definition of reality. As already pointed out, in *contrasting* reality with particular, logically determined contents, we inevitably limit it, artificially transforming it, too, into a particular content; and at the same time, we deprive reality of all definite meaning, making it utterly formless and void: a limitless and indefinite 'all' is nothing. Our argument would be completely meaningless if the word 'reality' did not, after all, denote something definite. Thus what we understand by reality must both transcend everything logically determined and yet be something determinate (obviously in some other, superlogical sense). If the peculiar nature of reality consists in always being 'this and the other', that constitutes its *uniqueness* which distinguishes it from all else and in virtue of which it itself is—on a different plane of being or in some different form—'this' and not the 'other'. Thus when expressed in a logical form, our apprehension of reality in its unique, super-logical nature necessarily acquires an antinomic character, involving a 'coincidence of opposites'. It is, precisely, in this that *docta ignorantia* consists. We must say 'coincidence' and not mere coexistence of opposites. Mere coexistence of different and opposed determinations is a familiar characteristic of all multiplicity, in so far as we subsume it under a unity external to it. But reality must be conceived as a certain primary unity, and therefore the opposites included in it coincide.

This argument is not an artificial device of abstract thought, repugnant to our legitimate striving for clear, simple and concrete thinking. It is only by means of such seemingly exaggerated and

---

[1] It would be more correct to say: determinateness is constituted by the fact that the law of identity (A is A) is unthinkable apart from its connection with the law of contradiction (A is not non-A) and the law of excluded middle (A must be either A or non-A). This is discussed more fully in my book *La connaissance et l'être*, ch. VI. Here those details can be omitted.

unnatural intellectual subtlety that we attain to true concrete thinking and get over the inevitable inadequacy of the abstract approach
to the subject.

In other words, it obviously follows from the foregoing that we
can truly apprehend the reality we are in search of only by embracing
it in one intellectual gaze in its two contrary aspects at once: both
as distinct from all particular determinate contents and as including
and interpenetrating them. It is precisely in this duality that the true
uniqueness, the super-logical character of reality consists. On the
one hand reality manifests itself as the inexpressible *remainder*,
the something absolutely simple which remains after the subtraction
of all particular contents, all the variegated multiplicity of the positive qualitative determinations of being; on the other hand the concrete essence of that which we apprehend as such a remainder is
not anything separate, not anything thinkable apart from all particular contents; it is the bearer of those contents, it possesses them, i.e.
embraces and interpenetrates them, and in that sense they co-belong
to it. These two different meanings of reality are two indissolubly
interconnected aspects of it, and their combination—a contradictory
combination from the abstractly logical point of view—manifests
the indivisibly single, truly concrete oneness of reality as such.

That which I call reality is obviously closely akin to what is known
in philosophy as the 'absolute' (as distinct from the relative). It
has been pointed out long ago that the idea of the absolute involves a
peculiar dialectic of its own: being 'other than' the relative, it cannot
have the relative outside itself, for then it would no longer be
absolute or all-embracing, but would merely be a particular alongside of the other, 'relative' half of reality. To be truly absolute, the
absolute must include its contrary: only as the unity of itself and the
relative is it truly absolute. On the one hand the absolute is the
'detached' (this is the literal sense of the word *ab-solutum*), i.e. it is
in principle qualitatively different from everything relative, but it
can be such only through including everything relative within itself.
Its peculiarity and uniqueness lies precisely in its being a concretely
all-embracing and all-pervading whole. The same antinomic bi-
unity constitutes the nature of reality.

This circumstance makes abundantly clear that the two permanent
tendencies of human thought, mutually opposed and yet formally
akin, are equally fruitless and mistaken. One of them finds expression in what may be called *rational metaphysics*, or 'dogmatic meta-

physics' as Kant described it. Rational metaphysics is an attempt to penetrate into the inmost core of being, to solve the riddle of existence and *logically* to define the inner, self-subsistent qualitative content of reality in its contradistinction to all that is empirically given and forms the external, visible picture of being. Human thought fancies that it discovers this hidden, detached 'inmost essence' by defining it now as matter, now as spirit or soul or as the duality of both, now as idea, as will, and so on. But whatever all these theories may regard as the true essence of reality, they are at one in trying logically to define and analyse it as something determinate.

The opposite tendency is exemplified in *positivism*. It is characteristic of positivism to deny that reality is something *sui generis*, different from the empirical multiplicity of events. Reality is simply identified with all the particular contents of being taken as a whole— i.e., according to my terminology, with the world of fact. This point of view is favoured by most scientists in so far as they try to philosophize, but it is also adopted in some purely philosophical speculations. Reality becomes as it were dissolved, loses all independence and ceases to be a special plane of being.

Agnosticism or phenomenalism occupies a middle place between these two tendencies. It admits that reality has a special nature of its own, but takes it to be unknowable, thus removing it from the field of philosophical thought. For the purposes of the present argument this intermediary position need not be considered.

In opposition to those two lines of thought which, though natural enough, unduly simplify the truth and therefore distort it, it is possible, on the strength of the foregoing reasoning, to recognize the truly concrete essence of reality as such and to formulate its unique character in quite a different way. It should not be either opposed to the particular, empirical determinations or isolated from them, or have some special, logically determinable qualitative content ascribed to it; there can be no question of defining it qualitatively, since, being everything, or the ground of everything, it cannot be anything particular and have a special qualitative content.[1] But at the same time it must not be merged

---

[1] It would not be difficult to show that all attempts to give an exact qualitative definition of the absolute or reality—all the abstract philosophical *isms*: materialism, spiritualism, voluntarism etc.—appear to attain their end only by unconsciously and illegitimately extending the notions of 'matter', 'spirit', 'will', etc. *beyond* their usual significance in virtue of which they designate something

with the empirical world and identified with simple external unity or the whole of its particular contents. We apprehend its uniqueness only through 'wise ignorance', *docta ignorantia*, i.e. through perceiving that it is different *in kind* from all particular positive contents of knowledge. And that means, we cognize it through detecting in it the antinomic unity of identity and difference, fulness and abstractness, which constitutes its super-logical (and therefore logically undefinable) being. If we try to reduce this super-logical correlation to its simplest abstractly-symbolical form—in so far as this is at all possible—designating reality as A, and all the rest, i.e. all its particular contents as B, we shall have to say that $A = A + B$, however paradoxical this may appear from the point of view of our usual, logically-mathematical thought (it is analogous, however, to the long-established mathematical truth that in the infinite a whole may be equal to a part). Another way of formulating the same relation is to say that reality is always greater than itself in whatever manner we may try to define it. It is detached, absolutely unique, heterogeneous to everything else, and yet it embraces and interpenetrates all that is. Being an all-embracing whole, it is more than that whole, for it has its own inner nature, distinct from all the rest. This is, at bottom, only another way of saying that, as already pointed out in chapter one, the element of transcendence, of going beyond itself is inherent in reality as such.

One of the most essential consequences of this is that reality does not exclude anything, does not make anything impossible (except the idea of absolute isolation and self-containedness of the particular). In the history of human thought some attempts to determine reality or the absolute in an abstractly-logical, unnatural way as an all-embracing unity have led to the conception of reality as a principle which engulfs all multiplicity and everything individual. Such e.g. was the system of Parmenides who denied the reality of multiplicity and change, and such to a large extent was Spinoza's system. Nietzsche aptly called Parmenides 'iron' in contradistinction to the 'fiery' Heraclitus. In preceding pages reality has been compared to the firm ground upon which we stand and in which we are rooted. This analogy is useful, but if taken literally it becomes thoroughly misleading. If we were completely plunged into a ground which

definite, in other words, something particular, constituted by its difference from everything else. That which claims to be the only all-embracing basis of everything in general *ipso facto* ceases to be anything determinate.

48

surrounded and interpenetrated us, we should be buried and dissolved in it, losing our individual being. The analogy of atmosphere is more appropriate. The atmosphere in which we are submerged, which surrounds and interpenetrates us is a lifegiving principle—an element through which we maintain our individual existence and the freedom of independent life. But this analogy too—as indeed every analogy—is inadequate: a living individual organism as such is something utterly different from the surrounding atmosphere; and if 'air' were the only reality, individual being would be just as unthinkable as if everything were solid 'iron'. The point is that no images taken from the material spatial world consisting of *partes extra partes* can, from the nature of the case, be adequate to the superlogical nature of reality. Even if such images are not taken as a basis for abstract logical thought, they certainly serve as its psychological starting point and lead the mind along the path of logical fixation. The superlogical nature of reality is better brought out by images borrowed from the realm of mental life. The all-embracing and all-pervading unity of personal self-consciousness does not make our mental life a homogeneous and immovable unity, does not destroy the multiplicity and changeability of its separate contents or even the inner opposition between them—on the contrary, it is the necessary general condition of their existence; in the same way the superlogical unity of reality is the principle that gives rise to the multiplicity of all particular and individual entities, to their living mobility and true independence. Reality is not an extensive whole which unites everything from outside only, but a unity which so interpenetrates its parts from within that it is, to a greater or lesser extent, present as a whole, i.e. in its true nature, in every one of them. It is on the basis of reality as such that everything particular and individual acquires a reality of its own. For to have a reality of one's own means precisely to participate—more or less—in reality as such, i.e. to share in its primary, self-contained and self-subsistent character. That which we call 'one's own' 'independent' being is not isolated being, cut off from everything else, absolutely self-contained and self-subsistent: such being is an unrealizable abstraction. Nothing of the kind can exist at all, and the illusion that it can is merely a result of spiritual blindness.[1] 'Independent' being participates in the

---

[1] This spiritual blindness is the source of the godless, or more generally speaking, nihilistic 'existentialism', so popular at the present day. When a man loses his spiritual endowment and is no longer conscious of the roots which

primary reality, is grounded and rooted in it; it discovers within itself the presence of the all-embracing reality, in which everything that exists participates also.

But this is possible just because reality is super-logical, and though distinct from everything singular and particular, includes it within itself and is therefore present in every portion of itself, imparting to it its own character of primary independent reality. In virtue of this correlation the particular and individual becomes, so to speak, derivatively primary, i.e. acquires in a derivative way the primacy of reality. This is the explanation of the vague, difficult and logically unanalysable idea of substance—of a certain 'something' which is distinct from all qualities and relations, from all particular determinations, and is their mysterious 'bearer'; it is an 'existent' which does not inhere in anything other than itself; Aristotle described it as 'first matter' (πρώτη οὐσία) and Descartes defined it as 'that which does not need anything else for its existence'. 'Substance' is in fact a manifestation of the superlogical nature of reality as it were at a single point or in a particular instance; substance has the same primacy as the all-embracing reality, but has it derivatively, through participating and being grounded in it. Later on more will be said about the bearing that this correlation has upon the nature and existence of man. At present I will only observe that it explains and is entirely in keeping with the religious doctrine of man as 'the image and likeness of God', i.e., of man as an entity that acquires primary and independent being through possessing in a derivative, analogous way the characteristics of his creator and source.

Philosophical reflection always tends towards one or the other abstract interpretation of reality—towards *monism* or *pluralism*. The type of thought exemplified by Parmenides and Spinoza, centred upon the synthetic, coherent aspect of existence, conceives

unite him with the super-individual all-embracing reality and, through it, with the world, he has nothing left him but his own precious existence and he becomes an 'existentialist'. Such self-centered 'existence' poised over a void is of course utterly tragic. But however tragic human existence may be in reality, the tragedy of the existentialist's position is simply an expression of spiritual devastation due to spiritual blindness. It would be easy to show (see above, I. 4) that taken in absolute isolation I cease to be 'myself', 'my' existence ceases to be 'mine' and accordingly ceases to be what we call 'existence'. Nihilistic existentialism is a spasmodic, hopeless effort to catch at a phantom, at something utterly unstable and groundless in the hope of staving off the fatal fall into the abyss of pure non-being.

reality as a continuous, homogeneous whole. The diversity and multiplicity manifested by the particular elements of being, coexisting and replacing one another in the process of change appear to thinkers of this type as a kind of illusion. But the very recognition of the difference between 'deceptive appearance' and 'true reality' is an argument against their main position, for it proves that multiplicity cannot be radically and unconditionally denied. Even as merely 'apparent' and 'illusory', multiplicity is not a zero, but a certain reality, however superficial, and somehow participates in existence. For Spinoza *natura naturata*, 'derivative nature' is the totality of particular 'modes' which are transitory states of one unchangeable substance, as it were accidental splashes of waves on the surface of one continuous ocean of being; it is introduced, so to speak, by contraband, from nowhere, and proves to be, on closer inspection, a kind of outer covering, an extraneous addition to God or Substance which, consistently with Spinoza's system, should be the whole of reality. The conception is artificial and obviously distorts the natural, spontaneous testimony of our experience as to the variegated multiplicity and living changeability of the particular separate elements of being; it also contradicts the decisive verdict of inner experience from which we know that each one of us has primary and independent being. But the artificiality of the theory does not save it from inconsistency: that which is openly denied has to be tacitly and surreptitiously admitted.

The direct opposite of the monistic view, but equally abstract and therefore unsatisfactory, is the pluralistic conception of the type of Leibniz's monadology. It splits up reality into an infinite multiplicity of absolutely independent, isolated and self-contained bearers—'monads'—which have the whole fulness of life in themselves alone and have no 'windows' for mutual interconnection. It is not hard to see that if this were really the case, the very idea of plurality upon which Leibniz's system is based, would be impossible: it presupposes that monads are open to one another's contemplation. A self-contained isolated monad would know nothing except itself, and would have to identify itself with universal being, i.e. conceive of that being as absolute unity. On the other hand, if some supernatural spirit could, contrary to the system's presuppositions, somehow see the plurality of monads, that plurality would be absolutely disconnected and indeed would not be a plurality as a synthesis of the manifold, but a disjointed collection of one . . .

one . . . one . . ., a monotonous repetition of pure isolated unity. Accordingly, Leibniz found it necessary inconsistently to amplify the conception of this absolutely disrupted multiplicity by the idea of 'pre-established harmony' between the monads. But harmony is by its very meaning an all-embracing and guiding unity of the manifold; and if it is externally superimposed upon the manifold instead of naturally forming part of it, the artificiality of the procedure is of no avail: the superadded unity coming from without—in the last resort, simply out of the blue—is in any case something real and therefore an inalienable constitutive element of reality. Thus it appears that plurality itself is unthinkable apart from unity: it is unthinkable both because it is a plurality of 'monads' or *units*, i.e. because the principle of unity construes the actual elements of which it consists, and because it itself is a *synthesis*—a plurality as interpenetrated and held together by unity.

The hopeless difficulties of the two opposite conceptions are removed as soon as it is grasped that reality, being superlogical, is an antinomic unity of opposites or, to put it in another way, is always something greater than itself and includes that which from the purely logical point of view, is different from it. This is why the all-embracing unity, while differing from the plurality of particular elements or determinations, contains it within itself, or, rather, generates it. The unity of reality, embracing everything, rises above the opposition between unity and plurality: it is the unity of unity and plurality. As all-pervading it is present as a unity at every point, thus transforming every point of being into a derivative unity and imparting to it its own primary, self-sufficient and self-contained character. Thereby the unity of reality generates within itself a plurality of substantially existent particular elements, without ceasing to be a simple and absolutely primary unity transcending everything particular and plural.

This brings us, as it were by another road, to the position indicated in the preceding chapter that reality does not lead us away from the world of fact, but, on the contrary, leads us to it, for it embraces it. The nature of that world as existing independently of us, indifferent, so to speak, to the mental gaze directed upon it, and confronting us as self-subsistent being, is in the last resort determined by the circumstance that the 'objective world' is reality *alienated from us in so far as it is an object of thought*. In stabilizing the contents of reality in a definite form of 'this and not that' thought inevitably imparts to them the character of self-subsistent being. The world of fact is simply a rationalized or logically crystallised part of reality.

If there were a *logical* opposition between reality and rational determinateness, the deeper we penetrated into reality, the further we would move away from the world of fact. But as already pointed out, the distinction between them is superlogical and irreducible to mere logical negation. That means that reality is super-rational, but not irrational; it is not irrational if only because it *does not exclude anything* and, therefore, does not exclude rationality. In this respect, as in others, it is not 'this and not that' but always 'this and that'; it is the unity of every 'this' with 'something other'. It recedes into infinite depths far beyond all that appears to us as the objective world, and, in contradistinction to it, is self-subsistent and immediately self-revealing; it is not outside us, for we ourselves are it or are in it—and at the same time it is the bearer and primary basis of the objective world. Embracing and penetrating the being of the subject, it also embraces and penetrates objective being which surrounds us as 'the world of fact'. That world, in spite of all its independence and alienation from us which constitutes its very essence, is, as it were, a superficial part of the living reality, fixed and rigid in its objectivity. It is somewhat similar to the bark of a tree or the shell of a nut—a hardened and comparatively separate outer layer built up by the resources of the organism itself. Therefore, although it stands over against us and is felt to be a limitation and an obstacle to the self-activity of the living forces of reality in us, it is a product of reality and is subject to its continuous creative and form-giving action. Reality is, thus, a unity of itself and of the objective world. This abstract and awkward statement is another expression of the fully concrete and practically important conclusion, partly indicated at the end of the preceding chapter: the path leading into the depths of reality, and as it were liberating us from the empirical husk of our existence in the objective world, proves to be a path that grows in breadth as well as in depth. Withdrawing from external contact with the objective world we once more approach it *at its root* and discover that its inner being is akin to us and connected with us. The two limited standpoints—that of mergence with objective existence and losing one's identity as a subordinate part of it, and that of ascetic rejection of the world and escape from it into the secluded depths of inner being—are superseded by accepting the world in its inmost essence through self-affirmation in the world-transcending depths of primary reality.

All this, however, is much too abstract. But, as already mentioned, indirect knowledge of reality obtained through contrasting it with that which can be expressed by a system of logical determinations may be amplified by a kind of intuitive description: we can so combine concepts that the inmost nature of reality, empirically given, but inexpressible by any one concept, may shine through them.

In many spheres of life, if we are attentive enough, we discover so to speak the actual presence of reality in its concretely superlogical nature.

3. Beauty. Reality in the aesthetic experience.

The first instance I propose to consider is not the most important, but the simplest and most obvious—the perception of beauty or aesthetic perception.

Our everyday attitude to our environment is either intellectually-utilitarian or subjectively emotional. In both cases external phenomena are apprehended as *facts* which in themselves, in their objective content, are alien from us (our attitude to other people will be discussed later). In the cases of intellectually-utilitarian attitude we regard them as useful and necessary or as harmful, or as indifferent; we have no intimate personal relation to them. But even when our attitude is emotional we clearly distinguish—at any rate if we pay attention to the matter—between subjective feeling and objective content. Facts evoke in us feelings of sympathy or antipathy, pleasure or annoyance, but in themselves they do not possess any of the qualities that characterize our experience with regard to them. The objective world remains for us a mere totality of recognized and logically determinate facts which as such have nothing in common with the inmost nature of our 'self'.

But against the background of this objective world, essentially indifferent to us and commanding only a cold recognition, there stand out facts of a different order; whether they be events in nature or products of human creativeness, they attract not our intellectual attention, but our inmost heart. We experience in them as such, in their own content, somewhat significant, some spiritual meaning, something akin to the intimate depths of our self; our perception of them is disinterested and has no relation whatever either to our practical needs or to purely subjective feelings. Such perception gives us a peculiar delight, further undefinable and called by us *aesthetic*. Facts that call it forth acquire a special and unique value for us. This is precisely what is meant by *beauty*.

But what exactly is beauty? May it be more closely defined and if so, how?[1]

The most appropriate definition of that which is called 'beauty' and is given in aesthetic experience is suggested by its *expressive* character.[2] To perceive something aesthetically means to perceive along with the sense-data and, as it were, in their depths, something else which is not sensuous. The beautiful is beautiful because it 'expresses' something, because it 'tells us' about something that lies beyond the definable data of sense; it thus indicates something *significant* which is absent from the content of our usual experience of the objective world. It is not merely a brute fact, meaningless and inwardly alien to us, forced upon us as it were from without and compelling us to reckon with it. On the contrary it 'charms' and captivates us inwardly by bearing witness to some final depth akin to our own being and full of meaning.

But what exactly does the beautiful 'express'? To an aesthetically sensitive and logically clear mind there is no point in asking such a question. If we could define in ordinary words, that is, in logical notions that which the beautiful stands for, we would, in doing so, *express* it in a way that was not aesthetic and thus make the aesthetic experience an unnecessary duplicate of the ordinary, logically expressible experience. The beautiful expresses precisely that which is *inexpressible logically* and for that very reason can only be expressed aesthetically. Attempts, unfortunately often made (for instance in criticizing works of art) to convey in prose, i.e. in words as equivalents of logical notions that of which beauty tells us, greatly impoverish, to say the last of it, and therefore distort the true meaning of aesthetic experience. The only way to speak of its content prosaically is to do so in terms of *docta ignorantia*, i.e. through contrasting it with the logically formulated and in that sense 'objective' contents, and recognizing that it is unfathomable and logically inexpressible. This does not mean, however, that we must sink into silence in

---

[1] The argument that follows is worked out more fully in my book *The Unfathomable* (in Russian), ch. VII, 2.

[2] This has been best expressed by Benedetto Croce in his *Estetica come scienza del' expressione et linguistica generale*, 1912.

mute delight at the message which the beautiful brings us. The conception of reality worked out in the preceding pages provides a philosophical form of expressing the inexpressible, the superlogical —and is in this respect analogous to that of which the aesthetic experience speaks.

The beautiful is that which by means of sensuous experience gives us a direct perception of *reality*. We find at times—most of us but rarely and in exceptional circumstances—that the hard crust of 'brute fact' and logical determinateness is in places so fine and transparent that reality shines through it and becomes perceptible. From the point of view of logical thought the beautiful is part of the world of fact—a beautiful face or body belongs to an 'organism', a beautiful landscape is part of the structure of the earth's surface, a beautiful statue, picture, edifice, symphony, entirely consist of the usual objective sensuous elements; but in aesthetic experience as such its content acquires an intrinsic value of its own and transcends the realm of mere fact. In the 'earthly' we become aware of something 'heavenly', akin to the inmost depths of our soul—to our self-subsistent and self-revealing reality. In virtue of this the beautiful possesses quite a special kind of obviousness: it neither requires nor admits of explanation and cannot be reduced to anything else, because it is not determined by its logical connection with anything other than itself; it is self-sufficient and has an inner unity which finds expression in what we call the harmony of its parts or elements. That means that the beautiful as such is, like reality, an all-embracing and self-contained whole which is present in its entirety in the particular and the limited. This combination of finitude and integral wholeness accounts for the significance of aesthetic *form*. Form is a configuration or combination of elements giving on a limited scale a unique and adequate expression—one of the infinite number of other possible expressions—to the all-embracing and therefore self-contained fulness of reality.

As already pointed out, this reality is akin to the one which we experience in the hidden depths of our own soul. Indeed, we have a right to say that it is *the same reality*—in so far as the principle of identity is at all applicable to reality (which, as we know, never is simply a 'this' in the strictly logical sense, but is always 'this and the other' in their indivisible unity). As an all-pervading and all-embracing unity, reality is one in essence and in that sense it is always the same in all its manifestations; but this does not prevent it being different in each one of its concrete manifestations and, like Proteus, appearing in ever changing forms.

Let us try to describe more accurately both the likeness and the difference between reality discovered in the depths of the inner experience, and revealed in aesthetic perception.

The expressiveness of beauty means that in it something 'inner' is expressed in the 'outer', in the sensuously-given. The 'beautiful' is experienced as having affinity with living, animate being, similar to our own, in which invisible inner life is somehow united with external, bodily form and incarnate in it. All that is aesthetically perceived contains a 'soul-like' element—a kind of inner life embodied and expressed in outer form much in the same way as our 'soul' manifests itself in facial expression, look, smile or speech. At moments of aesthetic experience we no longer feel lonely, for we enter into communion with something in the external world which is akin to us. That which is external to us ceases to be a part of the cold and indifferent objective world, and we are conscious of its kinship with our own inner being.

At the same time, however, an essential difference remains. Although the beautiful is 'soul-like', we know that it is not a real, living 'soul'; and even if for a moment we fall into such an illusion, we are aware that it *is* an illusion. We know that a statue as such is simply marble or plaster, that a picture is a combination of daubs of paint on canvas, that a mountain landscape is a geological formation which is not conscious of its own grandeur—in short, we know that the 'something soul-like' expressed by the beautiful has not the specific property of mind or spirit—the property of being-for-itself or of being a real subject. Only in the case of beautiful human exterior we often (in erotic experience) fall into the natural error of confusing the impersonal 'soul-like' something expressed by the sensuous image with the real living soul of its bearer, and discover our mistake much later—for instance when we find out that a woman's 'celestially' beautiful face belongs to a sinful or insignificant creature.

The circumstance that aesthetic experience is in this sense illusory and the prevalent tendency to confuse the conceptions of reality and of the world of fact (see Chapter I) lead to the vague and false contention that aesthetic experience as such is an illusion. According to the theory of *Einfühlung*, highly popular a short time ago, aesthetic experience consists in our transferring to the object, or reading into it, our own subjective feelings. This theory has no objective foundation whatever and is a typical example of artificial interpretation put upon the immediate content of experience; besides, it is based upon a gross confusion of thought. Immediate experience does not show a trace of the mysterious process of transferring our own inner states to external objects; on the contrary, it clearly bears witness to the objects' action upon us. Besides, the feelings which we ourselves experience in perceiving 'the beautiful' essentially differ from the objective content of aesthetic experience. Although that content partly 'infects' us and is transferred from the object into our mind, we have at the same time feelings which are clearly distinct from it. This is clear if only from the fact that every aesthetic perception—even that of the tragic, the gloomy, the terrible, the disharmonious—delights us, i.e. contains an element of joy and pleasure. A clear and cultivated mind always clearly distinguishes between the actual content of the aesthetic experience and the subjective feelings which it calls forth.

The whole of this false and artificial theory is based on the assumption that everything analogous to our inner conscious experience must be either logically identical with it, or be a mere illusion; and since inanimate objects of aesthetic experience unquestionably have no 'soul' of their own and are not conscious of themselves, the conclusion seems inevitable that such experience is merely our own subjective 'impression' transferred in an illusory way to the object.

Unprejudiced description of the nature of aesthetic experience clearly points to something very different, and instead of trying to make facts fit in with our preconceived ideas, we must try to find words and ideas adequate to the content of the experience in question. As already pointed out, in aesthetic experience there is clearly revealed to us a certain reality which lies as it were behind the sense data and is, as we say, 'expressed' by them. And we are aware that this reality is akin to the reality revealed to us in the depths of our own inner experience and is, so to speak, on the same plane with it. At the same time we are aware of the reality apprehended in aesthetic experience as *impersonal*: its relation to the sensuous material expressing it is different from the relation between our inner world and our expression of it. Aesthetic reality has no personal centre of self-consciousness, no personal expressive activity: it does not deliberately express itself, but is involuntarily expressed; in short, it is something other than 'mind' or 'inner life'.

58

It is precisely this difference that confirms the argument of the preceding chapter that reality, though akin to the subject's inner life, goes far beyond it as the all-embracing ground of being in general. In aesthetic experience reality in the sense just indicated manifests itself obviously and unquestionably—we break through the hard shell of 'objectivity' both in the hidden depths of our own self and in the external world around us, and come into contact with the inmost living core of being.

4. Reality in the experience of communion

Let us now consider quite a different realm of being in which we also find concrete empirical insight into reality as distinct both from the objective world and from my inner subjective being. I am refering to the fact of communion.

At the beginning of the present century philosophical literature was greatly concerned with the question as to how we apprehend the mental life of others, and what are the grounds of our belief in it. Strangely enough, classical theories of knowledge by-passed that problem. Tremendous efforts of thought were spent on discovering the grounds for our belief in the existence of an objective world outside our consciousness, but no attention at all was given to the question as to the source and ground of the conviction that there exist other minds than our own. Hume's universal scepticism does not touch upon it; 'all-destroying' Kant, by declaring that the criterion of truth is its universally binding character, tacitly admits that the recognition of a plurality of mind lies at the basis of his whole theory of knowledge. Solipsism—i.e. the conviction that only my own existence is certain, however inevitable from the standpoint of scepticism and subjective idealism, was carefully avoided.

Nevertheless, the prevalent idea that we have only an indirect, mediated knowledge of all that is external to us has eventually led to inquiry into the grounds of our belief in the existence of other minds. The first hypothesis that suggested itself—that of 'inference from analogy'—was easily shown to be untenable. According to that hypothesis, in perceiving facial expression, speech and behaviour of certain objects, and knowing from our inner experience that those external signs are connected with mental life, we infer that the objects in question have mental life, and thus apprehend them as 'animate'. The decisive argument against this absurdly artificial

59

theory is that inference from analogy entitles us to transfer some *general* characteristic from one object or class of objects to another, but is inapplicable when a fact by its very definition is unique. The assertion that I transfer by analogy the characteristic of consciousness from myself to external objects thus presupposes the very point at issue, namely, that 'consciousness' is a *general idea* applicable to a number of individual events; according to the original premise it should be conceived as something essentially unique, i.e. coinciding with my 'self'.

The German psychologist Lipps attempted to replace this fallacious view by the theory of 'animation' or 'feeling in' (*Einfühlung*) analogous to the theory discussed with regard to aesthetic experience. In meeting with another mind we become as it were infected with mental contents which enter our own mental life, but bear the specific mark of being forced upon us from without—and it is in this that our experience of their belonging to another mind consists. A criticism of this theory would be largely a repetition of what has already been said apropos of the aesthetic theory of *Einfühlung*. It has been disproved once and for all by Max Scheler in his *Wesen und Formen der Sympathie* (1923).

Since the theories that our knowledge of other minds is mediated and indirect are untenable, the only alternative is to admit that we have a specific direct perception of the mental life of others. That view was worked out in different forms by Scheler and (before him) by N. O. Lossky. Their main contention is indisputably true, but needs further elaboration. At present, however, we must not attempt this, because the subject has only been mentioned here in order to introduce another problem—that of *communion*, (which alone can help us fully to grasp the subject).

Communion is more than mere perception of another mind, and is different from it. An external object recognized by me as 'an animate being' does not cease on that account alone to be similar to other objects. For a slave-owner a slave, though an animate being, is simply one of his tools; similarly, people to whom we are indifferent —for instance passers-by in the street, though animate, interest us merely as moving objects and our sole concern is not to run into them, exactly as it is with street traffic. Finally, an enemy on the battlefield is simply a living force to be made harmless or destroyed. Such an 'animate being' is grammatically designated in the third person: it is 'he' or 'she', by analogy with 'it'. As such a 'he', an animate being is in our experience *wholly included in the 'world of objects'* and presents no special interest.

The position is radically changed in the case of *communion*, even of the most superficial kind. When we speak to a person, shake hands, or even when our eyes meet in silence, that person ceases to be an 'object' for us and is no longer a 'he' but a 'thou'. That means he no longer fits into the frame-work of 'the world of objects': he ceases to be a passive something upon which our cognitive gaze is directed for the purposes of perception without in any way affecting it. Such one-sided relation is replaced by a two-sided one, by an interchange of spiritual activities. We attend to him and he to us, and this attitude is different from—though it may coexist with—the purely ideal direction of attention which we call objective knowledge: it is real spiritual interaction. Communion is both our link with that which is external to us, and a part of our inner life, and indeed a most essential part of it. From the abstract logical point of view this is a paradoxical case of something external not merely coexisting with the 'inward' but of actually merging in it. Communion is at one and the same time both something 'external' to us and something 'inward'—in other words it cannot in the strict sense be called either external or inward.

This can still more clearly be seen from the fact that all communion between 'I' and 'thou' leads to the formation of a new reality designated by the word 'we'—or, rather, coincides with it. But what is 'we'—the term described in grammar as the plural of the first person, the plural of 'I'? In the strict and literal sense 'I' can only be in the singular: I am unique—a second 'me' would be merely an uncanny and never fully realizable fantastic idea of 'the double'. Nothing in the world, and not even God Himself can make *my own self* plural. When abstract philosophy speaks of many selves, it removes me from my true element—reality—and in a derivative way transfers me to the alien sphere of the world of objects; instead of me myself in my true being, it deals with the self in the third person, i.e. as 'he' which of course easily admits of the plural 'they'.

And yet, since language has produced the word 'we', instead of being content with 'I and thou', there is a profound reason for this: it expresses the fact that 'I and thou' is not a mere plurality or togetherness of two separate events, but is also a certain unity, and a unity somehow akin to the unity of *myself*. 'We' is not the plural of 'I' but is a certain *widening* of the 'I' spreading beyond its primary

61

and, so to speak, its natural limits. The consciousness of 'we' is for me the consciousness that somehow I exist *beyond the confines of my own self*.

The impossibility of expressing the relation in question in clear logical terms, or, what is the same thing, the fact that we are bound to express it in terms which are logically contradictory—testifies that we have to do here with something super-logically concrete, a 'coincidence of opposites' accessible only to *docta ignorantia*. In other words in the case of 'we', and therefore of 'thou', we have to do with *reality* in contradistinction to the 'objective world'. In communion or actual apprehension of another personality not through the cognitive gaze but through vital contact, we come into touch with the mysterious depths of living reality, no longer merely in our inner life, but outside us.

In every meeting between two pairs of eyes one reality sends a message to another through visual and auditory impressions, and the other 'answers'; something essentially hidden, inward, supermundane, comes out and not merely makes a contact, but actually interacts with another bearer of reality and, however partially and superficially, unites itself with it. This is different in principle from mere natural interaction between parts of the objective world such as two billiard balls colliding. It is as though some invisible feelers reached out from the depths, and if only for a moment touched other feelers stretched forward to meet them.

The general nature of such a meeting admits of an infinite number of variations; it is saturated with moral and aesthetic qualities which deeply affect our inmost being. We often 'like' a person 'at first glance', he 'appeals' to us, satisfies us, calls forth a feeling of approval; another one we dislike, feel antipathy for him, disapprove of him. Repeated meetings result in the peculiar fact, incomparable to anything else, of 'human relations'. Those relations may be solidarity, friendship, love, or antagonism and hostility, provided they do not lead to complete alienation and indifference, and reduce a living 'thou' to an indifferent object, a 'he'. As a rule human relations are complex and combine intimacy and solidarity with antagonism and all kinds of 'friction'; being a part of our life they are changeable, dynamic, have a history of their own and pass through a number of stages and sometimes of stormy developments. Artistic literature of all centuries is concerned with describing this infinitely complex, rich and dramatic world of human relations. Side by side

62

with purely personal relations which preserve their character of living, spontaneous expressions of personal dynamism, and are fluid, changeable and unformed, there are others which assume stable forms having the appearance of objective fact independent of us; they are subordinate to rules and as such constitute our social environment—beginning with the family union and ending with the state and legal norms. Surrounded and interpenetrated by all the multifarious inter-human relations we live not only in the physical, but also in a special psychical world, common to us all. Although, as just pointed out, some of those relations become stabilized and form a world that appears to be independent of us, we are conscious that at bottom it is the world of our own spiritual life in its collective aspect; it is the totality of individual inner lives, intertwined into a certain indissoluble unity. Spiritual culture or spiritual life of a society at a given epoch, which forms the true substratum of 'history', is just the super-individual aspect of the spiritual life that lies at the core of our own personal being. This clearly shows that *reality* is given us not only in the form of 'my inner life' as the reality of my 'self', but also in a super-individual form as the unity of many individual subjects.

There must of course be no romantic personification, both false and pernicious, of this super-individual spiritual reality—no converting it, as Hegel did, into an 'objective spirit' which dominates individuals much in the same way as do the 'brute facts' of the objective world. We must be clearly aware that in the last resort it is a life that springs from the living depths of our own selves and is created by us, but in so far as it is a common life concretely expressed in interhuman relations, it remains a super-individual reality. It constitutes for us a world of its own—the world of history, politics, social customs and spiritual culture, as distinct from the whole of the natural world. In virtue of this, our scientific knowledge is concerned with two heterogeneous and essentially irreconcilable domains which, though impinging upon each other, cannot be brought into one common system of ideas (however frequently the hopeless attempt to unite them may be made)—natural sciences, and sciences dealing with the socially-historical and spiritual life (*Geisteswissenschaften*, as the Germans call them). These two spheres are irreconcilable because in dealing with 'nature' we are concerned with the world of objective fact as such, and in dealing with the world of history we have to do with reality which is only partly 'objectified'. In order to see more clearly the unique character of the domain of inter-human relations we must understand how deeply and firmly this super-individual reality is rooted in the inmost essence of our 'self'.

From the purely concrete and practical point of view the super-individual basis of individual existence is perfectly obvious. A self-subsistent and absolutely self-contained individual 'I' is an un-realizable abstraction. Self-consciousness or awareness of oneself as an entity which we come, later, to call 'I' arises in early infancy, not merely through distinguishing oneself from objects of the external world apprehended as not-self, but also through the infant's dim awareness of the bond between itself and its mother. In actual fact there can be no 'I' apart from its relation to a 'thou'; in the order of psychogenesis, a rudimentary 'thou' expressed by the mother's affectionate gaze or the warmth of her embrace is as primary as the rudimentary 'I', and this correlation, growing more pronounced and assuming different forms, is preserved throughout life. Even a man sentenced to life-long solitary confinement lives by the memory of his near and dear, hoping that they, too, have not forgotten him—i.e. lives by his relation to 'thou'. Even a hermit in the desert, solely concerned with saving his own soul, lives by being centred upon God and connected with Him (that, too, is a special connection with a 'thou' which shall be discussed elsewhere) and also by the conviction that in seclusion and solitude he can best develop his love for men and take part in their salvation. And, *vice versa*, the most extreme and hardened egoist, despising and hating other people, in his proud reserve lives by his rebellion against them, by his alienation from them, by hatred and contempt—and this also is, negatively, relatedness to others. In short there is no personal existence and no situation which does not, in one way or another, include a relation to some 'thou'.

But this is not all. It may be objected that although the relation to a 'thou' is an integral part of human existence, it does not affect the actual inner being of the self which is unique, inexpressible, hidden from the eyes of another (of a 'thou') and in that sense, isolated. This, indeed, has been stressed in the preceding pages. The only reason why the conception of the self as an absolutely self-contained point or sphere has been rejected as untenable is that, as we have seen, the very nature of the self consists in its being rooted in reality as such; but in that sense, every 'self' has a special root of its own, lying in secret depths inaccessible to another person's eyes. This finds concrete expression in the consciousness that all real communion with a 'thou', however intimate, cannot fully exhaust my 'self' and that the most essential part of me forever remains solitary and inexpressible. In primitive epochs man was not aware of this, and found complete realization in social life, pouring himself out, as it were, into a collective whole; but that was solely because he was not acutely conscious of his personality. As that consciousness develops, the sense of man's metaphysical solitude grows stronger.

This argument is essentially true: we cannot put the whole fulness of our 'self' into any empirically realizable communion, and it is extremely important to recognize this, for only thus can we grasp the unique nature of our own being as inner spiritual life. Anticipating what is to follow, we can say that we are wholly open only to ourselves—and to God. Distinction must be drawn, however, between the practical empirical realizability of communion and the metaphysical structure of personal being which shows that personality or 'the self' is in its very essence a member of a communal multiple unity, a co-partner of 'we'. A closer analysis of the nature of our 'self' clearly shows this to be the case—however much it may conflict with our habitual ideas. It has been already shown that the self is the bearer or subject of the inner life as a self-revealing, to-itself-given reality; this reality is immeasurable in depth and unlimited. In that sense we are aware of our 'self' as something absolute. But at the same time we are aware of it, both in its inner being and in so far as it belongs to the world of objects, as something particular, limited, conditioned. A mind that ascribes absolute significance to itself, and is aware of itself as a true and therefore only centre of reality as a whole, suffers from a morbid, unnatural perversion of the normal self-consciousness. The normal self combines absoluteness with relativity, infinitude with limitedness. 'I' as the subject, i.e. as the bearer of self-revealing reality, am aware of myself as a particular manifestation of reality in general or as *one* of its manifestations. I am, as it were, surrounded by the ocean of reality transcending the limits of my inner life. But this 'self-revealing reality' is necessarily conceived as having a personal centre or existing in the form of a subject; hence, in being conscious of myself as *one* of such subjects, I think of myself as a member of a many-centred system of reality, as a partner in a 'kingdom of spirits' (leaving aside for the moment the conception of God as the absolute centre of this reality). As already said 'the self' is not a self-contained point, but a kind of root going into the infinite depths of the soil. The classical metaphor used by Plotinus is however more appropriate: 'I' am a leaf on a tree; outwardly separated from other leaves and touching them only accidentally (e.g. when a gust of wind brings the leaves together), I am united to them *from within*, through the branches and the tree trunk, and am a member of this multiple unity (cp. the Gospel simile of the vine and the branches, or the image used by St. Paul of persons as members of a single organism of the Church). The important point is that this multiple unity is *interpenetrable from within*, so that a multitude of outwardly separate bearers of reality inwardly, in their final depth, form an unbroken unity: the leaves are nourished by the sap that penetrates the whole of the tree, and have a common life.

Accordingly, the 'thou' which outwardly I merely 'meet', and have only superficial and accidental contact with, inwardly co-belongs to my own being as a further expression of it lying beyond its boundaries. And for that very reason primary reality has the power of revealing itself not only *to itself*, or of being a self-conscious 'I', but also *to another*, i.e. of assuming the form of a 'thou', and there-fore, of 'we'. It may well be that outwardly 'I' and 'thou' on their empirical side, never wholly reveal themselves to each other, and that therefore the 'we' cannot in fact completely include the 'I'; but such impossibility of perfect mergence of two or of many into one is due to the circumstance that it is only in their invisible and unfathomable *depth* that they are truly interpenetrable and form an unbroken organic unity.

'I' always remain a unique, unutterable reality, not fully ex-pressible in any empirical communion; and yet I am but a leaf or a branch on the general tree of the collective humanity, a member of the kingdom of spirits. This is confirmed by the fact that, as already pointed out, the more individual and spiritually deep a person is (e.g. a man of genius), the more 'universally human' he is, the more he expresses that which is the common property and the common essence of all. The ultimate, fullest and deepest communion takes place not on the surface of our being, not through our external relation to others or a decrease in our individual uniqueness; it takes place in invisible depths and is an involuntary result and expression of our personality as a whole. In its true inmost essence my 'self' forms part of 'we' and co-belongs to the same ultimate ground. Accordingly, all external communion, all empirical relations between 'I' and 'thou' are an actual, though incomplete and inadequate expression of this inner mutual interpenetrability of the kingdom of spirits. Reality can have for me the form of 'thou' and reveal itself to me from outside solely because it is akin to me from within and merged with my own being.

Nothing could be more false, more contrary to the true nature of man—and therefore more pernicious—than the prevalent idea of the human soul being shut in and isolated.[1] We have already seen in another connection that 'the soul' is not circumscribed from within, but is able to look outwards as well as inwards at the reality which is revealed to it from within. It is in contact with that reality and imperceptibly passes into it, finding in it its own continuation. But that reality is 'the kingdom of spirits'. The fact that I belong to it and truly realize myself only through a living union with it is brought home to me by every spontaneous and not purely utilitarian meeting with a fellow man. For, being a 'thou', he speaks to me of *my own self*, is akin to me, and I see that there is the same life in him as in me. True, this correlation stands out with final, overwhelming clarity only when living knowledge reaches exceptional intensity and becomes true love. But a vague beginning of it is contained in every liking, however fleeting, in every true meeting with any 'thou', and in that sense it may be said that *potency of love* is the very essence of human life.

The peculiar nature of the self-revelation of reality in the form of 'thou' must be clearly recognized. At first sight it might appear that reality reveals itself to another—i.e. to the knowing subject—in every act of cognition. But there is a profound difference in principle between the subject-object relation in and through which reality reveals itself to us in the form of objective things and events and the way in which it manifests itself in the I–thou relation. In the first relation, reality as an 'object' is something absolutely dumb and passive; the whole activity of 'discovering' it belongs to the subject

[1] The wholly unnatural individualism and mutual segregation between men in modern society provides a psychological basis for this idea. On the other hand the tendency of socialism and communism towards a compulsory socialization of human life is based upon the same false conception: the view of society as a chaotic mass of isolated individual units leads to the demand forcibly to mould them into a single mechanism in order to stop blind anarchical conflicts between individuals. In truth, however, free and spontaneous intercommunion is an essential property of man's inner being.

who directs his cognitive gaze, as if it were a ray of light, upon the object and makes it accessible to himself without anything happening in the object; our knowledge is successful precisely in so far as we discover the content of the object as it actually is, independently of our cognitive processes. The discovery of a 'thou' is quite a different matter; it does not form part of 'objective knowledge', and this is why our knowledge of other minds appears to be problematic. A 'thou' does not passively stand before me, dispassionately submitting itself to my inquiring gaze; on the contrary, there takes place here a true active meeting between two entities. Leaving aside for the moment the consideration that I too reveal myself to the other and become a 'thou' for him, and concentrating on the nature of the 'thou' as such, we must admit that the whole activity proceeds from the 'thou' and that his 'knowableness' depends upon his own activity. It is not I who discover a 'thou': it reveals itself to me. It itself sends out as it were an invisible emanation that invades me, and when I have absorbed it, I have come to know the 'thou'.

In contradistinction to the knowledge of objects this kind of knowledge can only be described by the word *revelation*. The word is generally applied only to religious life. In theological literature it designates either the authoritative original source of faith, e.g. the Holy Writ or the tradition of the Church, or, in a primary and deeper sense, the manifestation ('theophany') or the revelation of God— the Word proceeding from God. I am well aware of the objections to using in a new sense a word that has a habitual and firmly rooted connotation. But I can find no better term to designate the extremely important and wholly unique fact in question. I merely ask the reader to remember that I take the word 'revelation' in its literal and most general sense. There is revelation wherever a living and conscious entity, as it were of its own initiative, *reveals* itself to another by acting upon it.

It is in such revelation that the nature of 'thou', and the way in which it becomes accessible to us, consists. A 'thou' is turned to me or directed upon me and affects me; it acts not blindly, as a physical object might act on my body, but by 'revealing' itself to me, that is, by 'speaking' to me about itself. It speaks even when it is silent. A look or a smile may be more eloquent than any words; lovers know this well, but all recognize it even in the most prosaic or fleeting social intercourse. 'To speak' in this general sense means to pour into another's mind if not one's very being, then at any rate a certain spiritual energy expressive of its true nature.

Thus reality is not only given in our own inner life, not only disclosed from without in aesthetic experience, but spontaneously reveals itself to us by its own activity as a 'thou'.

5. *Reality in moral experience.*

There is another sphere in which we have a highly significant experience of reality: we meet it as it appears in our own spiritual life. It has been shown in Chapter I that 'the soul' is not shut in, but in its innermost essence comes into contact with, or passes into, something which is neither itself nor the world of objects; it can as it were direct its gaze towards its own inner depths. The general idea of reality as super-cosmic being has been arrived at through following this line of thought. But in addition to a general and indefinite consciousness of reality as such, we also have in our inner experience a specific apprehension of it as a determining factor in our spiritual life.

Our inner life in general has the property of spontaneity or freedom; as a rule, we feel that our mental states, desires and actions somehow arise from the centre of our own being and are generated by what we call our 'self'. This feeling constitutes the general primary nature of that which we describe as 'free will' and without which we cannot imagine our inner being at all. Our life as subjective or as proceeding from and belonging to a 'self' is determined by it, and to a superficial observer it may appear that this applies to the whole of our inner life. Closer analysis shows, however, that this is not so. In cases that have a vital, decisive influence upon the whole course of our existence, we experience at times something very different and feel that some of our mental contents are not our own creations, but come—and sometimes tempestually rush—into our inmost heart from without, from a sphere of being different to our own. And we are aware of that sphere as far exceeding us in power and significance. Such a character attaches for instance to every profound passion of which we say that it 'gets hold of' and 'possesses' us.

The power which thus invades us is sometimes felt to be alien to our real self or even actually hostile to it, enslaving it by violence. This is true of every dark and blind passion against which we struggle

—sometimes successfully and often unsuccessfully; in the latter case we submit to it, as it were, against our will. This is the nature of all vicious, criminal motivation, of all power of evil in us. But sometimes, on the contrary, this invading and overwhelming power is felt to be a reality akin and therefore friendly to us, a powerful ally helping us to realize our own ends and innermost strivings. This is the case, for instance, with all creative intuition in artistic or scientific work, or in solving problems of practical life. The solution, which we have been seeking so painfully and in vain comes to us unexpectedly as a gift, and is as it were 'suggested' to us. Goethe says of intellectual creative work: 'no efforts of thought help us to think; good ideas come to us suddenly of themselves, as God's free children, and say: here we are.'

In religious life the same thing is expressed by the idea of 'grace': spiritual peace, joy, the power to overcome low desires or the depression and despair that possess us—all that we have been vainly trying to attain by our own efforts suddenly comes to us either without any effort on our part at all or as a result of prayer, i.e. of turning to God as a higher, transcendent reality.

But the chief instance that brings out the point at issue is the unique character of the so-called moral experience. As Kant pointed out, in it we are aware of something—an action or a mental attitude —as absolutely binding, as that which ought to be. Whatever we may think of the ethical theory built by Kant upon this basis, there can be no doubt that his actual discovery of the categorial uniqueness of the *ought* is an immortal achievement. What is the meaning of 'ought'? It is not something that I wish, but something that is commanded or prescribed to me, and prescribed unconditionally, i.e. without any reference to the subjective ends and values of my life. The command issues not from some external authority or power, for, in virtue of my freedom, I could refuse to fulfil such a command; no, the command has the character of inner authoritativeness or persuasiveness, i.e. of self-evidence: I know from my inner experience that I *ought* to do something, ought to behave in a certain way; in that sense the command is 'autonomous'—I myself freely recognize it, or, as Kant interprets it, I myself put it to my empirical ego—thus admitting that the ego which issues the command is distinct from the empirical ego to which the command is addressed. When I say to myself 'I ought', I really say to myself 'you ought', i.e. my empirical self appears as a subordinate entity, receiving the command. Thus even according to Kant the higher, commanding self as 'the intelligible ego' belongs to the super-empirical, super-cosmic reality.

This duality of the self will be discussed later; at present it should merely be observed that Kant's identification of the source of the imperative with the ego is ambiguous, and is a defect of his theory. It is true in the sense that the command does not force itself upon our mental life *apart from* its inmost personal centre—the self—but passes through it; it does not, however, proceed from the self as an isolated entity. I do not issue the command, I merely *apprehend* it as unconditional, i.e. as self-evidently authoritative. Its source is obviously something different from me; it is not external to me as some alien reality, but it differs from me in the sense that my inmost self participates in it and acts as its organ and messenger. In religious terms, the 'autonomy' in this case is theonomy: *my* conscience hears the voice of God and passes His command to my empirical will.

This religious interpretation of the moral life is essentially correct, but it would be a mistake to regard it as a direct description of the immanent content of moral experience. Some people have a keen and clear moral sense but no religious experience, and deny the very possibility of it. What is immediately given in moral experience is a general awareness of a transcendental command addressed to our will and apprehended as issuing from the same depths in which our inner life is rooted. Contrary to Kant, our 'intelligible ego', or, to speak more simply, our conscience is not the supreme authority, but only a kind of intermediary which is freely and from inner conviction in complete accord with that authority. It is, so to speak, a living and active receiver and transmitter, through which we are subordinated to a different and higher power than ourselves.

Is it possible to define more closely the nature of that authority, or the specific way in which it acts upon us? The moral category of 'ought', discovered by Kant, undoubtedly has a certain primacy about it and cannot be reduced by logical analysis to anything more primary. This, however, does not rule out the possibility of describing it in greater detail and thus bringing out its nature more clearly.

The 'ought' has the character of an imperative or command. To say that we ought to do something, to act in a certain way is the same as to say that in so doing we submit to an inwardly perceived and recognized command. But a command is only thinkable as an expression of someone's will addressed to another will and calling for obedience. To whose will, then, do we submit in carrying out a moral command? It obviously cannot be our own will, nor the will of another human being (for in that case the command would not be absolute).

If we put aside for the moment the assumption that it is the will of God, the only alternative is to say that it is a *subjectless* will. It must of course be distinguished from an impersonal will, for 'impersonal' means 'elemental'. In that sense only dark, blind passion is impersonal—and it is the direct opposite of moral will. Moral will is subjectless simply in the sense that we cannot indicate its bearer: we are conscious of it in the impersonal form of 'ought'.

But how is this possible? An analogy with a kindred sphere of life may help to make it clearer. Jurists say that in submitting to the law of the state we submit to 'the will of the lawgiver'. But it is quite immaterial whether the actual human being (or, if the lawgiver means the parliament, a number of human beings) who expressed that will, is still alive. The lawgiver may have died long ago and ceased to have any will at all, yet his law holds good all the same. Created by a human will, it continues acting as an impersonally-objective will. A moral command has the same nature, except that it does not spring from human will, but acts from the first as 'subjectless will'. On the other hand, however, the idea of a will which is no one's will or has no real bearer, is unthinkable.

The conclusion at once suggests itself; it is not an abstractly logical conclusion, but merely an indication of what is immediately given in experience. A moral command is an expression of *the will of reality as such*—of the transcendent spiritual sphere in its all-embracing unity and, therefore, in its absoluteness given us in the inner experience. The 'categorical imperative' or the unconditional sovereign will is the will of the absolute principle. This must not of course involve any personification of reality as a subject which 'has' will. We have seen that reality is not directly given us in the form of a subject and that moral commands are apprehended as subjectless; true, in the experience of communion reality manifests itself as a kingdom of spirits or a coherent multiple unity of minds, but that kingdom as a whole has no all-embracing subject of which we have direct experience. Reality therefore *has* no will as a personal subject has; rather, it *is* a will, or manifests itself in moral experience *as* a will. This will, though subjectless, is not an abstraction, but something concrete. Reality as self-revealing (and, accordingly, revealing itself to us), self-contained and self-subsistent *life*—taken in its all-embracing unity—appears in moral experience as *will*.

The unconditional character of the moral command is, thus, an expression of the absoluteness of reality itself; and the primacy of reality is manifested here in a new way—namely, as *supremacy*. Reality is not merely an all-embracing concrete unity, permeating all multiplicity of which it is the ultimate ground; it is also the first source of all existence, manifesting itself as a power which ideally rules over it and appears as an absolute value, as a holy will, i.e. a will that demands obedience.

This will gives rise to a unique kind of necessity. That which 'ought' to be is not necessary in the sense of inviolable causal necessity: since the will of reality acts through our 'self' and our freedom, we always can (and unfortunately, very often do) refuse to submit to it. It acts upon us not in the form of irresistible compulsion, but of appeal and persuasion. On the other hand—and this is merely another expression of the same thing—the necessity of the 'ought', in contradistinction to the natural necessity—is inherently self-evident and convincing. Every causal tie is in the last resort merely a connection between facts: A is connected with B; if we succeed in explaining that connection through establishing its intermediary links (A is connected with B because it is connected with C, which involves B), the explanation ultimately rests on the recognition of the fact that *this is so*. The actual connection between one thing and another remains incomprehensible; it stands for something that is given as a fact, as an existing and externally compelling arrangement. We are bound obediently to accept it without understanding its inner significance or having any spiritual insight into it. The 'ought' is, on the contrary, experienced as inwardly binding—as something the necessity of which clearly follows from the very nature of the case. That which ought to be manifests itself as something that depends upon *meaning*: it is grounded not in the brute obviousness of fact, forced upon us from without, but in self-evidence wholly transparent to our mind and completely convincing. This kind of inner convincingness is identical with the primary aspect of value (objective or unconditional value as distinct from the subjective, or the merely pleasing and attractive). The conception of objective or unconditional value is only another way of expressing that which by its nature, self-evident to our spirit, 'demands' realization and, being supercosmic and dynamic, strives to manifest itself in the empirical world. It does so through attracting our spirit which, having once seen its inner convincingness, becomes its willing mediator. The conceptions of 'absolute value' and of 'a higher reality', akin to the inmost depths of our spirit and imparting being to it, as well as something of its own unconditional character—are correlative. Unconditional value and primary reality conceived as a will addressed to our own will are one and the same: manifesting itself empirically through inwardly appealing to our spirit which is irresistibly drawn to it, this reality is experienced by us as 'that which ought to be'. From the point of view of external necessity our spirit remains free and may respond or not respond to this appeal; but once the primary reality has taken possession of us from within, i.e., has appeared in its final self-evidence, it becomes an absolutely irresistible almighty power, coinciding as it were with the inmost essence of our own self (as noted in Kant's conception of autonomy). When Luther expressed the effect of his religious conviction upon him by the words '*Hier stehe ich, ich kann nicht anders!*' he gave a classical formulation of the inner certitude and omnipotence of the higher reality in moral experience. Man's capacity for superhuman achievements in the cause of truth and goodness in spite of his 'natural' frailty is a living testimony to the invincible power of the supreme reality which enters into him and acts through him.

Thus, in moral experience 'reality' as distinct both from the world of fact and from our own personal life stands out with special clarity. The category of 'ought' is a sign that clearly marks the difference: we contrast that which ought to be with that which actually is. Accordingly, the world of fact does not exhaust all that is accessible to our spirit and claims recognition; over and above that world there rises a higher kind of reality demanding a far more unconditional recognition. Reality is real not merely because it bears witness to its own actual presence, but because it is felt to have a *right* to be real: it bears its own ground in itself and in virtue of this *demands* to be realised on the empirical plane. It is experienced as the legitimate, rightful and in this sense primary reality. In that respect it is more real, or real in a deeper sense, than the world of fact.

This character of reality is clearly seen by contrast with our own mental life. Our feelings and impulses are arbitrary, unjustified, ungrounded: if I feel something, or want something, I do so 'for some unknown reason' or, more correctly, without any reason at all. Our mental states as such are rather like soap bubbles or will o' the wisp. They somehow arise out of nothing and pass away into nothing again. In Chapter I it was argued that the life of the subject is not 'subjective' in the sense of being illusory or unreal. But in quite a different sense, namely in the sense of being *groundless*, it can and must be described as subjective. Reality as we find it in moral experience is the direct opposite of this: it is objective—not in the sense of belonging to the world of objects, but of being firmly grounded in itself and inwardly necessary. In recognizing this we are aware that it is far more real and has much greater depth of fulness than my own mental life. Thus, in moral experience reality is most obviously manifested as the *ens realissimum*, to use a scholastic term.

Ancient philosophy as represented by Plato drew a distinction between true being (τό ὄντως ὄν) and apparent being, and Aristotle worked out the doctrine of degrees of reality. Centuries later, Thomas Aquinas built up the whole of his philosophical system upon that doctrine. Modern philosophy rejects the conception as self-contradictory; it knows only the simple, absolute distinction between 'is' and 'is not' and admits no possibility of degrees of being. Most of the hopeless difficulties which beset modern thought may well be said to have their source precisely in this simplified conception.[1] Moral experience provides one of the most clear testimonies to the fact that there are degrees of reality—i.e. that qualitatively different forms of being may manifest a greater or lesser degree of stability, fulness and depth and be more or less rightful, or 'well grounded' in reality.

6. *Reality as life. The unity of the actual and the potential*

Let us now sum up. Reality in its superlogical concreteness is the all-embracing and all-pervading unity which is the ground and source of the multiplicity and the independence of everything particular. The special ways in which its unique character manifests itself in the experience of beauty, of intercommunion and of moral life have been briefly indicated. We have seen that reality is something to which, in spite of its unfathomableness, the conception of *life* is pre-eminently applicable—life as self-revealing being and as a dynamic, creative, self-transcending principle which somehow

---

[1] The doctrine of the degrees of reality reappears, however, in Bradley's system (*Appearance and Reality*).

contains even that which is not actually present in it. The likeness and the difference between this absolute life and our own inner life must now be considered more closely. This is necessary because all experience of reality is given us directly or indirectly through our inner experience, i.e. through our mental life. The essential points of difference between reality and the subjective life have already been mentioned, so that now the points of similarity should be examined; and this, incidentally, will throw a new light upon the differences.

The ancient philosophy established the position that 'like is known by like'. Whatever value this may have with regard to external, objective knowledge, it is unquestionably true in reference to the inner experience. It is obvious that in the inner experience we cannot possibly come upon anything like a stone or some other material object—upon anything that has definite, perceptible outlines and exists in a fixed, ready-made form. Whatever we may find in it will be similar to the rest of our mental life: it will have the characteristics of life—dynamism, activity, or at any rate be the creative source of these characteristics. In short, reality given in inner experience is somehow analogous to the further unanalysable element called 'life' in contradistinction to everything immovable, passive and fixed. This is why the word 'reality' is preferable to the word 'being': 'being' is generally taken to mean the opposite of 'becoming', and indicates something already achieved and in this sense fixed and immovable. However incomprehensible and undefinable the nature of reality may be, it obviously is something living and not dead. Or, to put it more exactly, it closely resembles the further indescribable nature of our mental life—else we should not be able to meet it in our inner experience at all.

At first sight it might appear that this statement contradicts one of the main tenets of the 'perennial philosophy', dating back to Parmenides and Plato, clearly formulated by Aristotle and systematically developed by Thomas Aquinas—namely, the position that actuality ontologically precedes potentiality, or that all 'becoming' presupposes as its ground the completed fulness of being. An influential tendency in modern thought emphasizes, on the contrary, the vital, dynamic, creative character of reality and identifies it with becoming and potentiality. Bergson develops his philosophy of 'becoming' as against the old Platonic conception of the ontological primacy of the eternal, complete and immovable being. Samuel

REALITY AND THE KNOWLEDGE OF IT

Alexander maintains that modern philosophy has 'for the first time discovered time' (in its ontological primacy). This trend of thought coincides with 'evolutionism' or the idea that being in its fulness is not primary, but is gradually created in the process of becoming, in which the greater, fuller and more perfect arises out of the lesser, the poorer and the rudimentary. 'Evolutionism' is in direct opposition to Plato's and Aristotle's contention that actual fulness is the condition of all becoming, and that the effect cannot contain more reality than the cause.

I am far from sharing this modern trend of thought and indeed altogether disbelieve in the possibility of radically-new discoveries in philosophy, subversive of ancient truths. The vital, creative and dynamic aspect of reality cannot coincide with the abstract idea of becoming, evolution, or temporal process as distinct from eternity, complete finality and fulness. As already pointed out, reality never and in no respect is merely 'this and not that'; it is always a unity of 'this and that'; consequently it cannot be simply identified with 'time' or with 'becoming'. The main tenet of Plato's metaphysics is that temporal being, as arising and disappearing again, stands midway between being and non-being and is therefore an imperfect form of being; this is so obviously true that no new 'discovery' can disprove it. Reality may include time, but only in such unity with its contrary—eternity and actual fulness—that 'becoming' ceases to be specifically distinct from actuality and assumes a new, trans-figured form. As already pointed out, reality in its fulness is distinct from our own subjective life—else we could not encounter it and have it in inner experience. It differs from our own life both by its primary character and by the fact that in it the element of life, creativeness, becoming is *qualitatively* different from what it is in our experience. This does not prevent us, however, from appre-hending it as a living and creative force, obviously unlike the dead, sterile and passive immobility of a stone or even the completed finality and timelessness of a geometrical figure.

The element of truth contained in the 'modern' view is not to be found either in its revolutionary insistence upon the absolute prim-acy of dynamism and 'becoming', or in its claim to have first made the discovery of time (the nature of time was discovered by Plotinus no less fully than e.g. by Bergson); that claim merely means that the modern man, completely enthralled by the element of pure becom-ing and the process of 'doing', has lost the power of apprehending

77

the ontological significance of the complete and the eternal. The only thing that is true in the view in question is this: the ideas of actuality and potentiality, of the completed and the becoming cannot, with reference to reality, stand in the relation of such entire subordination of the second to the first and be so separate from each other as the thought of antiquity took them to be; though, indeed, this applies only to one tendency of Greek thought, the most strictly logical and uncompromising; in Plato's later writings an opposite tendency is already noticeable, and Plotinus works it out quite definitely.

Since reality is the unity of 'this' and 'the other', it must be regarded as an irreducible superlogical unity of creativeness and completedness, of becoming and eternity. The element of creativeness, life, activity is not merely a derivative manifestation of a different, already completed, immovable and eternal being: on the contrary, it is just as primary as it. Reality as being, and reality as creative activity simply coincide; an analogy of this—though of course an imperfect one—is provided by our 'self' the very being of which consists in the fact that it 'lives', i.e. does something, or has something happening within it. In other words, reality creates not only something other than itself; primarily its creativeness consists in *its creating itself*. Reality *is* creativeness. If it be asked who or what is it that creates, the answer can only be that such a question is out of place. It presupposes a categorial distinction between the subject or 'substance' as the bearer of reality and the activity that proceeds from it, but such a distinction is inapplicable to the superlogical nature of reality.[1] On the other hand, however, reality creates itself not by 'evolving' (which means the greater and the more perfect arising out of nothing, or out of something infinitely small and poor) but in such a way that 'becoming' is the realization of that which in another aspect already *is* from all eternity. The end here coincides with the beginning, and the 'evolution' is not a movement along a straight line into a hitherto non-existent distance, but, as it were, an unfolding in the order of time of that which on the plane of eternity forever is.

In other words, reality in virtue of its very nature cannot be *either* pure actuality *or* pure potentiality; it is both the one and the other in their indivisible unity. Reality is actual fulness, but a fulness

[1] This correlation is expounded with extraordinary depth and subtlety by Plotinus in the discussion of 'the freedom and the will of the One' (Enn. VI. 9).

which consists in activity, i.e. which creates itself and *is* self-creativeness. And, reversely: reality is activity, creativeness, becoming, but it contains this aspect within itself and is not subsumed under it: it is both the source and the eternal bearer of all its achievements. Creativeness does not here presuppose a final end beyond itself, inexistent as yet and to be realized. On the contrary, the purpose coincides with its creator, the end coincides with the beginning. Hegel truly says that 'in teleological activity (i.e. in creativeness) the end is the beginning, the consequence is the ground, the effect is the cause; that which already is, comes into being'.[1] Reality is *life*, i.e. activity, creativeness, a process of continuous becoming; but it also is *eternal* life, i.e. a life which from the beginning and at once contains the fulness of all that it actively realizes within itself. In its final completeness or eternity it is free from all that imparts to creativeness the character of a temporal, gradual process, but it contains the essence of creativeness—creative activity. As already pointed out, the basic feature of reality is its super-temporality, and that means completed all-embracing fulness, having time and activity within itself.

This combination, or, rather, this unity, of completed fulness and creative vitality makes reality an ideal for us who are bearers of potentiality and of becoming as a process of gradual realization. That which we strive for and are conscious of as an end to be achieved, and therefore as still not in our possession, is already present in its entirety in reality. And whatever we may be seeking, whatever our particular ends may be, in the last resort we strive for one thing only: for the fulness and completeness which we feel to be inherent in reality from the first as forming its very nature; we long ourselves to become the eternal all-embracing life. That longing is unrealizable and self-contradictory in so far as it is conceived and pursued within the forms and limits of our subjective being, which is potential and evolving; potentiality *as such* cannot, while remaining itself, acquire actuality and completed fulness. Insufficiency, dissatisfaction, groundlessness and longing for completion form the essence of our subjective being as such—in so far as we are confined within its limits we seek for what Hegel called 'a bad', i.e. a never realizable infinity. So long as we try to find the fulness of being in things determined by our subjectivity, such as wealth, power, fame, unruffled enjoyment, we are possessed by insatiable

[1] *Logik*, vol. III.

thirst: however much we may have, the demand for increase, the painful longing for the ever alluring and ever elusive 'more' poisons our existence.

The position radically changes when instead of striving for something external which is to give us completeness and fulness in spite of all our subjective limitations, we begin to seek reality *inwardly* and try to approximate to that in which it differs from our subjectivity. True, this aim is also unrealizable and the path leading to it is also endless. But each new stage attained changes our being qualitatively and transmutes our potentiality into partial actuality. We avoid the *logical* and therefore absolutely unreconcilable contradiction between the potential and the actual and enter the path of their superlogical combination which qualitatively transforms our nature. This path is open to us because our being cannot be wholly reduced to pure potentiality, but is only thinkable as a potential actuality, i.e. as containing from the first a germ of actuality. Purely human subjective activity is guided by subjective values and a longing for something which would complete our being in its groundless subjectivity; it differs from *creativeness*, in which our activity is a medium for the fulness of the self-subsistent reality, and is directed not towards 'our own' ends, but to that which the eternal, completed and creative life wants and demands of us. It is not only in moral activity in the specific sense that we realize that which is 'demanded' of us and is experienced as the power of the higher trans-subjective reality itself; in artistic, scientific, and every other kind of creativeness the end we strive for is not our own subjective invention, but is felt to be an objective value, i.e. something which ought to be; our will submits to a higher will—to the will of reality itself seeking self-realization (this will be discussed more fully in Chapter IV, 6). It may be said that, thus understood, the category of *ought* is characteristic not only of the moral life in the strict sense, but of human life as a whole: it betokens our inner connection with reality as a creative force, our subordination to it, and it indicates in what way reality rules over us and acts in and through us.

These considerations throw a fresh light on the kinship between reality and the nature of our own inner life. Our activity can serve as a means for the creative activity of reality solely because it is essentially the same in kind. It has the property of spontaneity, of being its own source, or, more simply, of *freedom*. True, our freedom is limited; we are conscious of being subject to forces external to us.

The external aspect of our existence forms part of the world of objects and is encompassed by it, occupying a definite confined place in space and time; hence, we can only act spontaneously within those narrow limits. Moreover, even our inner life does not wholly belong to our own 'self' as the spontaneous centre of activity: a great deal in it is not our possession but, rather, possesses us, or merely 'happens' within us and is not created by us. Yet, in spite of all these limitations, a creative spontaneous centre does exist in us, and its being consists in activity, i.e. in the reality of free spontaneous creativeness. There is something in us which we call our true self, transcending our empirical existence, both inner and outer, and acting—or able to act—as its judge, teacher and guide;[1] and in so far as we are that self, we are a true likeness of reality as such. Since reality has nothing outside itself and is pure creative actuality, it is pure spontaneity, absolute freedom. In contradistinction to us, reality is spontaneity through and through, and accordingly the conception of freedom can be only applied to it in a different, analogical sense—on the principle of *docta ignorantia*. In our human usage freedom, like all other notions, is defined negatively: it is the opposite of 'non-freedom' i.e. of constraint or determination from without. But in the case of reality, freedom, spontaneity, primacy is *all*, and therefore has a different, inexpressible meaning. The only, more or less suitable description of it would be 'primary life' or 'self-creation'. It would indicate that reality is not only that which it actually *is*, but also that which it 'wants' or 'ought' to be and which it creates within itself. In this respect, in spite of the profound difference between reality and ourselves, we perceive that it is similar to what we, in a limited and derivative way, are in our inmost being. For we, too, are in the last resort that which we create in ourselves; we build up not only our surroundings, but our own selves as well. This is precisely what is implied by the creative process of spiritual growth and self-education, apart from which there can be no personal inner life. We, too, have the inexpressible property of being *primary* and generating our own content. According to the general principle laid down in the preceding chapter, 'to have' (outside oneself) and 'to be' that which one 'has' is in this case one and the same. Distinguishing reality as such from ourselves, but 'having' it and being inwardly connected with it, we 'are' it and

---

[1] Cp. Kant's 'intelligible self'. The subject will be discussed more fully in ch. IV and V.

possess (in a derivative way) its characteristics. The property, common to us and to reality as such, of being primary creative activity, may also be called *spirit* or spiritual life. For spirit is not anything ready-made, is not 'substance', and is not even an 'entity' whose being could be distinguished from its vital activity; creative life is not its property, state, or attribute, but its very essence; the conceptions of life and of the living, of creativeness and the creator coincide. That which spirit strives for and lives by forms its very nature.

Thus in our inner experience the primary and absolute reality is revealed to us as on the one hand transcending and dominating us and providing the ultimate ground and meaning of what we call our 'self', and, on the other, as so intimately akin to us that only in and through it we find that which constitutes our own being.

CHAPTER III

The Idea and the Reality of God

*

1. Reason and faith. The problems of religious experience

A reader who has given any attention to the preceding chapters has probably more than once asked himself what is the relation between the enigmatic notion of 'reality', essentially indefinable in the usual logical way, and the universally recognized idea of God, clear and concrete to the religious consciousness. In some respects these two ideas seem alike and in others quite different. Does the author intend to replace the conception of God by that of 'reality' and to modify the generally accepted idea of the Divine so as to make it fit in with his conclusions? or is there room in his system for the living God of the religious consciousness, side by side with what he calls 'reality'?

So far I have intentionally avoided the subject of 'God' and in dealing with inner spiritual life have left out that sphere of it which is called 'the religious life'. The time has now come to make myself clear.

It would be intellectually dishonest to confuse or simply to identify reality with that which is meant by the term 'God'. Bradley wittily remarks that a person who identifies the ideas of 'the absolute'[1] and 'God' finds himself in the tragicomic position of a dog that has two masters and helplessly rushes from one to the other, not knowing which to obey. I have not the least inclination to find myself in this predicament, especially since, apart from all its logical difficulties,

[1] It has already been mentioned that, roughly speaking, reality corresponds to what is more often called 'the absolute'.

it often leads to serious and dangerous error. The point is that, as we shall see later, reality is the source, among other things, of that which we recognize as sin and evil in human life, and if only on that account cannot possibly be simply identified with God.[1]

But before discussing the relation between the idea of God and that of reality, and the place which that idea can occupy in the metaphysical system here indicated, it is necessary to answer a preliminary question as to whether it is possible to reason about God at all and make Him the subject of philosophical reflection. The answer remains doubtful in spite of the stable tradition going right through the history of philosophy ancient, mediaeval and modern, down to the German idealism and our own day. 'The God of the philosophers' (as Pascal used to say) generally remains in some of his essential characteristics so different from 'the God of Abraham, Isaac, and Jesus Christ', that one cannot help suspecting the philosophers of using the name of God—with conscious or unconscious mendacity —to designate something quite alien to religious consciousness and incapable of satisfying it. No one has expressed more powerfully than Pascal the conviction that pure thought and religious faith are *toto genere* distinct. The depth of thought and the artistic excellence of expression makes his reflections on the subject rank with the greatest achievements of the human mind. The reader will not complain if I begin by discussing them. This is what Pascal says:

'La distance infinie des corps aux esprits figure la distance infiniment plus infinie des esprits à la charité, car elle est surnaturelle.

Tout l'éclat des grandeurs n'a point de lustre pour les gens qui sont dans la recherche de l'esprit.

La grandeur des gens d'esprit est invisible aux rois, aux riches, aux capitaines, à tous ces gens de chair.

La grandeur de la sagesse qui n'est nulle sinon de Dieu est

[1] The identification of reality with God is the basic error of pantheism. The usual opinion that pantheism identifies God with the objective world is mistaken: *such* pantheism has never existed (a suggestion of it may, at best, be detected in the first helplessly-naive sketch of it in Xenophanes). The Stoics, and Spinoza even more so, carefully distinguished the metaphysical ground or the primary basis of universal being—something similar to what I call reality—from the empirically given 'objective existence', and it was only the first that they identified with God. Spinoza expresses this by speaking of *natura naturans* and *natura naturata*.

invisible aux charnels et aux gens d'esprit. Ce sont trois ordres differents de genre . . .

Tous les corps, le firmament, les étoiles, la terre et ses royaumes, ne valent pas le moindre des esprits; car il connait tout cela, et soi; et les corps, rien.

Tous les corps ensemble et tous les esprits ensemble, et toutes leur productions, ne valent pas le moindre mouvement de la charité. Cela est d'un ordre infiniment plus élevé.

De tous les corps ensemble, on ne saurait faire réussir une petite pensée: cela est impossible, et d'un autre ordre. De tous les corps et esprits, on n'en saurait tirer un mouvement de vraie charité; cela est impossible, et d'un autre ordre surnaturel.'[1]

The same idea is summed up in the famous dictum 'Le coeur a ses raisons, que la raison ne connaît pas'.

Thus for Pascal faith which reveals to the human soul the living God is achieved in quite a special way which he calls 'l'ordre de charité' or 'the heart' and which has nothing in common with reason, being separated from it by an 'infinitely greater infinity' than thought or reason is separated from inanimate bodies.

It is obvious for every religiously-sensitive mind that this idea contains a profound and indisputable truth. It is equally obvious, however, that as thus expressed it is bound to raise the gravest doubts. To begin with, the analogy between the unsurmountable dualism of faith and reason and the Cartesian conception of the dualism of 'minds' and 'bodies', so convincing to Pascal (and to the ordinary common sense view in general), is far from convincing to us who have been enriched by the discoveries of modern psychology and philosophy of nature. If 'bodies' are in the last resort immaterial bearers of energy or of some dynamic force, and 'mind' or consciousness has for its concrete basis a certain vital impulse, there must be an inner connection between the two in spite of the chasm which apparently divides them. But this is only by the way: the chief point is that if the impassable gulf between thought and the religious consciousness were a fact, no theology would be possible, even in the most elementary sense of a simple intellectual expression of faith, i.e. there could be no clearly-conscious faith. Besides, the assertion that such a gulf exists would be self-contradictory: it would be impossible to understand how in that case Pascal could

---

[1] Pascal, *Pensées*, ed. Brunschvicq, No. 793.

express his *awareness* of the absolute heterogeneity between faith and reason in words that combine a profound intuition of the heart with a perfect rational clarity of thought. Obviously Pascal himself does not draw such extreme conclusions from his thesis.

If, however, his thesis cannot be accepted in the form in which he has expressed it, a conclusion of the utmost importance follows forthwith: the inaccessibility of the domain of faith to reason involves the same kind of dialectic as does the relation between supra-rational experience of concrete reality and rational knowledge. The domain of faith is super-rational, and categories of rational knowledge are inapplicable to it; but this does not preclude us from giving a conscious account—through concrete description and transcendental thought—of that in which the domain of faith surpasses that of rational knowledge (cp. Chapter II, 2). Hence it follows that however deep the chasm separating faith from reason may be, it is not impassable: at a certain depth there must be a connection between these two heterogeneous spheres. This is confirmed, too, by the fact that human mind is intellectually or spiritually capable of embracing and surveying the chasm at a single glance, i.e. of combining both domains in the unity of its consciousness.

These general considerations, however, are not sufficient. To return to Pascal's thesis, the truth of it might be expressed in a modified form as follows: the domain of faith is absolutely unfathomable, for it is heterogeneous to 'pure reason' as such. It is not quite clear what exactly Pascal means in this connection by *esprit* (reason). Very probably he means by it what elsewhere he calls *esprit géometrique* or the faculty of purely intellectual contemplation, i.e. of the contemplation of ideal forms and relations. Those intellectually apprehensible forms and relations constitute as it were the external structure of being, while truths of faith reveal themselves at a deeper level. Pascal himself opposes pure reason—*esprit géometrique*—to another reason which he calls *esprit de finesse*. The latter may be defined as the faculty of finding one's bearings in the complex whole of existence not directly determined by its ideal structure. It is the aspect of reason in virtue of which it has flexibility, plasticity, 'subtlety', i.e. the faculty of adapting ideas to the complex and logically unanalysable content of being, apprehended only by experience. By admitting a special *esprit de finesse* Pascal overcomes the one-sidedness of the rationalistic ideal of philosophy established by his senior contemporary, Descartes—an ideal which strongly appealed to his own scientific and mathematical genius. The idea that all the truths of philosophy must be 'deducible' and capable of logical proof has warped philosophical thought for centuries and is perhaps not wholly outlived yet.[1]

This *esprit de finesse* ought to embrace the experience which I have called 'living knowledge' as distinct from dispassionate objective knowledge—the experience in which reality reveals itself to us from within, through our co-belonging to it. Now, such experience undoubtedly includes religious consciousness, given in the 'experience of the heart'. Its truths, inaccessible to 'pure reason'—*esprit géometrique*—might still be accessible to the *esprit de finesse*. Of course 'the experience of the heart' precedes intellectual intuition both psychologically and in reality. But once it is reached (by the path of 'faith' which alone leads to it) reason has a chance of interpreting and expressing the content of it by its own means, i.e. in notions.

It is precisely at this point that the true meaning of Pascal's contention about the utter heterogeneity of faith and reason (*coeur* and *esprit*) becomes apparent. He maintains that religious experience is *toto genere* distinct from all other, 'earthly' experience that lies at the basis of the usual rational interpretation of the world and of life. The experience of faith is a miraculous meeting with the absolutely transcendent and super-cosmic reality of God, flight into an utterly different dimension of being, foreign to all other experience—'*le surnaturel*' as the Catholic thinkers call it; there is bound to be an impassable gulf between religious experience and the usual

---

[1] Strange as it may seem, the philosophical school of English Empiricism, opposed to Cartesianism, has not introduced the necessary correction. Having recognised experience as the source of knowledge, it narrowed down the conception of it to merely sensuous experience, i.e. to the apprehension of the particular and therefore temporal being. It has thus rejected the very notion of metaphysical or ontological knowledge. The idea that in the actual depths of being there are correlations accessible to intellectual intuitition as, so to speak, 'eternal facts of being', discoverable by experience, has remained foreign to it. This truth was first expressed not by a philosopher, but by the great poet and sage Goethe in his highly original theory of knowledge. According to him cognition reaches its final end when it discovers certain 'primary appearances' (Urphänomene) and must humbly recognize that it can go no further; all attempts at further 'explanation', i.e. at rational understanding, remain vain and objectless. The merit of stating this in clear logical terms belongs to the remarkable French nineteenth-century philosopher-mathematician Cournot, who argued against Cartesian rationalism.

THE IDEA AND THE REALITY OF GOD

interpretation of the world and of life. Neither the purely rational knowledge nor our ordinary practical wisdom can grasp or fathom 'the experience of the heart'.

It is, of course, quite indisputable that religious life contains, in fact, an element of the 'miraculous', apprehensible only in the emotionally-irrational way in the 'experience of the heart' and alien not merely from sober, purely intellectual knowledge, but from all philosophic thought as such. This is due to the fact that religious life is the totality of the believer's purely personal experiences, i.e. of processes and events, so to speak, of lyrical or dramatic nature, determining the relation of the human heart to God. In so far as religious experience has the character of such personal and as it were accidental—i.e. unconnected with the rest of our knowledge— 'meetings' with God as an absolutely unique and individual Being, and involves changes in our relation to Him and in emotions connected therewith, it remains inaccessible to intellectual generalization and does not fit into a philosophical pattern of the world and of life. This is the final limit of all 'philosophies of religion'. Faith in this sense is indeed an independent and self-sufficient sphere of life, having an experiential certainty of its own; it neither needs nor allows of any explanation. Thus a lover in the arms of his beloved finds all the spiritual fulness of life that he needs and that is possible for him, and neither can nor wants to 'reason' about his love, or seek to explain and to justify it.

And yet religious experience includes another element as well. We are conscious that in it the ultimate depths of being are revealed to us. But ultimate depth or primary ground is a *universal*, all-determining basis, necessarily connected with all other contents of reality accessible to us. In other words, religious experience includes an element of that living knowledge, common to all our inner life, which may be called *metaphysical experience*. In religious experience we are aware of God as an individual concrete being to which we stand in a personal subjective relation, and at the same time we are aware of Him as eternal, all-embracing and omnipresent, as the absolute ground of all existence. In this capacity He is obviously indissolubly connected with all that is.

The same correlation may be elucidated in another way: our ordinary 'earthly' experience forms a certain general picture of the world and of life, and, as we have seen, this objective picture is unthinkable apart from its basis—apart from the supercosmic sphere of the all-embracing *reality*, immediately revealed in the inner 'metaphysical' experience. This brings us back to our starting point: 'God'—whatever we may actually mean by the term—certainly does not coincide with the idea of reality, but is intimately connected with it. Religious experience has an aspect in which it coincides with metaphysical experience; and if we are to give a philosophical interpretation to the idea of God, we must go further along the path that has led us to the domain of 'reality'. However heterogeneous the particular contents of experience may be, they all have an aspect in which they are merged in one all-embracing experience of reality, apart from which philosophy itself is unthinkable; that experience is akin to Pascal's 'knowledge of the heart', though it does not entirely coincide with it.

The same conclusion is reached by showing that a sharp dualism between the 'supernatural' (*surnaturel*) and the 'natural' is untenable. It cannot, of course, be denied that there is a duality between 'earthly' or 'natural' being, familiar to us from our general experience, and its 'supernatural', 'divine' and 'miraculous' aspect revealed to us in religious experience. But the point is that the so-called 'natural' being is also in the last resort, derivatively supernatural: the 'supernatural' principle interpenetrates it through and through. The connecting link between the transcendentally-supernatural and the 'natural' (in which the supernatural is immanently present) is *reality* as the basic innermost element of being. This is why philosophy, or conceptual knowledge of being is not separated from religion by an impassable gulf, but is organically connected with it— and also why a philosophical understanding of religious experience and its object, God, is necessary. Philosophy must of course recognize that its possibilities in this respect are inevitably limited. In the apprehension of God saints and mystics will always be wiser than the most profound philosopher because, as just pointed out, they alone are able to grasp their object in its concrete fulness and perceive not only its general nature, but its individual, personal aspect, inaccessible to philosophical thought. Hence in religious life there always remains something 'hidden from the wise and prudent' and revealed only unto 'babes'. With this reservation, however, philosophy has a right to believe that in virtue of the ultimate unity between human spirit and reality as such, the 'heart' and 'the intellect', in spite of all the difference between them, are destined for harmonious co-operation.

This, however, does not exhaust our subject. The discussion has so far proceeded on the tacit assumption that religious experience and the idea of God obtained through it are perfectly definite and univocal. In using the word 'God' we imply that at any rate the general meaning of it is understood by everyone alike. The variety of religious beliefs, however, bears witness to the contrary. The question is, what kind of religious experience and what idea of God are we to start with in trying to reach a philosophical apprehension of God.

If for the sake of fairness and completeness we proceed inductively, by enumerating all the historical forms of the idea of God, the content common to them all is in danger of dissolving in sheer indefiniteness. If we leave out of account faiths in which, as in the original Buddhism, the idea of God is altogether absent, and attempt to generalize such different religions as ancient paganism in its many varieties, Judeo-Christian and Mahometan monotheism, Brahmanism, Confucianism, Taoism, and all the innumerable multitude of the so-called primitive religions, the idea of God common to them all will be scarcely more than a name. At best it will be possible to say that 'God' is a vague object of 'worship' or of a specific feeling of fear—something for which the German theologian, Rudolf Otto, invented the term *das Numinose*. This idea is too indefinite to be philosophically useful.

If on the contrary, for the sake of definiteness, we start with religious experience that has already found expression in dogma, e.g. with the Christian faith, we shall be renouncing unprejudiced freedom of thought, for we shall be replacing immediate religious experience by uncritically accepted dogmatic teaching about God; obviously, every definite confessional idea of God, and the corresponding type of religious faith inevitably contain an element of theological doctrine accepted on the authority of tradition. Philosophical apprehension of God would lose all meaning if it simply coincided with 'dogmatic theology' as a rational and systematic explanation of a particular definite set of religious ideas.

For an independent thinker the only alternative is to start with his own personal and immediate religious experience. Of course this involves the danger of accepting that experience with all its limitations and subjectively-individual peculiarities as a criterion of truth. And indeed, many 'philosophies of religion', especially at our epoch of the decay of religious culture, provide an alarming example of philistine paltriness and conceit laying claim to be universally binding. In order to avoid this danger as far as possible one must, while preserving independence of thought, try to enrich and deepen one's religious experience by learning from 'the masters of the craft' —saints and mystics; it is essential to develop a kind of religious sensitiveness or good taste.[1] This, of course, does not cancel, but merely diminishes the risk of our experience being subjective and limited. But the mere fact of an experience being limited does not prevent its being trustworthy, so long as no exhaustive fulness is claimed for it: even a short-sighted person may clearly see at any rate the objects nearest to him. As to subjectivity, its significance must not be exaggerated; the danger of it, after all, threatens human knowledge throughout, especially in the spiritual domain, where individual peculiarities of the subject play a greater part than in sciences based upon external experience. All human knowledge runs the risk of being one-sided and distorting the truth because of the knowing subject's particular interests and habits of thought. Psychology proves that even our perceptions are determined by thought —and thought, if only because it is bound up with the level of the subject's development and the structure of language, bears the impress of a certain intellectual and spiritual culture. Accordingly, it must be honestly admitted that our religious and philosophical thought is determined both by traditional religious culture and by the general spiritual outlook of the period. This does not preclude, however, either sincere striving for objective truth or the possibility of approaching it. Only those who start with the assumption that religious faith is not a real *experience*, i.e. not an intuitive apprehension of reality, can believe that the inevitable element of subjectivity deprives judgments about God of objective significance and value. In the domain of religious thought (as indeed of all thought about spiritual realities) bold striving after objective truth, and faith in the possibility of attaining it are perfectly justified if combined with humble recognition that all human achievements in this respect are relative.

How then are we to interpret the idea of God revealed in the immediate supra-rational experience of faith, and what place are

---

[1] Bergson's standpoint in his book *Les deux sources de la morale et de la religion* may be taken as a pattern.

we to give it in the general scheme of reality indicated in the preceding chapters?

2. God as a reality of inner experience

Starting with the meaning which the word 'God' has for most religious minds and not as yet defining it more closely, we must say in the first place that God has a direct and immediate relation to 'reality' and is but indirectly related through it to the world of objects; He certainly does not form part of that world. In a sense this is taken for granted in the usual conception of God. He is conceived as existing 'outside' the world as a supercosmic, transcendent Being. This is why pantheism—at any rate in so far as it is supposed to identify God and the world—is always regarded as 'atheism', i.e. as a denial of God's existence.

In another respect, however, the prevalent type of religious thought tends to conceive God as a reality existing outside us, as an *object* the existence of which has to be intellectually established. In the judgment of faith 'God exists' the word 'existence' is used much in the same sense in which it is applied to objects or to the world as a whole. In that case objective reality is conceived as falling into two distinct halves: the world, and the super-cosmic God. Ancient and mediaeval thought definitely localized God 'above the heavens', i.e. beyond the utmost boundary of the fixed stars. The Copernican revolution, and especially modern physics, which makes a concrete picture of the universe altogether impossible, rule out this naive conception; and yet in some other and more subtle sense, the prevalent type of religious thought still takes God to exist as objectively and, so to speak, in the same kind of way or on the same plane of being as the world, though externally to it. The dispute between religion and atheism takes the form of arguing whether there are grounds for admitting 'the existence' of God, i.e. of including Him among objects of our knowledge, proved to exist outside and independently of us. Thus the classical theological 'proofs of the existence of God', e.g. most of those used by Thomas Aquinas, are inferences from the world's structure; they are intended to show that in studying nature we are compelled to admit the existence of God as the 'first mover' or 'the first cause', or the source of the world's purposive character. God is conceived as so to speak the foundation of the world-structure and in that sense as possessing categorically the same character of objective being as the world—just as the foundation and the building upon which it rests are equally subject to the general laws of physics.[1]

In opposition to this prevalent type of religious thought it must be urged that God belongs to the sphere of 'reality', as distinct in principle from 'the world of fact' and therefore cannot form part of that world, even if it be taken to include the super-cosmic realm. If 'to exist' means to form part of the world of fact, faith and unbelief—paradoxically enough—must agree in denying this predicate to God. True, they will understand such a denial in different ways and draw totally different conclusions from it. Unbelief identifies the world of fact with reality, or, in other words, takes it to be all-inclusive; accordingly, to exclude God from it is the same as to say that He is a human invention, a fiction—just as to deny the existence of winged serpents is identical with saying that they are imaginary. From the point of view of faith, on the contrary, it will simply mean that the word 'existence', which implies belonging to the world of fact, is inapplicable to God, because it gives a wrong idea of Him; the negative judgment does not in the least affect the value or the truth of the idea of God.

This argument is not an idle refinement of logical thought or an indulgence in pedantic subtlety. It is of decisive significance for interpreting the very essence of religious faith. It takes the sting out of the atheists' main contention. The whole point of atheism is that in our direct experience of objective reality we do not encounter any such object as God and that all we know about the world gives us no sufficient grounds, to say the least of it, for inferring the existence of God, which is therefore an unjustified hypothesis. The first part of the argument is unquestionably true, and with regard to it, faith really agrees with unbelief. The possibility spoken of by the mystics, of coming into direct contact with God in and through experience, is in any case something utterly different from a sober recognition of His presence in the familiar, everyday world of fact equally valid for all. But however incontestable the assertion that God does not form part of the world of objects may be, from the religious standpoint it is as irrelevant as the notorious remark of a Soviet airman that in his flights into the stratosphere he never met God. The

---

[1] Thomas Aquinas's doctrine of the non-identical but 'analogical' meaning of the term existence as applied to different realms of being implies quite another trend of thought, but we can leave this aside for the present.

THE IDEA AND THE REALITY OF GOD

second part of the argument is that scientific knowledge does not justify the admission that God is the world's creator and architect. Recent developments in science have shattered the prevalent mechanistic view of the world, on the strength of which Laplace defiantly declared that 'he never had need to postulate the existence of God'; science is now rather inclined to admit a purposive organizing principle at the basis of the universe. But this is only one of the possible scientific hypotheses, relative and uncertain as all hypotheses that allow of no experimental verification; and besides, from the point of view of purely objective knowledge, world's purposiveness always remains limited, and is accompanied by events and processes that are obviously irrational and elemental. No one would venture to affirm the purposiveness of earthquakes, hurricanes, or volcanic eruptions; Voltaire's religious doubts in connection with the Lisbon earthquake of 1755 remain unanswered. Catastrophes and disasters in social life produce an even stronger impression of irrationality. The experience of recent years taken at its face value, powerfully suggests that the world of human life is senseless, chaotic, unrighteous and irrational, and that the ultimate ground of the universe, however it may be conceived, is infinitely remote from even the most general and elementary characteristics presupposed by the popular idea of God.

But what does it all mean? It means one thing only: God cannot be found—cannot even be sought—on the paths of external experience and rational thought which lead us to dispassionate recognition, or as it were to a cold and sober registration of 'objects': God may and must be sought only on paths that lead to actual living meeting with *reality*. Since reality is not a dumb and passive object of our cognitive efforts, but something that reveals itself to us through its own activity, we can repeat the old and generally recognized religious truth that God is not an 'object' directly accessible to knowledge, but becomes accessible only through *revelation* in the general and literal sense of that term (see Chapter II, 4).

Hence it follows that if, and in so far as, the idea of God can be substantiated at all, we can reach it, in the first instance at any rate, only by means of inner experience. For it is only in inner experience that we come into direct contact with reality and that it is revealed to us. In moral experience and in the experience of communion (the 'I—thou' relation) we meet reality or come upon it as it were from

94

without; but our awareness of this is only possible on the basis of a previous inner experience of reality, or else already contains such experience. This is why the experience of 'the knowledge of God' or, more exactly, of meeting God as a reality has the character of primary self-evidence and, as such, is completely independent of any other knowledge, of all that we think or know about the nature and structure of the objective world, and indeed of the whole domain of thought and reason. In this sense Pascal is perfectly right in saying that it is a leap into a different sphere, a totally other order of being, inaccessible to *esprit* or pure reason. Experiential apprehension of God is so direct and immediate that our conviction of His reality is in no way affected by the possible difficulties of reconciling it with our knowledge about the world of fact. However great those difficulties might be, the problems of 'theodicy' do not in the smallest degree undermine the self-evidence of our actual apprehension of God. On the other hand, all rational 'proofs' of the existence of God in so far as they are at all possible and truly convincing presuppose that we already have the *idea* of God, attained in quite a different way.

St. Augustine was the first clearly to grasp that the reality of God was different in kind from all objective existence, and therefore could only be attained through inner experience as a revelation. Describing his previous doubts and the way he overcame them, he says: 'And I said "Is Truth therefore nothing because it is not diffused through space finite or infinite?" And Thou criedst to me from afar; "Yea verily, *I am that I am*". And I heard as the heart heareth, nor had I room to doubt, and I should sooner doubt that I live than that Truth is not.' (Confessions VII, 10).

This seems to contradict the indisputable fact that we may, and indeed often do, apprehend the Deity through external experience as well, for instance in connection with events in our own life or in nature. There is no doubt that the awakening of religious consciousness is often furthered by external shocks—by such facts as the death of people we love, or a sudden collapse of all our hopes and plans, or by the menacing or beautiful natural phenomena that overwhelm us by their superhuman grandeur, and so on. Yet as already pointed out, the outer experience in such cases is not merely 'objective knowledge', but only an external stimulus either for awakening for the first time an inner experience of the invisible reality, or for recalling a previous experience of it. The 'knowledge of God' acquired in this way is reached not through the sense organs or the intellect, but through 'the heart', i.e. the inmost essence of our being to which a certain supra-cosmic, *supra-objective* divine reality is revealed from within.

True, there may be different ways of interpreting religious experience of this kind. Martin Buber has rightly pointed out that the fundamental difference between monotheism and pagan religions lies in the fact that a pagan apprehends every striking event of the external world as the direct action and expression of a special deity, whereas a monotheist sees in it merely an indirect manifestation of the one God whom he apprehends more adequately in the inner experience of moral and spiritual life. To repeat: in both cases religious apprehension is an inner experience of 'the heart', but in the first case it is entirely bound up with a particular external impression and qualitatively determined by it, whereas in the second the experience called forth by an external impression is interpreted with the help of richer and more profound experience, acquired in the depths of the spirit, independently of anything external. Which of the two is nearer to truth? From what has already been said it is clear that there can be no question here of truth and error in the usual sense of correspondence or lack of correspondence between our ideas and objective facts, but only of the greater or lesser fulness and adequacy of the self-manifestation of reality, i.e. of the revelation of God. This is another instance of the correlation in virtue of which we can only have objective (i.e. truly justified and self-evident) knowledge of God in a *religiously* determined form, i.e. in the form of knowledge dependent upon the type and the level of our own religious development. In any case, in our experience—the experience of people of our spiritual culture—the religious element contained in our impressions from the surrounding world can only be expressed as a consciousness of 'something divine', of some indirect action or manifestation of the divine principle; it does not take the form of true 'theophany', or the actual appearance to us of God Himself. It is only in the inner experience detached from everything external, only in the inmost depths of the heart that we meet God, and, in however vague a way, come into contact with Him, unutterable as He is and distinct from all else. Only one impression external to our 'self', or, rather, transcending it, can form part of this experience—namely, intimate communion with the mysterious supercosmic depths of another personal spirit, stirring the depths of our own 'self' hitherto concealed from us (this is the meaning of theophany not only in the coming of Jesus Christ, but also of every meeting with manifestations of true holiness). Such communion opens to us the recesses of our own spiritual being, leads us further and deeper into ourselves. Only left alone with my self, and apprehending in silence and darkness through the inmost reality of my inner life the infinite depths of reality as such, can I 'meet' God and have experiential knowledge of Him.

But what is it we meet on those inner paths of the soul and may be entitled to call 'God'? So far our argument has been purely hypothetical: *if* there is God, *if* the idea of Him is well grounded, its source can only be the inner experience of reality and not—at any rate not directly—the experience of the objective world. *If* God is, He is somehow related to reality.

The actual and immediate religious experience says—apart from any arguments and proofs—that God *is*. As already pointed out, a philosophical justification of the idea of God cannot possibly mean an attempt to substantiate it by abstract considerations *apart from* religious experience. It can only mean interpreting that idea, i.e. elucidating as far as possible its content, and connecting it with other data of the inner experience, already familiar to us. In doing so we must endeavour to renounce all the familiar abstract definitions of God, all that we have learned from hearsay, and seek to discover by experience the aspect of reality which we would be justified in describing by that traditional name.

3. The idea of God and the self-evidence of His reality

It is advisable to begin with the subjectively-psychological, or, more exactly, the subjectively-spiritual aspect of the problem—in other words, to start from the only primary source of knowledge in this sphere—the pure 'experience of the heart'.

Our self or 'soul' is conscious in two respects of its poverty and insufficiency, of the inherent tragedy of its existence. On the one hand, in so far as it attains true self-consciousness, it is inevitably aware of its solitude and homelessness in the world of fact in which it is bound to participate and to which it is largely subordinated. 'The world' is a certain self-contained order of things and events, the course and arrangement of which are independent of our personal needs, hopes and desires, and indifferent to them. Our cherished desires remain unfulfilled, our hopes are shattered by the implacable course of events, our wordly fate to a large extent depends not upon ourselves or our own will, but upon external circumstances and incomprehensible sequence of facts ruled by laws that are alien to us. Man is supposed to have gained power over nature, but this power is distinctly limited: he has not yet learned to deal with a number of elemental calamities that threaten him, and indeed, on sober reflection, is not likely ever to avoid them completely. It is sufficient to recall that all our proud scientific achievements are powerless against the 'chief enemy'—inevitable death. Besides, it is not only the world of external non-human nature that is alien and hostile to man. The cold 'objective' sphere felt by us as a power opposed to the demands of the spirit includes, paradoxically enough, the collective world of human society and communion; strange to say, our will often proves to have even less power over it than over physical nature. Thus, the state with all its activities is, in the words of Nietzsche 'the coldest of all cold monsters'; the same character attaches to all the 'public' side of social life. The experience of history has taught us that the power of '*this* world' over us is increasing rather than diminishing. Even on the plane of purely personal relations we constantly find that the mental life of others confronts us as a 'brute fact', indifferent to our inner being, or limiting and repressing it. In all these respects our inmost self is in opposition to the blind course of events in the natural and the objectively-human world. In one way or another that which we call happiness—the satisfaction of the innermost strivings that form the very essence of our soul—remains unrealizable, and human life, even the most successful outwardly, is to a great extent a series of failures and disappointments, and continuous unsatisfied longing. The perennial dream of human heart—to harmonize the external course and structure of life, both social and personal, with the vital aspirations of the human spirit is doomed to remain a 'utopia'.

On the other hand, when we try to escape from this hostile or indifferent world into our inner life and seclude ourselves within it, we discover to our horror and dismay that the blind forces alien or opposed to our inmost being overcome us even there, in our own soul. This is the most tragic and enigmatic fact of our existence. We resemble a country waging a constant, bitter and hopeless war against an enemy far more powerful than it, and at the same time being devastated by a civil war. As already pointed out, the specific 'subjectivity' of our mental life consists in its *groundlessness*—in the fact that our desires, feelings and moods arise in us of themselves, independently of the directing central will of the 'self'. Those anarchical elements bring confusion and conflict into our life and often entice us into ways leading to destruction. Freedom or spontaneity which forms the very essence of our inner life is very far from being true self-determination; to a great extent it is anarchy enslaving us to blind, irresponsible forces. Our position resembles that of a man driven hither and thither by gusts of wind and constantly losing his direction as he walks across a shifting bog, ready to engulf him at any moment.

The calamities that thus beset us both from without and from within clearly indicate what it is we need. We need a friendly protecting power which would save us both from the ills caused by the blindness and indifference of 'the world' and from the fatal blindness of irrational forces dominating us from within. In order to save us from the world, this power must be able to compensate us for our sufferings in it by satisfying the true and primary needs of the heart; that means, it must be akin to our inmost being, so that we could feel at home in it, finding shelter and perfect contentment. But this is only possible if it contains all that constitutes our being as persons, for everything impersonal is alien from us and cannot be our refuge and home. And in order to save us from ourselves this power must be not merely stronger than we, but must also have its self-evident—and in that sense absolutely secure—ground in itself, instead of being blind and groundless as we are; it must be absolutely supreme. No purely subjective power, no friend or protector as subjective as ourselves could save us, for he would suffer from the same defects and limitations as we, and, bewaring of them, we should have to fall back on the shifting ground of our own selves. But a personality free from subjectivity is *super-personal* and is not to be met with in the empirical world. It super-logically combines the characteristics of personality and of absolute self-groundedness and objectivity, in the sense of absolute intrinsic value (cp. Chapter II, 5).

Our first and immediate reaction towards such a power is the awareness that it saves and protects us, granting us the peace of security and complete inner satisfaction or happiness; we stand in the same relation to it as a weak, helpless and suffering child does to its loving father or mother. Even in the case of a child the happiness

99

of the relation lies in trustful self-surrender, in joyful readiness to renounce one's own will to a being felt to be wiser and more stable than oneself; the same thing is true to a still greater extent of our relation to the absolute being that saves us. We only find the longed-for salutary basis of our personal being when we renounce self-centred subjectivity and transfer our centre of gravity to that higher reality. Accordingly, our second reaction towards it (second in the order of discussion, but first as the necessary condition of the second) is a completely disinterested recognition of its supremacy and intrinsic value, without any reference to ourselves and our personal needs—a disinterested joy in its perfection.[1]

The unique reality to which we stand in this twofold relation as to the only power that truly saves and protects us, and as to an object of worship and an absolute value, bestowing upon us the joy of disinterested admiration and self surrender—is precisely that which we call 'God'. This implies that the basic 'attributes' constituting the idea of God follow from the apprehension of Him as a reality revealed in our inner experience, and therefore from its relation to our inner being. All the rest—the conception of God as the creator and ruler of the world, the faith in His omnipotence, in short, all that is concerned with God's relation to the objective world—is derivative and, from the point of view of pure experience, more or less problematic. God is immediately revealed to me only as forming the indivisible unity of 'God and me'.

We give the name of God to the supreme and ultimate reality which, as the primary source of all that is real, is absolutely self-subsistent. It is, on the one hand, the only absolutely secure basis of our being, and, on the other, as having supremacy and absolute value, is for us an object of worship and loving self-surrender; in virtue of this, the good or the morally binding is experienced as the command or the will of God—cp. Chapter II, 5—and therefore as

[1] In this connection one is reminded of the famous dispute between Fénélon and Bossuet as to whether we should love God and obey Him disinterestedly, or look upon Him as the source of our own salvation. The issue is hopelessly confused by the fact that both sides regard as logically contradictory and incompatible that which in actual religious experience is given as an indivisible super-rational unity. The dispute is settled beforehand by the words 'he that findeth his life shall lose it and he that loseth his life for My sake shall find it'. God is for us both the power that saves us and the object of admiration and complete self-surrender, so that the very conceptions of 'self-seeking' and disinterestedness are inapplicable to our relation to Him; the simple name for this relation is *love*.

the condition of our salvation. In the inseverable unity of these two main attributes God reveals Himself as the only reality in and through which our self or soul finds its true realization.

But does He truly reveal Himself to me? What objective grounds have I for recognizing Him? So far reference has only been made to man's need for such a Being, but sober reason teaches us the bitter truth that a great deal of what we need is, unfortunately, not given us. Is not the admission of the reality of God a comforting fairy tale, or the fruit of wishful thinking? That is what the voice of 'common sense' tells us. The direct answer given by religious consciousness to this question is contained in the already quoted words of Pascal '*le coeur a ses raisons que la raison ne connaît pas*'. From the 'experience of the heart' we know for certain that in the end no heart's longing remains unfulfilled—that the reality we yearn for comes to meet us and to grant our need. The truth of the great words 'seek and ye shall find, knock and it shall be opened unto you' is always justified by religious experience.

But, contrary to Pascal and to the widely prevalent opinion, it is precisely at this point that the 'experience of the heart' is seen not to be separated by an impassable gulf from the domain of 'reason,' if the latter be understood in the deep and broad sense of metaphysical experience or philosophic intuition of reality. That which has just been stated in religious terms as the 'need' of the human heart and its satisfaction can also be expressed in a purely objective way by analysing the meaning of reality which is both super-rational and expressible in a rational and therefore universally-binding form.

To begin with, setting aside for the moment the doubt as to whether our religious need can be rationally justified, let us be quite clear about one thing: that *need itself* is in any case not a subjective invention, but a self-evident and ineradicable part of our inner being, i.e. of our reality. Unbelievers are aware of this too, in so far as they are able to give themselves an honest account of their inner life. True, there are a number of people who imagine that they can live perfectly well without inner spiritual support, but this is sheer illusion, dispelled by every more or less serious trail, or indeed by simply looking back at one's life and seeing how unsatisfactory and meaningless it is within the limits of 'purely human' existence. In so far as man is conscious of himself as a certain inner reality at all (cp. Chapter I, 2) he is also conscious that this reality of his 'self' is inherently unstable and in need of support from without. Either he feels that he is hanging over an abyss, and loses the sense that life has any meaning, or he succeeds in finding an absolutely secure support in the reality we call 'God'. *Tertium non datur*, or *datur* only in the ostrich policy of shutting one's eyes to the true nature of the human being.

Now we can go on to deal with the doubt itself. It is disposed of, to begin with, by the distinction that has been established between reality and the world of fact. We see once more that atheism and religious doubt arise from mistakenly including the being of God in the empirical world to which it does not belong. The doubt is based upon the conviction that we must clearly distinguish genuine, objective recognition of facts from mere imagination. But this applies to the empirical world which stands over against our subjectivity as indifferent and implacable 'brute fact'. The whole point is whether the same relation holds in the domain of *reality* to which the idea of God belongs.

The history of philosophical thought contains an instructive instance of a naive confusion between these two domains with reference to this very question. So acute a thinker as Kant in criticizing the so-called ontological argument for the existence of God (the argument that with regard to God idea and reality inevitably coincide) did not scruple to illustrate his thought by a distinctly vulgar, as Schelling rightly remarked, argument *ad hominem*. Kant said that a hundred imaginary thalers are 'ideally' not less than a hundred thalers in my pocket, but 'really' the difference between them is very considerable. At first glance the argument seems unanswerable, but Hegel took away the force of it by remarking that the whole question is whether God may be compared to a hundred thalers.

For indeed, the point is not whether God is 'in my pocket' or merely in my imagination (or in someone else's pocket!), and not even whether external experience, alien to the needs of our personal inner life, confirms the fact that God 'actually' exists, i.e. forms part of the world of objects. The point is whether we have a right to ascribe to 'reality' attributes which constitute for us the idea of God, or, what is the same thing, whether we have a right to recognize that idea as a reality.

A general characterization of reality has been given in the preceding chapter (Chapter II, 6). On the one hand reality is somehow akin to our inner life and is generically the same, so that we have it in the sense of belonging to it; on the other hand it completes our subjectivity and groundlessness by its unconditional self-subsistence, inner convincingness and absolute value. Reality itself, at any rate in a certain aspect of it, possesses the attributes which 'experience of the heart' finds in the idea of God, and in this respect is something divine. This accounts for the element of truth contained in pantheism—namely, in its religious apprehension of God as all-embracing and all-pervading, as the immanent basis of all that is.

But this formless and elementary awareness of reality as the supercosmic and, in certain of its manifestations, 'divine' ground of existence is insufficient. To begin with, reality may—as already mentioned—appear as a hostile power, groundless, destructive and 'anti-divine'. Besides, the apprehension of reality as such leaves out of account the profound generic difference between our own being as persons and all the rest of existence; consequently, it gives no satisfaction to the 'heart'. The question, then, is, whether in its innermost depths reality possesses in a form adequate to our heart's need, the two attributes we are in search of. In other words, can we find in reality the true ground of ourselves as persons—something which has all the positive content of human personality and at the same time can remedy the groundlessness and subjectivity of the purely human personal being? This is only a different way of formulating the two basic characteristics which constitute for philosophic thought, based upon metaphysical experience, the meaning of the idea of God.

In seeking to answer this question we must not be again misled by the habitual confusion between reality and the world of fact. It is not the case of discovering in the alien, unknown and indifferent to us external sphere of existence something that we need and that could only be present in it, so to speak, by a lucky chance. We are concerned with the sphere of being to which we ourselves belong and of which we know beforehand that, broadly speaking, it is akin to our inner conscious being and is the ground of it. In other words, we are concerned with the sphere of being which both transcends us and is immanent in us. By considering the immanent aspect of it we can discover its true nature.

It has been made abundantly clear in the preceding pages that reality as such is closely akin to human personality and provides or may provide its ultimate ground. But at the same time reality as it directly manifests itself in experience has so far appeared to us as something impersonal, as a kind of spiritual 'atmosphere' diffused in all being and forming its general basis. This is true of reality in the aspect most immediately accessible to us, but, from all that has been said it follows that reality has also a dimension of depth, or, rather, that 'depth' is the very essence of it. Metaphysical experience —experience gained through the profoundest insight of which our self-consciousness is capable—shows that the aspect of personal being, with all that is involved in it, belongs to the inmost core of reality and must be recognised as its centre and primary source. Thus 'reason', i.e. the interpretation of metaphysical experience, is seen 'to agree with the experience of the heart' which, apart from any reasoning, simply 'meets' God as a personal Being.

The only completely adequate 'proof of the existence of God' is the existence of human personality taken in all its depth and significance as an entity that transcends itself. The very consciousness of the tragedy of human existence, that so often leads to unbelief, provides, if fully thought out, a philosophical justification of the reality of God. If man is aware of himself as a person, i.e. as a being generically distinct from all external objectival existence and transcending it in depth, primariness and significance, if he feels like an exile having no true home in this world—that means that he *has* a home in another sphere of being, that he is, as it were, a representative in this world of a different and wholly real principle. Socrates proved the existence of God by the following argument: if our body is merely an infinitessimally small part of matter existing in the external world, how can we believe that by some lucky chance we are the only bearers of reason which does not exist anywhere outside us? This argument is irrefutable; it must only be freed from its purely intellectualistic (and consequently naturalistic) setting. Indeed, how could our spirit, our personal being, form part of the universe if it did not spring from a certain general, primary sphere of being which had the same properties as it? This is not simply an ordinary inference from the consequence to the ground. It is an immanent apprehension of a universal principle in ourselves, more primary than we are, and in this sense transcending us. It is an intuition that I as a living subject, standing over against the world of fact as such, am not a self-contained entity springing from nowhere and as it were floating above all being, but am a *reality*, i.e. am rooted in and nurtured by reality itself.

It is usual to accuse religious consciousness of 'anthropomorphism'. This accusation is just when we arbitrarily interpret natural phenomena as the play of man-like forces and, e.g. populate woods and rivers with nymphs and satyrs, or regard thunder as the expression of Jupiter's wrath. But in dealing with a human personality as such, it is impossible to apprehend it as a reality without recognizing that it has its roots in reality, i.e. has the same ontological basis as it. This consideration coincides at bottom with man's awareness of himself as an 'image and likeness of God'. In the book of Genesis this awareness is expressed by the statement that 'God created man in His own image and likeness', i.e. it presupposes the existence of God as a previously recognized basic fact and is derived from it; this is quite natural in a religious epic, which takes the reality of God as its starting point, but philosophically the position must be expressed in the reverse order, starting with the immanently-given nature of man. On the basis of inner experience, which convinces him that as a personality he transcends the natural world and is qualitatively different from it, man is aware of himself as 'an image' or a manifestation on earth of a supercosmic principle different from all earthly existence, primary and absolutely valuable—i.e. God. In and through being aware of himself as merely a derivative and imperfect manifestation of this supercosmic principle, man is aware of the reality of his primary source and archetype; he knows the fulness and primacy of the reality apart from which he himself, as its particular, derivative, and imperfect manifestation, is unthinkable. Metaphysical experience of God is in the last resort the apprehension of the absolute ultimate ground of the human spirit—of the ground which in its absoluteness transcends man as an empirical entity.

That which in religious terms has been called the need and the longing of the heart manifests itself on the purely logical and rationally expressible side as the consciousness of *limitation and insufficiency*. In so far as we are conscious of something as limited and insufficient, we are aware of the completeness which it lacks. As Descartes rightly observed in his so-called anthropological proof of the existence of God—analogous, at bottom, to the argument just stated—the idea of the infinite is more primary than that of the finite. Verbally, 'the finite' seems to be a positive idea, and 'the infinite'—to be an idea based upon a simple negation of finitude, but in truth the reverse is the case: 'the infinite' is the primary, positive idea of universal fulness, while the finite is a derivative negative notion constituted by the characteristic of incompleteness, limitation. This refers of course not only to the quantitative relation between the finite and the infinite magnitudes, but also to the qualitative and axiological relation between the imperfect and the perfect, or, generally speaking, between everything apprehended as insufficient and unsatisfactory and the criterion by comparison with which it is recognized as such.

The apprehension of the reality of God is, thus, immanently given in the apprehension of my own being as a person, in so far as, in recognizing my being and essence as qualitatively different from the whole of the natural world, I am at the same time aware of myself as insufficient, imperfect, incomplete, unstable and groundless. The relation between my inner being and the world of fact is such that my need and insufficiency is one thing, and the satisfaction of it—quite another, by no means guaranteed to me (my needing 'a hundred thalers' in no way implies that I have, or ever shall have them); but the relation between me and reality, in which 'to be conscious' is the same as 'to have', is such that the idea of insufficiency, by presupposing the idea of *that which I lack* testifies that I possess the very thing in which I am deficient. Just as in mathematics a fraction presupposes a whole, so in the inner contemplation of reality the poor and imperfect way in which I possess the supreme and absolutely valuable principle inherent in me, bears clear witness to the reality of the Absolute Personality which transcends me and is the absolute primary basis of personal being. It is sufficient for me to be fully conscious of myself in all my uniqueness as a true reality in order to have a sure apprehension of God. 'If only I saw myself, I would see Thee'—*Viderim me, viderim te* (St. Augustine). This too is the meaning of the words which Pascal heard in his heart in the midst of his doubts and struggles: 'Be of good cheer: you could not seek Me unless you had already found Me'. We could not be aware of our insufficiency, could not need God and seek Him, if we were not a reflection, however poor and imperfect, of that which we lack and are in search of. It is the presence and action of God in us that compels us to seek God outside us. At bottom, I can as little doubt the reality of God as I can doubt my own reality. Moreover, in the ontological order, God is more certain for me than my own self, for He is the condition of that which I apprehend as my true nature; it is only in the order of knowledge that I am the starting point of my own recognition of God's reality.

Thus 'reason' in the last resort, contrary to Pascal's opinion, understands and confirms the arguments of 'the heart'. This should not be taken to mean that reason is the supreme court of appeal, verifying and sanctioning with its authority the voice of the heart. No, reason in its knowledge of God is as it were merely another side or aspect of that voice. The comparison that has just been made between the self-evidence of God's reality and mathematical and logical self-evidence (e.g. of the correlation between part and whole, or the finite and the infinite) is not altogether applicable. For purely intellectual contemplation it is sufficient to strain one's intellectual attention; the perception of God's reality, however, is not a purely intellectual contemplation, but a *living intuition* and requires a different and more profound kind of attention: our whole being must be directed upon reality. The very possibility of this shows that 'heart' and 'reason' are in the last resort inseverable in the unity of our spirit. The apprehension of God—and of reality in general—does not consist in our actively gaining intellectual possession or 'catching' a passive object, but on the contrary in *His* action upon us and in us. The apprehension of God is not a vision of Him (leaving aside the rare and exceptional instances of highest mystical intuition) but rather 'hearing His voice' in our heart, the presence and action in us of His unfathomable and unutterable essence—an actual experience of Him. All rational 'proofs' of God's existence are only secondary, derivative explanations of this experiential apprehension of God; as Hegel aptly remarked they are 'movements of thought accompanying the soul's ascent to God.'

This explains why the reality of God, though self-evident, is extremely difficult to recognize. Even in the case of intellectual contemplation, e.g. in mathematics, self-evidence is attained with the greatest difficulty (the truth of a geometrical theorem, once solved, is self-evident, but the solution presupposes intense efforts of attention in discriminating the disjoined elements and their inter-connection, and is in the first instance possible only for a mathematical genius); this is still more the case with the living intuition of God. As already pointed out, even the perception of the true reality of my 'self', of my inner conscious being as a special realm of its own, in contradistinction to the usual perceptions of my mental life against the background of the world of fact, is a comparatively rare experience, felt to be a kind of revelation. Still more rare and difficult is the perception of my real self in all its depth and significance,

THE IDEA AND THE REALITY OF GOD

revealing its absolute transcendent ground, God. The great psychologist of spiritual life, Augustine, has expressed this with the insight of genius: 'Thou hast always been with me, but I have not always been with myself.'

The idea of God, then, is made intelligible through recognizing that it is correlative to our own essence and existence. This of course is merely the first step on the theoretically endless path of the knowledge of God, but the path itself is the only right one. Although nothing has so far been said of the so-called 'essence' of God, this omission is due not to any defect in the argument, but to the super-rational nature of the subject under discussion. It is a truism of theological thought that the essence of God as such is unfathomable and that we can only apprehend God in His relation to us and to the world. This generally recognized truth may also be expressed in a different way in connection with what has already been said. God, as we have seen, belongs to the domain of reality and not to the empirical world. Accordingly, He shares in the super-rational nature of reality. But reality, as we know, never is 'this and not that', it always is 'this *and* that'—a unity of itself and its opposite. Therefore God not only reveals Himself to us as, but actually is, 'Himself and the other'—is an indissoluble unity of Himself and of that which is distinct from Him. According to the teaching of traditional theology the knowledge of God's nature as it is in itself, in isolation from all else, is unattainable for man (at any rate in his earthly life); but it is not merely unattainable in fact—it is unrealizable because the very conception of such isolated and self-enclosed nature of God is inconsistent with His super-rationality, i.e. the true fulness of His being. We can only approach it by means of antinomic knowledge, that is, conceive of it as a certain reality the nature of which, though different in principle from all else, consists in the totality of its relations to all else, so that this 'else' also somehow co-belongs with it.

It is only because our thought is discursive that we can distinguish at all between 'God as such' and 'God's relation to everything else': in the super-rational reality one is inseparable from the other. We have been concerned so far with the idea of God as such; now we must consider His relation to 'all else'. In accordance with what has been said, this 'all else', for religious and metaphysical experience, is in the first instance 'myself', or in other words, human spirit. Thus in the order of discussion, the subject of 'God' is followed by the subject 'God and man'.

THE IDEA AND THE REALITY OF GOD

In dealing with that subject it is advisable to start not with the unfathomable nature of God, wrapped in impenetrable mystery ('the cloud of unknowing' in the phrase of an anonymous English mystic of the fourteenth century), but with the more familiar and accessible to us nature of man.

CHAPTER IV

Man and God

*

1. The twofold nature of man and the idea of God-manhood

What is man? This question is no less vital to our whole conception of life than the question of the meaning and existence of God. Indeed, it is the same question approached from another side.

It has been shown in Chapter I that man belongs simultaneously to two worlds and is as it were their meeting point. On the one hand, man is a natural being, a specimen of the animal kingdom. Through his body and his mental life, in so far as it is determined by bodily processes and subject to natural laws, man forms part of nature or, to put it more generally, of the world of fact. On the other hand, through his consciousness as a self-revealing reality existing in and for itself, man forms part of quite a different world—the world of reality—and is rooted as it were in its depths. In his spiritual blindness man may deny or fail to notice this duality, and regard himself merely in his external aspect, as an insignificant particle of the world of fact; philosophical theories that express this view may be widely prevalent; but unprejudiced phenomenological analysis conclusively proves that man attains the normal fulness of his being only through simultaneous participation in both these worlds. It is this that constitutes the fundamental distinction between man and animal. An animal is nothing but a 'natural' being, i.e. a being cognisant of 'this' world only and entirely belonging to it; man, though forming part of 'this world', transcends it, for he has another, non-worldly aspect which differentiates him from this world. This is why a naturalistic conception of man is unable to account for such fundamental and primary characteristics of human existence as knowledge, morality and creative activity. Conscious and deliberate cognition, even in its most elementary form determined by utilitarian motives, presupposes a subject-object relation which already is 'above' nature: it transcends 'the world of objects', and cannot be interpreted as merely a natural event, if only because it preconditions the very idea of an objective world. That idea—correlative to the idea of a subject—presupposes an element of transcendence which can only be attained through our participation in the all-embracing reality (see Chapter I, 5). The definition of man as a 'thinking being' tacitly admits that in the act of 'thought' man transcends the sphere of the empirically given. In a similar way the ideas of good and evil, right and wrong are distinct in principle and qualitatively different from all that merely *is* as a fact, and arise from our participation in a sphere that transcends the world of objects and is heterogeneous to it. Finally, any creative conception—a striving to realize something new and still non-existent—also presupposes that our self or spirit is not limited to the world of fact, but contains an aspect distinct from it, out of which the creative idea is born—as it were a kind of subterranean layer from which creative activity springs. Thus in every conscious action man opposes to all that is merely empirically given something else which transcends it, and thereby manifests the fundamental duality of his being.

But this duality is not confined to the distinction between man as an empirically given part of the objective world and man as a spontaneous inner reality. Even reality as actually present in him is recognized by man to be insufficient to satisfy him and inadequate to his true nature. The reality of which he is conscious within himself is, to begin with, incomplete, partial, and only potentially infinite, i.e. capable of expansion, and secondly—and that is the most important point—it is elemental, chaotic, *groundless* (it is this that, as we have seen, constitutes the 'subjectivity' of the inner life). Man feels the need for an unconditionally stable and self-subsistent ground for his existence, and that ground is precisely what we call God; and this need—or the consciousness of one's insufficiency— also forms part of man's very being.

The most adequate answer to the eternal question 'what is man?' consists, in the first instance, in pointing out the *differentia specifica* in virtue of which man is capable of judgment and evaluation. This and this alone constitutes his difference in principle from an animal and from all that exists simply as it actually is. Man is an entity capable of withdrawing from all that exists as a fact (including his own actual existence), of considering it from outside and determining its relation to something other, which is more convincing to him and is primary and authoritative. Man's being consists in *transcending*, at every moment of his conscious existence, all that is given as a fact. Apart from such transcendence, *self-consciousness* that constitutes the mystery of man as a personality is unthinkable. In the act of self-consciousness man looks upon himself and passes judgment upon himself, thus having himself both as the knower and the known, the valuer and the valued, the judge and the accused.[1]

It is only from this other sphere rising above all actual existence that man can draw guidance and power for his activity in 'this' world; and apart from its practical significance, this super-cosmic reality is as it were a permanent base to which man can always retreat for shelter and true self-realization. Human life is a struggle and interaction, a balance perpetually disturbed and re-established, between these two spheres of his being—the factual and the ideal— their indivisible, but ever distinct bi-unity. When the balance is destroyed and this bi-unity ceases to be the basis of life, personality either gradually dies away, or there takes place a terrible and mysterious act of suicide, of which man alone is capable: his inner reality, severed from its natural primary basis, becomes its own mortal enemy and puts an end to his empirical existence.

The final basis, transcendent centre and primary source of man's reality is God. We are therefore entitled to say that man's relation to, or connection with God is the determining characteristic of man's very being. That which makes man human—the principle of *humanity* in man—is his God-manhood. Our further discussion of the problem of man must explain and justify this contention. At present only a few preliminary remarks will be made.

As we have seen God is, in the first instance, that which man needs—a principle which is lacking to man and therefore transcends him. Apart from this consciousness of transcendence the idea of God is unthinkable. On the other hand, as belonging to the domain of reality God shares in its super-rational character. He therefore always is 'other and greater than Himself', or, in other words, His own being and His relation to everything else form an indissoluble

---

[1] Cp. the already mentioned difference between Kant's 'intelligible' and 'empirical' ego. Even a naturalistically-minded thinker like Freud is compelled, as a subtle and conscientious psychologist to recognize in man a special aspect of '*Ueber-Ich*' (super self).

unity; all abstract distinctions between these two aspects are inadequate to their true super-rational nature. This can also be expressed by saying that as the primary source and centre of reality God interpenetrates the whole of it, sending forth His rays, as it were, through its all-embracing fulness. Since man also belongs to the domain of reality, God in this aspect of His Being interpenetrates man too, is present in him and therefore immanent in him. Accordingly, in so far as man is a reality, God—or more exactly the divine principle—constitutes the very nature of man. God's transcendence and immanence do not simply coexist, but form an indivisible super-rational unity. This becomes apparent at every attempt rationally to explain their correlation as reflected in the human nature.

To repeat—God is apprehended by us as fundamentally and intimately akin to man in that which constitutes the unique and unutterable essence of the human 'self'. Since I apprehend this ultimate depth of reality only in transcending my own self, God appears to me as 'another person', as a 'Thou' which I meet and to which I stand in the specific relation of inter-communion—in the relation 'I—Thou'. This is the essence of the purely religious attitude as such. But it is evident from the first that the similarity between our relation to God and to any other 'thou'—to 'thou' in its usual sense—coexists with an essential and all-important difference. I meet an ordinary human 'thou' so to speak accidentally, from outside, as a bearer of reality whom I come across in the external world of fact. True, closer consideration shows (see Chapter II, 4) that this external meeting presupposes a certain primary inner connection, but such connection refers to the general 'I-thou' relation and does not alter the accidental and empirical character of the meeting with a particular individual 'thou'. But the apprehension of God as a 'thou' takes place only in the inmost depths of my 'self'—on that final and essentially solitary level of it on which I am invisible and inaccessible to any one except myself—and God (as Kierkegaard rightly insisted). I meet God only in the utter solitude in which I meet death. And that means that it is not a 'meeting' in the usual sense of the word, but is a manifestation of my abiding and indissol-. uble bond with God. God reveals Himself to me from within, in the last depths of my solitary self—or I reveal myself to Him. Communion with God is quite a different way out of my isolation and seclusion than through the relation to human 'thou's. God is for me a 'thou' which completes me and is other than myself, and yet lives in the depths of my own 'self'. In order to meet Him I need not, so to speak, withdraw from myself, leave the intimate home of my soul, as I have to in meeting my fellow men—I must, on the contrary, retire into the most secret chamber of it. (It is not surprising, therefore, that minds, guided solely by rational conceptions applicable to the world of fact, and imagining that 'the soul' is limited in depth, regard communion with God as merely a subjective illusion or an abnormal' splitting of personality'). God is a 'thou' which is the inmost ground of my own self. In this connection the familiar words 'outside' and 'within' lose their usual significance. God is not only 'outside' and 'within' me at the same time: He is 'within' me as a reality external to me and transcending me, and I am aware of Him as the inner basis of my being precisely in so far as He is different from me.

The same kind of dialectic is involved in the idea of God as the absolute value or the Good, voluntary submission to which saves me from the subjectivity and groundlessness of my own being. In so far as we express this aspect of God in rational terms, He is not primarily a 'thou', not a being similar to me, but directly opposed to me—just as the earth on which I rest, or the air which I breathe, are bound to be quite different from me who needs them. And yet, heterogeneity in this case means something very different from what it usually does, for as we have seen, only something intimately akin to me as a person can give meaning to my existence and be a real basis of it. This should not be taken to mean simply that heterogeneity in one respect is compatible with kinship in another respect. That which distinguishes God from me is precisely that which is apprehended in the experience of the heart as necessary to me, because it corresponds and answers to the ultimate depths of my own personality—namely, His primary self-groundedness, His character as the supreme Good and the highest value, the source of the world's meaning, in short, His absolute and pure spiritual objectivity in contradistinction to the groundless subjectivity of my own being. In this sense, God is super-personal as the absolute bearer of all that is positive in the idea of personality, but free from its 'subjectivity' or defectiveness. God is the unity of personality and absolute objectivity—unimaginable in the creature; He is Holiness itself, the Good, the Truth in a personal form.

There is an old question, insoluble in its strictly logical form: is God subordinate to the good, or the good to God—i.e., is the good that which God arbitrarily wills, or on the contrary, does He and can He will only that which is good in itself? This question is solved in the living religious and metaphysical experience through the awareness that God *is* the Good from the very first; the Good appears to us here not as an abstract idea or a self-subsistent general norm, but as coinciding with the living God Himself. This is the very essence of religious consciousness as distinct from consciousness guided solely by the abstract conception of the 'ought'. This super-rational relation between me in my subjectivity and God's spiritual objectivity, apprehended by us in a living and personal form, has its only analogy in true erotic love—particularly in the feminine aspect of it, in which the objectivity, strength, stability and authority lacking to the loving soul is embodied in the masculine principle and found in the living personal image of the lover. Herein lies the profound truth of the ancient symbolic comparison between the relation of the human soul to God and a loving woman's relation to her lover or husband. Like a woman, a believer first fully *finds himself* in his true depth and fulness through voluntary surrender to a superior and different principle.

Man in his ordinary empirical nature, as 'simply and only a man' is smaller, less valuable and significant than he truly is as a self-conscious inner reality. It may paradoxically be said that he is a man—in contradistinction to an animal—precisely in so far as he is conscious, or at any rate vaguely aware of this discrepancy between his 'merely human' nature and his true being. But that means that God Who transcends me both as being *outside* me and as belonging to quite a different sphere of reality, is deeply and intimately *immanent* in me and akin to me in His very transcendence. That which I lack and which I find only in Him is, in a potential form, the inmost essence of my own self; I can seek and can find final satis-faction in the object of my search, only because potentially I from the first possess that which I seek—indeed, because I *am* that which I seek. In the words of Plotinus: just as we could not see the sun if our eye were not similar to it, so we could not seek and apprehend God if we were not akin to Him.

Thus, in considering the two attributes which constitute for us the idea of God, we find that God is, on the one hand, a transcendent Being which we oppose to our 'self'; we are related to it as one reality to another, which is numerically and qualitatively different from it. On the other hand, this very relation forms part of our own inner being and is immanent in us, so that in speaking of our 'self' we mean by it a reality unthinkable apart from that relation and bearing an imprint of that to which it is related.

This super-rational character of the idea of man's Divine manhood constantly misleads rational thought into giving a simplified and therefore distorted interpretation of it, or into replacing it by unreal and artificial constructions.

It is useful in this connection to consider the main theories prevalent in the history of human thought with regard to the nature of man.

2. The idea of the absolute transcendence of God and the insignificance of man

One of the most ancient and widely prevalent conceptions of the relation between man and God is that which determines the Old Testament religious consciousness; it has been accepted by Christianity and, in a somewhat different form, is characteristic of classical thought. It is the conception of man's insignificance in the face of God, or, in philosophical language, of the absolute separateness and heterogeneity between God and man.

The genetically-psychological origin of this idea is the feeling of fear (in the usual, general sense of the term)—fear of the unlimited, overwhelming power of God. God is conceived as the autocratic, despotic and infinitely powerful lord of the world, before whom man is utterly impotent and insignificant, compelled to unconditional obedience—a slave and will-less instrument of an omnipotent master.

The primitive crudeness of this conception is modified by the Old Testament prophets, and religious consciousness is enlightened and ennobled. On the one hand, God is conceived as the bearer of the objective moral principles of goodness and justice, demanding their realization from man, and terrible only for those who violate His laws; on the other hand He is regarded as a master who loves his slaves and is concerned for their welfare, as 'the father' or 'the husband' of His people (both husband and father being taken in the old patriarchal sense of an autocratic, though loving, master). In this more refined consciousness the idea of God's transcendence is fully preserved: He is absolutely external to man and acts upon him from without. The idea of God's heterogeneity to man is preserved also, though it is softened and completed by the admission, as it were, of blood-relationship (as between father and children) or close intimacy (as between husband and wife). And in so far as God is conceived as the bearer of the moral principle, His supreme will, while remaining autocratic, ceases to be arbitrary, and man's obedience to it is determined no longer by blind fear, but by fear, the meaning of which is explained by the voice of conscience. In the last resort man's obedience to the will of God is due not to fear of a dreaded power, but to a heart-felt repulsion from evil and voluntary submission to the captivating power of holiness.

This conception of God's transcendence and heterogeneity to man, determining the prevalent religious consciousness, includes another element inherent in the very nature of religious consciousness as such. It is the element of *humility*, indissolubly connected with *penitence*. Human soul is permeated with the sense of dissatisfaction with its present condition, with its inability 'to save' itself by its own means and to satisfy its true and deepest needs. In other words it is profoundly conscious of the radical opposition between itself and God as the supreme and self-subsistent reality and absolute holiness—the only truly stable basis of its being. Man sees that he can only be spiritually healthy and normal if he renounces himself and humbly surrenders to the absolute Holiness. This attitude follows from man's ontological essence, i.e., is completely justified by purely objective philosophical analysis. Every doctrine that rejects humility and self-surrender to the higher transcendent principle is false, morally wrong, and practically deleterious. This must not, however, prevent us from admitting that in the Old Testament religion the motive of humility assumes a specific historical form of compulsory obedience to an external cosmic power, autocratic and absolutely alien from man.

The same must be said about the Old Testament doctrine of man as the image and likeness of God. At bottom, likeness never is a purely external and accidental relation: it presupposes a certain inner kinship, i.e. partial ontological identity. But in the Old Testament conception, stress is primarily laid upon that aspect of the relation in which the 'image' is both numerically and qualitatively different from the original, and likeness holds between two separate and in other respects utterly heterogeneous realities. God fashioned man out of clay, as a kind of figure similar to himself; and although that figure is animate, the disparity between it and its maker is as great as that between a pot and the potter. This absolute heterogeneity constitutes the original religious meaning of the idea of the creation of man and the world by God (the derivative metaphysical meaning of that doctrine may for the moment be left aside). The consciousness of man's essential and actual impotence and insignificance finds its culminating expression in the idea of man as a creature, as wholly made by a different Being and brought into existence by a Will alien from his own. The fact that this insignificant, ungrounded, absolutely derivative and dependent creature has nevertheless a certain likeness to its Creator is the only positive thing about it—the only indication of its connection with the source of its being.

Summing up, it may be said that the predominant note of the Old Testament religion is that of God's absolute transcendence; the opposite motif of His immanence in man begins to break through, but does not gain ascendency.[1]

In classical thought man was not conceived as a creature, i.e. as a wholly derivative being, dependent upon the higher reality which gave rise to him; on the contrary, the likeness between God (or gods) and men was of determining significance and was recognized as true kinship. The difference between them was confined to the fact that gods were immortal and had great (though not unlimited) power, and men were mortal and impotent. Intermediate beings were thought to be possible: there were demi-gods born of marriages between gods and human beings; in the mystery cults it was taught that men could attain communion with the divine substance and thus acquire immortality—a doctrine which received a philosophical expression in Plato. In short, gods and men were conceived somewhat like a higher and a lower race of the same genus. Nevertheless, the naturalistic character of the Greek religion and the absence of a moral bond between gods and men led to a pessimistic sense of man's impotence and insignificance, imparting a tragic character to his existence. 'Of all that breathes and crawls on the earth, nothing is more ill-fated than man' (Homer). 'Man's life is like a shadow seen in a dream' (Pindar).

[1] Transcendence is here taken to mean absolute separateness and heterogeneity. It is therefore compatible with the sense of (as it were spatial) nearness of God and His presence upon earth (e.g. in the 'tabernacle of the law' among his people); this too is characteristic of the Old Testament, and perhaps of all primitive religious consciousness.

The world of classical antiquity may be said to have felt the immanence of the divine principle in man, or at any rate its organic nearness to him; it had as it were a presentment of the idea of God-manhood, but this did not save man from the sense of his hopeless weakness and nothingness in the face of the omnipotent divinely-cosmic reality, indifferent to him. Only in the Platonic conception of the transcendent ideal world, super-cosmic and yet akin to human soul, the true meaning of God-manhood was foreshadowed.

Christian faith is essentially the religion of salvation—of man's salvation from his nothingness and from the tragic impotence of his earthly existence. It is the culmination of the prophets' awareness of the moral bond between God and man, and of God's nearness to us as a loving Father under whose protection we find the ultimate satisfaction of our perennial needs. The centre and basis of that faith is the perfect God-man Jesus Christ—true God and true man in one person—through communion with whom man is liberated from his nothingness as a helpless created entity and acquires the power of becoming 'a child of God' (John 1, 12). Fundamentally, Christian consciousness is a harmonious combination of transcendence and immanence in the relation between God and man. Man may and must be 'deified', that is, he must enter into complete inner communion with the divine principle as the only true and ultimate ground of his being; but this can only take place if there be intense and clear awareness of the divine principle transcending man's purely creaturely and non-divine nature. Man must renounce his self-centredness and find the basic point of his life in God, instead of in himself as a merely natural entity. Man finds his real, higher self only by renouncing his self-willed, non-divine natural being, and freely submitting to the will of God as a transcendent reality, which alone bestows upon him the fulness of *his own* reality. Thus man's nothingness and hopeless impotence apart from God give way to greatness and salvation when he realizes his true and higher nature through surrendering himself to God and being interpenetrated by Him—that is, through becoming divinely-human.

Historically, however, this super-rational, indivisible but distinct bi-unity of the transcendently divine and immanently-human principle in the concrete fulness of human nature was recognized chiefly in the form in which it was conceived in the Old Testament religion—the stress being laid on man's nothingness as a creature and on God's absolute omnipotence. In other words, the idea of God as completely transcendent and different from man largely superseded the super-rational idea of the indivisibly-harmonious unity of transcendence and immanence in the relation between God and man. It is remarkable—and tragic both for Christian thought and for the destinies of Christendom—that St. Augustine, whose religious genius and mystical insight clearly revealed the presence of God in man, was, as a dogmatic theologian, chiefly responsible for the prevalent conception of man's utter worthlessness and insignificance in the eyes of God.

The Augustinian tendency, worked out in the struggle against Pelagianism, in which the idea of man's self-affirmation as an independent positive reality found its first expression, remained on the whole predominant in Christianity. The difference between the ascetic and the mystical trends in Christianity is largely based upon the difference between the consciousness of God as absolutely transcendent, and as immanent and essentially akin to man. In so far as Christianity (beginning with the Alexandrian school) has adopted certain aspects of classical religious thought, especially of Platonism, it tends to counterbalance the motif of transcendence by a 'humanistic' idea of the dignity of man as a godlike being. (Already St. Paul in his speech to the Athenians quotes the saying of an ancient poet 'we are His kind'). In so far as the Incarnation is conceived by the Eastern Fathers as an event of general ontological significance, their view tacitly admits the inner bond between God and man. The theology of St. Thomas Aquinas, determined by Aristotelianism, insists in a somewhat different form upon the positive value of natural created being (including man), pointing out that the very essence of created reality, as derived from God, bears an immanent impress of His perfection. Besides, in recognizing and preaching its own divinity as the human expression of the Holy Spirit, the Church was bound, if only on that ground, to proclaim the divine, or divine-like dignity of the human element as represented by it, while preaching at the same time the Augustinian idea of man's nothingness and of the necessity of absolute submission to the transcendent Deity. This strain of semi-pelagianism in the Church doctrine called forth a reaction: Calvinism, one of the most influential trends in later-day Christianity, revived in an extreme form the stern Old Testament conception of the absolute transcendence of God and insignificance of man. But the dialectic involved in the very fact of the distinct and yet indivisible duality of man's divinely-human nature has led, ironically enough, in the process of historical development, to the result that the Calvinistic type of man, believing in his preordained and certain salvation and thus, so to speak, in his immanent deification, has helped to build up the new humanistic culture based upon man's creative activity and self-determination. (It will be remembered that the ideas of the inalienable rights of man and of self-determination as the basis of social life—i.e. the principles of modern humanistic democracy—are the historical progeny of puritanism). Another and correlatively opposite expression of the same dialectic is Jesuitism, which came into being at the same time as Calvinism. Starting with the demand for absolute slavish obedience to the transcendent will of God—especially as embodied on earth in the authority of the Church—it also became a powerful influence in bringing up a new type of men of creative will, ready to shoulder the responsibility for mapping out man's social destiny.

In traditional Christian thought, then, the motif of God's transcendence definitely predominates over that of His immanence in man. Man as such is either completely impotent or only capable of evil: everything good and positive descends upon him from above as grace, and is the activity in him of the Divine power distinct from him. This state of things is taken to be the result of the Fall which has destroyed the former, divinely-planned solidarity and intimate bond between God and man. Such a view renders less contradictory the position of theologians who extol the greatness of the Creator by comparison with the weakness and imperfection of His creation—like people who would praise the creative genius of an artist by pointing out the insignificance of his works as compared with his personality. In the doctrine of the Fall man's nothingness and the complete opposition between his nature and God is regarded as man's own fault, for he has distorted his own being as originally created. But the idea that man's very nature is radically changed owing to the Fall (fundamental for Augustinian theology and Protestant doctrines determined by it), does not really affect the more primary conception of man's fundamental weakness and insignificance as a created being. For although his present condition is the result of the Fall, the very *possibility* of the Fall follows from his nature as such in its absolute contradistinction to God—namely, from its inherent frailty. In his classical system of theology Thomas Aquinas, while admitting the positive value of creation in so far as it is Divine creation, expresses the idea that man's nature is essentially the same both before and after the Fall, and, in view of man's weakness as a creature, includes the capacity and tendency to sin (restrained in paradise by a special supernatural faculty granted by God as a *donum superadditum*). Thus man's ontological being is clearly and definitely declared to consist in his createdness, and all kinship between man and God, all immanent presence of the divine principle in him is ruled out.

It has already been pointed out that the sense of God's transcendence is not only a legitimate, but a necessary basis of normal human consciousness. Man loses his spiritual balance and his truly human image, if he has no humble consciousness of his natural sinfulness and weakness and no desire to overcome the subjectivity of the merely human element in him (of that which Nietzsche called 'human, all too human'); he must find the basis of his existence in God as the supreme and absolutely-valuable principle of being. Man's pride in imagining himself sinless, 'good by nature' and omnipotent is the main error and spiritual disease of the present age; with regard to it, the traditional church doctrine of man's sinfulness and impotence apart from God is a necessary and salutary truth. In so far, however, as God's transcendence and His difference from man are conceived purely rationally, in opposition to the principle of immanence and kinship, the living basis of the relation between God and man is undermined, and indeed the very essence of Christianity as the religion of God-manhood is lost sight of.

This is particularly clear in the domain of ethics. If man is worthless and insignificant—merely a neutral specimen of created natural being—why should love for God imply love for man? On what ground can, in that case, every human personality as such be regarded as sacred? How could have Christ said that to feed the hungry, give drink to the thirsty, visit the sick—in short, to satisfy even a purely material need of man as a natural being—means to manifest love for God? The sacredness of the human being as such reveals itself, in the first instance, as the sacredness of another, of 'one's neighbour', and the commandment to love him and help him in his material need is based upon this. From the point of view of moral training this commandment is quite understandable, for as a purely natural entity, divided from God, every individual is inclined egoistically to ascribe absolute value to himself alone. Man's physical and mental individual nature is self-centred, so that everyone is liable to think of his own needs only, and be indifferent to the needs of others. In doing so, we shut ourselves in our natural being, separated from God; in thinking about others we overcome our isolation, and manifest the activity of the spiritual principle in us. But this by no means exhausts the significance of the Christian commandment of love for one's neighbour. Self-sacrificing service to others, if rendered simply for the sake of ascetic exercise in overcoming one's natural inclinations and developing one's higher spiritual powers, implies a pharisaical and anti-christian attitude. True love for one's neighbour means direct awareness of something sacred and God-like in him—awareness, in virtue of which we must be considerate and attentive even to the corruptible created vessel that contains this holiness, and respond to a man's earthly needs. But man's holy and God-like essence is the same in my neighbour as in myself. In a different way—not through concern for my earthly needs—I must respect and watch over the higher spiritual principle in me, and respect in my own self the holiness of human personality as such. And this holiness is only explicable as the immanent presence of God, or of a principle proceeding from God and constituting that which is deepest and most real in man as a person. Christianity is the religion of worshipping God not as opposed, but as deeply akin to man. Christianity is the religion of humanness.

Accordingly, every religious tendency to affirm God's absolute transcendence and heterogeneity to man conceals a danger of indifference to human personality—the danger of *inhumanity* (this can be plainly seen in Mahometanism—the type of monotheism in which Divine transcendence in its pure and abstract form is expressed most forcibly). This danger was not clearly manifested in historical Christianity because the original Christian idea of God-manhood, and therefore of the sacredness of man, remained in force, though pushed into the background. That idea found support in the conception, inherited from classical antiquity, of the intrinsic value of natural cosmic being, including that of man.

And yet the profound crisis of Christian thought at the time of Renaissance—a crisis that mankind has not got over yet—was due to the fact that the Christian idea of God-manhood, of the inner kinship and nearness between God and man, insufficiently understood in the Middle Ages, was taken up and developed in a distorted form by an intellectual movement hostile to Christianity, or indeed to religion in general. The tragedy of modern European history is that the idea of man as divinely-human has, paradoxically, found fuller realization through a tremendous revolt of man against God.

3. Non-religious humanism and its inner dissolution

Although the conception of the indissoluble bond and kinship between God and man received but an incomplete and one-sided expression in traditional Christian theology and in the practical life of Christendom, its concrete religious meaning, acting like leaven upon human mind in the course of fifteen centuries, made man for the first time in his history conscious of himself as a *personality*. It taught man to recognize in himself a certain higher, absolutely valuable principle, in virtue of which he belongs to a different order of reality than the rest of the world and is called to creative self-determination and to the task of making life more perfect. It has for the first time developed in man a *humanistic* consciousness in the broad sense of the term.

There was a moment in the spiritual history of Europe, on the threshold between the Middle Ages and the modern era, when this humanism had a chance of developing naturally on the soil which gave rise to it, that is, within the Christian tradition itself. The widening of the intellectual horizon, the new influence of the classical world, especially of Platonism as the loftiest expression of its religious attitude, a new awareness of the greatness of creation— all this led to a deeper understanding of the Christian idea of God-manhood, and suggested that man had a positive religious value as the image and the child of God, as the bearer of the divine principle in the created world. This type of 'Christian humanism' found its highest philosophical interpretation in the teaching of the Cardinal Nicolas of Cusa, and its intellectually-religious expression in the work of Erasmus and Thomas More, in German and Dutch mysticism of the fourteenth and fifteenth centuries, in the teaching of St. Francis de Sales as well as in the type of piety akin to his.[1] Had this movement been a historical success, there would have been no rupture between Christian faith and non-religious humanism, and

[1] The historical development of this type of piety in the sixteenth and seventeenth century France is expounded in the remarkable eight-volumed (unfinished) work by Henri Brémond, *Histoire littéraire du sentiment religieux en France*.

the whole spiritual history of the Western nations might have developed in a different, a healthier and more harmonious way. This was not destined to be: the spiritual evolution of mankind took the form of going from one extreme to another. The cult of man inspired rebellion against the ecclesiastical tradition and finally against Christianity and religious faith as such. The meaning of this sudden change is clearly expressed by the transition from the Christian Platonism of Nicolas of Cusa to the anti-theistic philosophy of his disciple Giordano Bruno. Antinomic *panentheism*, the justification of the world and of man through the perception of the indivisible, though distinct, bi-unity of the Creator and the creature was replaced by a pantheistic deification of the world and a cult of the 'heroic fury' (*heroice furore*) of man conscious of himself as an earthly god. Since the time of the Renaissance the spiritual life of Europe entered the phase of fierce, deadly struggle between two faiths—the faith in God and the faith in man. An unbroken line of development goes from Giordano Bruno and the atheists of the Italian Renaissance right down to Feuerbach, Marx and Nietzsche.

There is no need to follow the numerous historical variations of the non-religious and anti-religious humanism born in the sixteenth century. It found its classical expression in the French eighteenth century enlightenment and in the optimistic humanism of the nineteenth century descended from it. The only thing of importance to us is to define its religious and philosophic nature. It consists in the deification of man. As a reaction against the one-sidedness of the traditional Christian view, faith in God appeared intellectually unjustifiable and spiritually wrong, for it was taken to be faith in a principle that enslaves man and hinders the self-determination and free creativeness to which he is called by his very nature. The vocation of man is to be an autocratic master of his own life and the supreme ruler of the world—this is the modern idea, unknown and impossible in former ages. As a fact of spiritual life it means that man became conscious of himself as an earthly god. Having lost and rejected God, he acquired faith in himself. Or, to put it differently, having lost the sense of the transcendent spiritual basis of his existence—the sense of God—man has substituted for the indivisible but distinct bi-unity of his divinely-human nature some vague mixture of the principles which he illogically tries to find in his purely empirical being. Recognizing only 'this' world, and himself as wholly belonging to it, he has come to believe at the same time in his own goodness and omnipotence, in his power and vocation to subdue, perfect and spiritualize nature, of which he is only a derivative part.

Hence the blind and, indeed, ridiculous—for it is contrary to all historical experience—comfortably optimistic faith in the certainty of a continuous moral and intellectual progress, in the easy possibility of realizing on earth the kingdom of reason, justice and goodness—that which the believers called 'the Kingdom of God'. Later on, the Darwinian theory further accentuated the purely naturalistic interpretation of human nature, declaring man to have descended from some ape-like creature in the course of a blind and purposeless process of evolution; instead of undermining the 'humanistic' faith, this was taken to be a confirmation of it. Vladimir Solovyov summed up the absurdity of this optimistic non-religious humanism in a bitterly ironical formula: 'man is an ape and *therefore* is called to realize the kingdom of goodness upon earth'.

The power of this blind faith has dominated thought for several centuries and is so great that so far it has easily recovered from the blows dealt to it by every conflict with the realities of human existence. The first blow was given it by the French revolution, when the reign of freedom, equality and fraternity was soon transformed into the reign of an infuriated bloodthirsty mob. A still more convincing argument against this faith has been provided by our own time, when the veneer of European enlightenment could no longer conceal man's untamed animal nature and the demonic forces of cruelty and contempt for the most elementary principles of morality. And yet even now non-religious humanism, though not so enthusiastically acclaimed as before, continues to dominate wide and influential circles in Europe and America.

Nevertheless, non-religious humanism is bound to break up, for it is being undermined by a fatal self-contradiction: it illogically combines faith in man's unlimited autocratic power as the supreme master of his destiny with faith in the duty to serve certain absolute moral values, independent of man's arbitrary will. The contradiction was smoothed over by the unproved optimistic assertion that 'man is good by nature' and that the realization of moral values satisfies his subjective natural strivings. It appeared that a rational man, like the God of the Christians *cannot* desire anything except the good. But what is to be done when the striving for the moral good and for the satisfaction of one's earthly desires, of the love of power and the unfettered freedom of passions, diverge and come into conflict? Non-religious humanism cannot give an answer to this question, for every answer would be self-contradictory. The classical humanism of the eighteenth and nineteenth centuries recognized the unconditional supremacy of absolute moral principles and the necessity of submitting to them, though it could not show any grounds for this conviction, or harmonize it with the view of man as a supreme master and earthly god. The worship of man was combined with an uncompromising reverence for the good, and with a puritanic morality. Such an illogical combination could not, however, from the nature of the case remain stable. Consistent deification of man as a natural being inevitably leads to amoralism: man as an unlimited autocrat is the master of his morals as well. This idea may be realized in two forms: by deifying either the collective or the individual man. On the one hand, it may be affirmed that absolute value and therefore unlimited supremacy belongs to the will of the collective—of the nation, of the majority, or of a definite class and that therefore the individual must unquestioningly obey that will, which transcends morality and is the source of it, being a kind of human embodiment of the Divine will. On the other hand, since man is only real as a particular individual person, it may be affirmed that the supreme value and autocracy belongs to the hero, the demi-god, a striking personality representing the higher species of man, whom the masses must unquestionably obey.

It is important to note in the first place that amoralism in both these forms is bound to be inconsistent. It is not a simple and complete denial of the category of 'ought', of the ideal and absolutely valuable, not a mere rejection of every criterion of good and evil, or satisfaction with what actually is; on the contrary, it is a stormy rebellion against man's actual condition in the name of an absolute ideal. While rejecting morality, it reverences and deifies some natural element of man's being. It is not mere cynical unbelief but, on the contrary, passionate, inspired faith—an unwilling testimony to the fact that the religious element and the worship of some absolute value is an inherent characteristic of human nature.[1]

Both the collective and the individualistic forms of amoralism

[1] Dostoevsky, a subtle psychologist of spiritual life, ironically remarks that man is so made that even if he wants to do some rascally trick he cannot be content until he invents some absolute sanction for his rascality. It is precisely this which shows that the spiritual element in man is ineradicable.

are represented in influential intellectual tendencies of the nineteenth century. The first form can be traced back to Rousseau who in his, as it were, deliberately ambiguous idea of *volonté générale* identified the will of the nation or of the majority with the universally binding will for the good, thereby ascribing to it sacred and unquestionable authority. The same idea determines Auguste Comte's 'religion of humanity', in which service of God is replaced by the service of a hypostacized humanity—*le Grand Etre*. Finally, the philosophy of Hegel, religious at its source, ends, in virtue of its pantheism, in a cult of the state as an earthly god and in the rejection of the moral claims of the individual as 'insolent'. Hegel's disciple, Marx, following Feuerbach, discarded the religious basis of Hegel's philosophy and declared God to be merely an illusory projection of man's own nature. Before he became a socialist, Marx called his theory 'real humanism'. Man must become master of his destiny not only in idea but in reality, in actual life.[1] How was this to be attained? For Marx the pivot of man's existence was economics, which is the most obvious expression of his carnal, material nature. Once man masters the economic sphere he will attain omnipotence and become in reality that which he is in principle—an earthly god. But he can only achieve this through collectivization, through welding individuals into a collective unit; this is the task of the 'proletariate' which thus plays the part of the chosen people, a new Israel. It is a collective embodiment of an earthly deity, called to realize the kingdom of God—the kingdom of the omnipotent man—on earth. The collective man as represented by the proletariate has all the attributes of an earthly deity: its will is the supreme and final court of appeal, the absolute criterion of the good. Not only its enemies, like the enemies of ancient Israel, must be mercilessly exterminated, but the individual human personality, which as such

[1] It is worth noting that the famous formula 'religion is opium for the people' has in this connection quite a different meaning in Marx than in its popular use by the bolshevists. It is not intended to imply that religion is a poison with which the reactionaries dope the people's will to freedom. Arguing against Feuerbach who dreamed of destroying the religious sense by denouncing it as illusory, Marx indicates by this formula that religion is a necessary and indestructible, though unreal, comfort and reassurance for humanity suffering from the slavish conditions of its present earthly existence. Religion will disappear of itself when man becomes true master of his destiny. This shows that from Marx's own point of view the attempt to destroy religion by political violence and persecution is futile.

is a reality opposed to the deified collective man, must be sacrificed to that Moloch and transformed into an ant in the human ant-heap, an insignificant cog-wheel in the enormous social machine. Moreover, since the collective man is deified in his earthly, carnal nature, his evil earthly passions—greed and class hatred—are regarded as creative forces which must be unleashed for the realization of the earthly paradise; amoralism thus becomes anti-moralism. Thus in Marxism the basis of non-religious humanism, namely the deification of man as a person, i.e. as the bearer of moral and spiritual principles, degenerates into a demonic deification of the carnal collective human element, soulless and depersonalized.

The other form of amoralistic humanism, more noble in its original conception—the deification of man as a concrete individual personality, isolated and self-contained—was first proclaimed by another disciple of Feuerbach, Stirner. Quite consistently he replaced the generic notion of man in Feuerbach's theory by the particular human being as a separate individual. The positive element in Stirner's doctrine consists in the idea (akin to Kierkegaard's religious individualism) that man's great and sacred true essence is to be found only in the inmost depths of his personal spirit, detached and isolated from the world. But owing to the naturalistic presuppositions of his philosophy, Stirner identifies this spiritual depth with subjectivity, i.e. with man's egoism and self-will, and therefore comes to affirm their supremacy and to deify man as a bold egoist. Man's highest dignity lies in his egoistic self-will, and morality is a pernicious and illegitimate attempt to suppress and fetter this free expression of man's inmost nature (this is the contention which Plato puts into the mouth of Callicles in *Gorgias*). A more profound and influential expression of a-moralistic humanism is, however, to be found in Nietzsche.

Nietzsche's starting point is the cult of heroic humanity—the glorification of man as the bearer of a higher, spiritual principle inherent in him, in contradistinction to the soulless human herd or the average man with his paltry, commonplace and non-individual standards of life. Nietzsche unconsciously gives expression to the true idea of the immanence of the divine principle in human spirit—analogous to Meister Eckhart's teaching about the divine 'spark' in the depths of the soul. But since Nietzsche completely rejects the idea of God's transcendence, his thought acquires the character of a titanic rebellion against Him. In subordinating man to God, religion enslaves man and conflicts with his noble higher nature. The ethics of love and compassion for men in their weakness and insignificance, and the demand to regard all human beings as equal, are the expression of the slavish spirit of the average man, anxious to assert himself through lowering the higher, aristocratic principle. Nietzsche starts by distinguishing two principles in man: in his actual condition man is a contemptible and insignificant creature, but potentially he is the bearer of a lofty divine principle; man is an imperfect, mis-shapen expression of a higher being as yet unrealized —of the 'superman'. The formula 'man is something that must be overcome' is a clear expression of the break-up of non-religious humanism. Nietzsche dreams of a being higher than the ordinary type of man; in terms of religious mysticism his dream might be expressed as the Christian ideal of the 'deified' man, permeated by the divine principle through and through. But since he rejects the transcendence of the divine principle, he can only express his dream as a self-contradictory hope that man will of himself, by his own power, ennoble himself and create out of himself a new and superior being—the superman. The fundamental ontological fact of man's divinely-human bi-unity—of his being both a weak creature and the bearer of the divine principle which transcends him—is replaced by the dream of man's self-transformation into a man-god.[1] But what is the criterion for distinguishing the superman (the man-god) from man who is worthless? Nietzsche's naturalistic philosophy prevents him finding such a criterion in any super-cosmic transcendent reality. The only alternative left him is to regard the superman as simply a new and higher biological species. Such a biological species can have only natural properties—self-confidence, force, self-will, daring, love of power. According to Nietzsche's own admission the real prototype of the superman is a shameless monster like Caesar Borgia or an ancient Teuton—'the blond beast'. Amoralistic humanism leads in the last resort, contrary to its primary conception, to *bestialism* and not to the ideal of a godlike being. In Marx the highest stage of human existence destroys personality, transforming man into an ant in a deified ant-heap or a wheel in a deified human machine; Nietzsche's dream of the man-god leads to sinking the spiritual human personality in the animal man. But an

[1] This is Dostoevsky's term by which, anticipating Nietzsche, he describes in *The Possessed* that whole type of thought, contrasting it with the Christian idea of the God-man.

animal is not a person—it is from its very nature merely a particular specimen of a genus, of a natural and elemental collective whole. Thus in Nietzsche, who hated gregariousness and mass principle above everything, the proud dream of individualism leads in its logical development to its own defeat. The final result of this suicidal dialectic was Nazism—a cheap and vulgar parody of Nietzscheanism. Combining the cult of the 'leader' ('the superman') and of the higher race with the cult of the omnipotent state and the mechanically-organized masses, it arrives by a different route at the same totalitarian collective idea as Marxism and in principle rejects personality as the bearer of the spiritual principle. The world has learned the practical consequences of this through bitter experience, which has very nearly put an end to the Christian humanistic civilization of Europe.

Thus the two different forms of a-moralistic and non-religious humanism have met with the same fatal end: in both humanism has destroyed itself. The historical epoch which began with the proud declaration of the greatness and supremacy of man, and set out to realize that principle, ends by denying it—by bringing about man's enslavement and reducing him to the animal level, by transforming him into a blind mechanized force of nature in which he loses his human image and essence. This is the immanent retribution for forgetting and rejecting the indivisible, but distinct divinely-human bi-unity of man.

The inner dissolution of non-religious humanism, long ago forseen by sensitive minds, has led to a kind of spiritual aftermath expressing itself in a curious intellectual attitude which may be described as 'sorrowful unbelief', highly typical of our epoch. It consists in a keen awareness of the difference and contradiction between the higher ideal principle which gives meaning to life, and the senselessness, ugliness and worthlessness of the lower, blind elemental forces in man and nature. It combines belief in the significance and the binding character of the Holy with disbelief in its objective power and reality, regarding it merely as an unstable and impotent subjective property of human spirit, having nothing in common with the rest of the objective world. From the standpoint of 'sorrowful unbelief' the task of man's life is the heroic defence, foredoomed to failure, of the higher spiritual principles against a hostile and omnipotent universe (Bertrand Russell's phrase). This attitude resembles the pessimistic outlook of the later Stoics, *'causa victrix diis placuit, sed victa Catoni'*. It has found its philosophical expression in the modern theory of *existentialism* (in its typical anti-religious form).

'Sorrowful unbelief' takes itself to be a mercilessly-sober apprehension of man's tragic destiny. Religious faith is for it a pitiful illusion, a result of cowardly and disingenuous thought, a kind of ostrich policy on the part of human spirit, and it prefers to it stern 'intellectual honesty', a phrase used by Nietzsche, whose early thought largely determined the spiritual attitude in question.

Sorrowful unbelief springs from the fact that man has lost the sense of transcendent reality as distinct from the world of fact, and therefore has transferred the supreme divine principle into the depths of the isolated human mind and subjectivized it. Thus the true transcendently-immanent, divinely-human bi-unity of human nature and existence is replaced by an inherent duality of the human spirit, rending man's nature in two, and by the sense that the spiritual principle as purely subjective is helpless in the face of omnipotent blind forces of nature. Sorrowful unbelief is a form of non-religious humanism—it regards the idea of God as a deceptive outer projection of the needs and aspirations of the human heart. But in contradistinction to the naive optimistic humanism—which replaces, as we have seen, the transcendentally-immanent bi-unity of God-manhood by a vague and undifferentiated unity or identity of the natural and the ideal in human nature—'sorrowful unbelief' regards man as hopelessly and irremediably divided in himself. It does not deify man as such, but recognizes all his blindness and worthlessness; from inner experience, however, it knows that in the depths of his nature there glows a divine spark, helplessly lost in it and coming from nowhere, since it has nothing akin to it in the whole of the universe. It does not worship God, but it worships that divine spark in the isolated human soul.

Sorrowful unbelief thus testifies anew that man's consciousness of being divinely-human is ineradicable. It unconsciously opposes to the banal optimistic humanism and to the a-moralistic demonic self-deification of man the Christian sense of the antinomic, and therefore tragic, truth of the divinely-human bi-unity. But at the basis of it lies the fundamental self-contradistinction of humanism: faith in man without faith in the reality of God as his source and ground. To regard the higher principle in man as his merely subjective characteristic is inconsistent with reverencing it and ascribing to it absolute value, or with clearly distinguishing between good and evil, between the higher, spiritual, and the lower, material principle. Sorrowful unbelief thought out to the end proves to be a kind of *religious faith*—limited by its dualism—somewhat like the faith of the ancient Gnostics in a God who, though all-merciful, is remote from the world and powerless in it. And the fact that the duality does somehow coexist in the human heart shows that, at any rate at that particular point of universal being, duality is bi-unity, and the ideal principle is a real creative force. The very fact of moral and spiritual heroism, of service to the Holy, is an instance of the action in the world, and upon the world, of the supreme transcendent reality of God. As already pointed out, man as a spiritual being is alien to the world and a helpless exile in it, precisely because his true home is in another and higher dimension—in God.

Sorrowful unbelief and its philosophical expression in existentialism is one of the most striking expressions of the tragic interpretation of life, characteristic of our epoch and, in general, of the last stage in the evolution of humanism. A tragic element is to be found in antitheistic Titanism (as represented both by Marxism and Nietzscheanism), for the *motif* of stern, unrelenting struggle against the historically given state of human existence as a whole is characteristic of it, too, though it inconsistently combines pessimism with an optimistic faith in an ideal future. The true meaning of the tragic principle in human life will be made clear later.

4. Antinomies involved in the relation between God and man

The historical survey of the two main ways of interpreting the relation between God and man—the theory of man's utter insignificance as a creature as compared with a transcendent God, and the opposite theory which deifies man as such—should help us to understand more clearly the complex nature of man's divinely-human bi-unity. The very possibility of these one-sided interpretations shows that the idea of man as divinely-human is essentially antinomic; this has not been sufficiently brought out in the preceding pages.

The general nature of the antinomy may be expressed as follows. The idea of God-manhood is that of the connection between God and man, or between the divine and the purely-human principle. This connection might be thought out consistently if the elements entering into it were two independent and self-contained realities,

133

i.e. if they could be conceived apart from their relation to each other. Thus, we can easily define water as a certain combination of hydrogen and oxygen, for both these chemical elements exist separately and each of them can be defined apart from its relation to the other.

But the case is different with regard to the relation between man and God. The very conception of man as such—of man as a being *distinct* from God—includes as its constituent principle man's relation to God. On the other hand, the idea of God is indissolubly connected with the idea of man and his experience of himself as a person. Thus, the connection between God and man is not a simply external, rationally conceived connection between two heterogeneous and mutually independent entities: they are unthinkable apart from each other. As pointed out at the end of Chapter III, the bi-unity of God-manhood is logically prior to the conceptions of God and of man. In order to avoid contradiction it is therefore necessary to distinguish between the secondary, derivative relation which presupposes the already formed ideas of God and of man, and the primary transcendental relation which gives rise to those ideas. Those two relations are on different ontological levels; failure to distinguish between them, and attempts to identify them lead to a hopeless confusion of thought.

The inherent antinomism of the relation between God and man shows itself in the dialectical working out of the one-sided or false theories that have been mentioned. If that relation be conceived as a purely external one between two different and mutually independent realities, we lose sight of man's divinity as a characteristic that constitutes the very idea of man (in contradistinction to animals and to natural being in general). If, on the contrary, 'divinity' be conceived as the attribute of man as such, as an immanent characteristic constituting his nature, we lose sight of the fact that man is only one member of the relation which presupposes the independent being of God as the other member of it—faith in God is rejected and man is deified. The aspect which is left out of account or denied proves its reality by secretly finding its way into the simplified theory and making it self-contradictory.

Let us again consider the traditional religious view, rooted in the Old Testament conception that man as a creature is a being distinct from God, existing outside of Him and standing in a merely external relation to Him. Curiously enough, this conception in one respect coincides with the naturalistic view of man which has now become the view of 'common sense': whether man is created by God or is a product of evolution, he is essentially a purely natural being, a psycho-physical organism forming part of the empirical world. Indisputable and obvious facts—apart from any theories—testify that man is a weak and insignificant being, inwardly and outwardly determined by natural forces, dependent upon heredity, the structure and functioning of his bodily organs, and subject to all the blind impacts of his physical environment. In all these respects man is obviously different from God. True, the religious view introduces one very important emendation: in spite of all, man is an 'image and likeness of God' and as such differs from purely natural creatures. The chief expression of this aspect of man's nature is that he has free will and is morally responsible for his actions. He must—and in principle, he can—freely fulfil the will of God; as God's image and likeness, he has something resembling God's primacy and spontaneity. But if man's creaturely nature be seriously taken into account, the resemblance will prove to be slight and in a sense illusory. Man has not sufficient power to carry out, freely and of himself, God's design concerning him and to fulfil the Divine will: he falls into sin, and in consequence his freedom becomes powerless, though it is not destroyed. This is Augustine's classical theory. The problems of sin and freedom will be considered more fully in the next chapter; at present it must be merely pointed out that man's sinful lack of freedom clearly manifests his creaturely impotence and worthlessness. The freedom still left to him is not a real freedom of will and action, but merely a certain ideal freedom of the spirit—namely, the power of recognizing and condemning his sinfulness and of feeling responsible for his impotence, although unable to overcome it.[1]

[1] That is how the position is formulated by the well-known American theologian R. Niebuhr in his subtle and penetrating work, imbued with the spirit of Calvinism—*The Nature and Destiny of Man*. According to St. Bernard's interesting theory (*De gratia et libero arbitrio*), man has *liberum arbitrium*, but after the Fall he is deprived of *liberum consilium* and *liberum complacitum*. The first—the faculty of consenting or not consenting to something, and of judging his own actions—is indestructible not only in fallen men, but even in sinners in hell, for it is the very essence of man as 'the image' of God. The last two—the freedom of choosing the good and of acting in accordance with that choice—were lost after the Fall, and through this the Divine 'likeness' (*similitudo*) which had been bestowed on man, was lost also. Cp. E. Gilson, *Théologie mystique de St. Bernard*, Paris 1934.

It is in this conception of freedom as powerless and illusory that the kinship between the religious doctrine indicated above and the naturalistic view of man becomes clearly apparent: Luther and Calvin are at one with Spinoza in denying human freedom.[1] This is perfectly intelligible. Nature does not know freedom, and man as a created and therefore 'natural' being is subject to nature's necessity. It must be admitted that this theory is quite a true expression of the actual structure of the human being in so far as it is a part of nature. Of course determinism must not be conceived in the old-fashioned mechanistic way which is obviously fallacious: man is not a mechanical complex of 'motives', not a balance, one side of which automatically inclines towards the most powerful motive, and not a passive and powerless product of external forces.[2] Simply as a living organism man is a manifestation of a certain central entelechy which forms and directs his life, spontaneously selecting some motives rather than others, and giving preponderance to one of them. The significance of spontaneity for the idea of freedom will be discussed later. It is immediately clear, however, that this entelechy itself is a blind natural force, though directed to a purpose. Ordinary will, inherent in man, and expressed in the consciousness that something is 'his own wish' is merely a reflection of the foreordained action of this psycho-physical entelechy, and in this respect man does not differ from an animal. The well-known argument of naturalistic determinists against the idea of freedom is that although man may do anything that he wills, he cannot *will* anything he wishes to will, and in a certain sense this is perfectly true. With regard to what men usually mean by their freedom Spinoza rightly says that the consciousness of being free is worth no more than a drunken man's conviction that he is 'freely' talking nonsense and behaving foolishly. And when a man acts under the influence of passion, he is himself

[1] Kant's theory that human will combines empirical necessity with 'intelligible' freedom is a blend of the naturalistic view with the Protestant religious tendency determined by Augustinian theology.

[2] Spinoza, in comparing human activity to the fall of a stone, says that if a stone had consciousness, it would think that it was falling to the earth because it willed to fall. This argument is an instance of the fact that even a thinker of genius may fall into obvious and easily refutable error. We do not know what a stone would think if it had a mind; but we know very well what we ourselves think when we fall like a stone, i.e. when we are conscious of being subject to the law of gravitation. We certainly do *not* think that we are falling 'of our own will'.

aware that he is acting not freely, but in obedience to a force which is blind and alien from him, though it lives in his own heart (the ontological meaning of such demonical possession will be discussed later).

To repeat: this pessimistic attitude towards human nature, the idea that the spirit of man is powerless against overwhelming elemental forces, and that his freedom as an objective active power is illusory, is to a certain extent true of human existence as it actually is. But if accepted without any reservations this view really denies the essential difference between the specifically human moral and spiritual activity and the blind, driving forces of nature—or indeed the very difference between man and other natural entities. All rational, beneficial and constructive activity issuing from man as such is regarded as impossible and illusory; outside the sphere of involuntary physiological actions and processes, man can do nothing but sin. This is the meaning of St. Augustine's famous phrase *non posse non peccare*. Man as such is a slave of nature and has no positive reality within himself; he is merely the bearer of the destructive principle of sin, and also, as it were, an empty point into which gracious forces may be poured in from outside by a transcendent God, the only true bearer of positive, actual and creative reality. Thus the sole positive basis of man's being is not in himself, but in a transcendent God, *toto genere* different from him. If consistently thought out this view deprives man's being of positive reality and renders it almost illusory. Of course Christian thought refrains from taking the last step on this path and proclaiming human existence to be pure illusion, as Hinduism does, for that would destroy its initial assumption of the absolute difference and duality between the Creator and the creature. But it would not be an exaggeration to say that it comes close to denying the purely *human* principle in man. Man is taken to be something like a vessel in the hands of the potter. He does not really *live* his life, but his life is merely an expression of the potter's activity in using him as a vessel or a tool. If he leaves 'the potter's' hands he can do nothing but fall to pieces.

But the idea of man as utterly impotent and entirely creaturely renders it virtually impossible for him to be aware of his relations to God and of his duty freely to carry out God's will: a vessel has no such awareness of the potter and does not need it in order to be what it is. St. Augustine as we have seen, recognizes in a limited sense man's spiritual freedom, but the very idea of the human spirit, presupposed by it, is inexplicable from his point of view.[1]

On the other hand, in this clear-cut rationalistic distinction between God and man the emphasis may be laid not upon man's creatureliness and therefore insignificance, but upon the true independence of his being as a reality external to and independent of God; in that case we fall into the opposite extreme—pure Pelagianism. Man is then conceived as a being grounded in himself; his will is his own, and is a real creative force, meeting and interacting with the will of God as a co-equal member of the relation, standing as it were on the same ontological level as God. Augustine quite rightly perceived the erroneousness and religious danger of this standpoint—however one-sided his own position might be. In denying that connection with God is a constituent element of man's very nature, Pelagianism implies a conception of man as an entity whose being and activity do not need God. It is the first step on the path to man's self-deification; its final stage is non-religious humanism and titanic rebellion against God, which, as already pointed out, has found its full expression in modern times. The Pelagian version of the dualism between God and man when worked out consistently leads, just like Augustinianism, to denying its own initial assumption—the clear duality between God and man. Augustinianism tends to abolish this assumption by belittling and almost destroying the reality of man, and Pelagianism—by belittling and destroying the ontological significance of God, so that ultimately God is regarded as an illusory projection of man's creative being. Augustinianism denies the independent value and existence of the world of human culture and history—of the spiritual world built up by the free creative will of man; consistent Pelagianism denies the subordination of that will to a transcendent principle and introduces,

[1] In contradistinction to Augustinianism, Tomism with its wonderful balance between spiritual motives, admits the independent being of human nature as a positive reality (e.g. the sphere of autonomous reason and moral will). This conclusion is arrived at through the doctrine of degrees of being and of the analogical use of the conception of being. And yet insistence upon the radical difference between the Creator and the creature leads St. Thomas, too, to deny the presence of the creative principle in man. But the ideas of creativeness and free self-determination are inextricably interwoven and together constitute the specific attribute of human nature; accordingly, human autonomy belongs on St. Thomas's view also, to a neutral, purely natural sphere and does not attain to the significance of truly supernatural reality.

instead, the fatal idea of basing man's existence upon his autocratic will—an idea that leads to a suicidal destruction of the true basis of man's spiritual being.

Thus in so far as the relation between God and man is conceived rationalistically as a relation between two separate and qualitatively different realities, we are driven to hopeless antinomies. Man ceases to be human in the face of God's overwhelming and omnipotent majesty; and he equally ceases to be human in losing his connection with God and thinking of himself in isolation from Him. The position is analogous to the self-contradictory and unrealizable erotic relation, alternating between slavish submission and rebellion, expressed by the well-known tragic dictum of Catullus 'nec sine te, nec tecum vivere possum'. The solution obviously is to be found in a super-rational synthesis of dependence and free and independent existence—not as an external combination (which is self-contradictory and therefore impossible), but in such wise that the two aspects should mutually determine each other and ultimately rest upon a certain unity as their common basis. Such a unity is suggested by the idea of God-manhood, which implies that the presence of God as a transcendent reality in man constitutes man's inmost being. In other words, God and man remain unrealizable abstractions so long as they are conceived as absolutely heterogeneous realities logically prior to the relation between them; they acquire a positive meaning only when conceived as indivisible but distinct aspects of God-manhood, as a truly primary principle.

But how can this be? Christian doctrine speaks of the perfect harmonious combination of the divine and the human principles in the One Person of Jesus Christ—true God and true man. But it conceives His personality as unique and from the nature of the case unrepeatable—as the result of the miraculous act of Incarnation that took place once for all, breaking in from without into the general order of cosmic existence. The idea that Christ is not man but God, wholly, essentially and in principle different from man, is firmly rooted in the minds of most Christians—to a certain extent against the exact meaning of the Chalcedon dogma about the unity of two natures in Christ, the Divine and the human, 'without division or confusion'. The main concern of the Christological teaching of the Church, resting on the conviction of man's nothingness before God, is to make the faithful conscious of their complete dependence upon Christ and not presume to equal themselves to Him. Whatever we may think about the theoretical implications of this position, it is no doubt perfectly right from the practically-religious point of view: the whole history of religious experience and of mystical ecstasies, in which man presumes to identify himself with Christ, testifies that such presumption is folly and fatal error. Although with God all things are possible, and God's ways are past finding out, historical religious experience testifies—apart from all dogmatic doctrines—that Jesus Christ was a unique, unrepeatable and miraculous personality. The perfect, stable and harmonious combination and balance of the Divine and human natures in Him, 'without division and confusion', is exceptional and in that sense miraculous—but does this imply that there can be *no other form* of combining these two principles in human personality?

To begin with, the experience of mystics of all times and nations bears witness to the contrary: they all say that, at any rate at exceptional moments of their life, they were conscious of the real presence of God in the depths of their heart.[1] The Christian doctrine as preached by one of its first exponents, St. Paul, sanctions and confirms this mystical experience: 'Christ living in me.' A perfectly orthodox meaning attaches to the well-known saying of the German mystic Angelus Silesius: 'Christ might be born a thousand times in Bethlehem, but if He has not been born in thy soul, thou art lost just the same.' The whole doctrine of the Holy Spirit, or of the Church as the body of Christ, presupposes the immanent presence of the Deity in the collective unity of the faithful. Furthermore, although insisting that the personality of Christ is unique, the Christian doctrine (and indeed Christ Himself) sets man the task of imitating Him and becoming Christ-like; that is the ideal of human life and the realization of man's true nature.

Deeper metaphysical reflection shows that in spite of the immeasurable difference between the average man and the God-man Jesus Christ, something 'divinely-human' is inherent in man's being as such; there is potentially present in it a certain divine element as its immanent constitutive principle. Far from conflicting with the Church doctrine of the Incarnation, it is its necessary

---

[1] The greatest mystic of Islam, Hussein al-Halladje (d. 922) was so intensely conscious of it that at moments of ecstasy he lost his purely human consciousness and, in uttering the word 'I', apprehended it as the 'I' of God Himself. This is the meaning of his enigmatic words 'I am the Truth', in which he repeated Christ's saying.

precondition: awareness of the potential divine-humanity of man as such reveals the metaphysical perspective in which the perfect Incarnation, without ceasing to be miraculous, loses its arbitrary character and fits in with the general meaning of human life and nature. Vladimir Solovyov has shown this most convincingly. The doctrine that God *became man* instead of incarnating in some other creature (in contradistinction to certain pagan doctrines according to which the deity found embodiment in animals) bears testimony to an affinity between God and man. This is the meaning of the dogma, directed against every form of Docetism and Monophysitism, that Christ was truly and really human, 'a new Adam', similar to us in everything but sin. Finally, the teaching of the Eastern Fathers that God became man in order that man might be 'deified', also presupposes affinity between the Divine and the human. If 'deification' of man is to be at all thinkable, the possibility of it must be inherent in man from the beginning. Human nature must combine an aspect in which man is a concrete being distinct from God with an aspect in which he is potentially at one with God and contains within himself the seed of Christ-like perfection.

The same conclusion is forced upon us quite independently of the Christological problem. Since connection with God constitutes man's very being, and at the same time, man can only find a basis for his existence in an external relation to a transcendent God, there must be, as it were, two different levels or layers in the human spirit itself. Only on that supposition can God's immanence in man and His transcendence be combined without contradiction.

2. *The duality of the human spirit. The uncreated principle of human nature*

It has been pointed out that mystics of all epochs and nations recognize the presence of the Deity in the human soul. Their experience confirms the conclusion we have just reached that man's nature in its relation to God is dual. Traditional religious thought in the narrow sense of the term regards the whole of the human being as a created entity, different from God in principle and existing as distinctly separate from Him; the relation between them is purely and entirely external. We have seen that this view, in so far as it claims to be exhaustive, leads to hopeless contradictions. But parallel to it there has existed throughout the history of religious speculation a type of thought which is called mystical. In so far as it is combined with monotheism (not only Christian, but Jewish and Mahometan as well—for instance in the Kabbalah and in the great systems of Arabian and Persian mysticism), it does not admit, as Hindu mysticism does, complete mergence of human personality in God. It preserves the difference between God and man and their separate being, and therefore recognizes a dual relation between them, both transcendent and immanent; in doing so it confirms the view that human spirit is so to speak on two levels: on one, God transcends it, and on the other, He is present in it as the immanent basis of man's nature. This conception of two planes, or, as it were, of two souls within man's inner being can be traced throughout the history of monotheistic mysticism and finds expression in a number of mystically minded poets.[1] It goes back to St. Paul, Tertullian, Plotinus, Augustine and Dionysius the Areopagite; it is found in Hugues and Richard de St. Victor; it forms the basis of Meister Echkart's teaching and of the kindred German-Dutch mysticism of the fourteenth and fifteenth centuries; it is clearly expressed by St. Theresa and St. Francis de Sales. I will confine myself to a few instances. The whole of St. Paul's doctrine about the indwelling Christ (or the Holy Spirit) presupposes the duality of the human soul; for in calling man to live in accordance with that aspect of his being in which he is the bearer of Christ or of the holy Spirit, it obviously distinguishes man as autonomous, from his inmost depths sanctified by the presence of God. Tertullian expresses the same correlation (in *De Testimonia animae*) by saying that whenever the soul 'returns into itself and acquires its natural health, it speaks of God', and that 'no human soul, *illumined by the light inherent in it*, can fail to profess God, although, o soul, thou dost not seek to know Him'. St. Augustine has already been quoted in another connection as saying that God lives in the depths of the human spirit, and that God 'was always with me, but I was not with my self'; this obviously implies the difference between the inmost 'self' and the 'self' capable of going away from it. This duality is very clearly expressed in German mysticism, which emphasizes the presence in the soul

[1] Instances of it are given in H. Brémond's book, especially in Vol. VII, pp. 48–59 and *passim*. Brémond calls the view in question 'le dogme fondamental de l'experience mystique'. See also Rufus Jones, *Studies in mystical religion* and V. Ivanov's brilliant article '*Anima*' in the German magazine *Corona*, Band V (1934–5), Heft 4.

of a special principle, distinct from its ordinary, familiar nature; that principle is designated as 'the highest in the soul', 'the core' or 'the last depth' of the spirit, 'the holy of holies' of the soul, or 'the spark' that lives in it (Eckhart). Likewise St. Theresa speaks of the 'spirit' or the 'centre' of the soul and insists that there is a real difference between 'the soul' and 'the spirit'. St. Francis de Sales calls this higher principle '*fine pointe de l'âme*', the point of unity between our spirit with the spirit of God'; he distinguishes between 'Sarah' and 'Hagar' in the soul, and regards the first, the higher part, as in a sense superhuman ('*en certaine façon surhumaine*'). Grace abides in it unfailingly without our being aware of it.[1]

It is important to note that this duality by no means coincides with the generally recognized distinction, referred to in the preceding pages, between man as a carnal being or a psycho-physical organism, and man's 'soul' or 'spirit'. On the contrary, the duality in question exists within the sphere of what in a general sense is called the 'soul': it is to be found within man's inner self-conscious being. A modern French poet, Paul Claudel, and the Swiss psychologist C. Jung—so far as I know, independently of each other—have called these two distinct layers *animus* and *anima*.[2] The correlation between them has been formulated with great expressiveness by Walt Whitman who says 'I cannot understand this mystery, but my mind repeats to me that we are two: there is my soul and there is my self'. These words may be taken as a starting point in discussing the subject.

What can be meant by the difference between my 'soul' and my 'self'? The answer is suggested by what has been said (Chapter I, 2–4) of the difference between my usual self-consciousness, expressed by the word 'I', and the awareness of my inner world as a wealth of reality abiding in and revealing itself to me (it will be remembered

[1] *Traité de l'amour de Dieu* quoted by Brémond, vol. VIII, p. 49 and f. Two images are used to symbolize this duality: the layer of the soul that is in intimately-immanent connection with God is sometimes called 'the highest point' of the soul, and sometimes its 'inmost depth' or 'core'. The first image is suggested by man's feeling that this aspect of the soul is of supreme value and by his regarding his spiritual struggles as something he can 'look down' upon; the second is due to the sense of the greater remoteness of this aspect of the soul from the outer world, and also to the awareness of it as the basis of human existence. The difference in symbolism does not affect the nature of the correlation.

[2] See also the above-mentioned article by the Russian mystical poet V. Ivanov.

that such awareness is comparatively rare and exceptional, and is of the nature of revelation or mystical experience). The 'I' is the pure subject—the subject of thought and knowledge and of autonomous primary will—a certain contentless point, the nature of which wholly consists in being 'the bearer' of my cognitive gaze and my volitions. But my 'soul' as a reality abiding within me does not confront me as an object in the usual sense of the term, and therefore differs from the whole of the 'objective world'; and yet I meet it in inner experience, and it is somehow 'revealed' to me within myself. Every attempt to define what I mean by 'my soul' in this sense shows that the usual categories of transcendence and immanence, or of subject and object are inapplicable to it, or that 'my soul' as a reality transcends them and in some way combines them within itself.

Accordingly, there is a fundamental difference in the relation in which my 'self' and my 'soul' in the sense just indicated stand to God. For me as a self-conscious subject God is a purely transcendent reality confronting me from without. Although, as we know, God does not form part of the world of fact, but is the reality beyond it, He stands over against me, is external to me and different from me, much as 'the world of fact is' (this explains why God is so easily taken to be part of it). But for my 'soul' as a reality revealing itself to me as the inmost depth of my being, God is immanent and dwells 'in me', while remaining distinct from me. Reality as an all-embracing and all-pervading unity cannot have anything outside itself. In it 'to have' and 'to be that which one has' coincide—and yet this is somehow compatible with the division of reality into various particular spheres. Therefore the relation of my soul as a reality to God may be equally correctly described either as God's presence in me or as my being rooted in Him. It is in this sense that God as a reality transcendent to me is the immanent basis of my own being.

This explains the correlation between man's two attitudes towards God—between mystical experience and the usual rationally-religious apprehension of God as a transcendent reality. It is exactly the same as the general correlation between reality and the world of fact (see Chapter I, 5). If the subject's cognitive activity is to be directed upon an external object at all, it is necessary that prior to and independently of such cognitive contact we should already 'have' the object in an *immediate* way; otherwise, the very idea of it—the idea of something existing outside us—would be impossible.

We 'have' the object, because we and it are from the first indissolubly interconnected in the all-embracing and all-pervading unity of reality; this is why we 'have' that which cognitively is *not given* us. and are aware of the object's existence when we are not perceiving it. The very conception of *transcendent* being is based upon this unity (cp. Chapter I, 5). Exactly the same argument is applicable to our relation to God—with the only difference that the activity directed upon Him is volitional and emotional rather than cognitive. The idea of God as a transcendent reality external to us, and of ourselves as subjective human spirits related to, or striving towards it, requires that in the first instance we should—not cognitively or subjectively, but *ontologically*, in our very being and essence—be in a primary indissoluble connection with God. Prior to any idea of a transcendent God, we must have the experience of Him as inseparable from the experience of our own being, i.e., must 'have' God in this sense immanently in ourselves. In so far as my soul is rooted in God, or bears God within itself, it passes on (for the most part without my being aware of it) this primary knowledge of God to the outer, superficial layer of my mind, to my rational self-consciousness. Only in virtue of this can my 'self', as distinct and separate from God, be derivatively aware of Him as a transcendent reality, be guided by Him, recognize its duty to obey Him, i.e. have a transcendent criterion in life. Mystical experience is, whether consciously or not, the basis of religious experience in the narrow sense of the term.

The same correlation that holds between the primary and the derivative knowledge of God applies to the bearers of that knowledge: 'I' as a self-conscious subject, a focal point, an autonomous being, am in a sense derived from the depth of my soul in which I am merged in God. Only because I *am* that depth, or because it lives in me, I am something other than a merely natural being—something other than a thing, than a totality of qualities and processes, or than simply an 'animate being'; only in virtue of this 'I am I'—a free agent, a primary centre of thought and will. I am usually unaware of it, and the kind of individualism typical of our age encourages me to forget or to deny it, but that does not alter the nature of the case. That of which I am conscious as myself is at bottom simply a reflected image or projection of my own depth—as it were a ray thrown out into the realm of natural objective being by the inmost divinely-human reality of my 'soul'. Precisely that which I experience as the essence of my 'self'—my spontaneity, my power of transcending all that is empirically given, of judging and valuing everything in the world, including myself as an empirical datum, my power of self-determination—is due to my being rooted in God, or to His presence in the inmost depths of my being. I am free and primary, I direct my life myself, I am a creative entity; indeed, creative freedom forms the very essence of my 'self'. But the fact of this free conscious existence as a 'self' does not arise, so to speak, of its own accord, does not give rise to itself. It is transcendentally determined from without, and springs from those depths in which God lives and acts in me. Through those depths God determines my being, but He determines it as *free being-for-itself*. The action of God in me does not destroy or hamper my freedom, but is its original source, and expresses itself in it. This brings us back to the main point: personality, 'the self', is not a self-contained and self-subsistent point or sphere, isolated from all else; its uniqueness as a 'monad' is constituted by the fact that it is a ray of the all-embracing reality, penetrating the very depths of my being. There lives in me, like 'a spark'—to use again Meister Eckhart's term—something that proceeds from the true primary source and centre of reality, God; and in virtue of this, my being acquires the character of subjectivity and becomes a self, a derivatively-primary centre of reality. The active power flowing from this deepest level does not stand over against me as an alien force affecting me from without, but on the contrary, flowing through the centre of my personality, or, rather, creating it for the first time, coincides with my own freedom. This constitutes the mystery of the *primary* relation between 'grace' and 'freedom': grace, 'a gift from above', is not the opposite of my freedom, but the source of it. The more firmly man is rooted in the transcendent depth of his spirit, and the more he listens to its voice, the more truly he is a person, a free and creative being. My freedom and the action of grace in me are not two heterogeneous forces external to each other; in their ultimate essence they are two aspects of one and the same living reality. They are, as it were, expressions of the 'masculine' and the 'feminine' principles of the primary 'androgynous' human nature; the 'feminine,' receptive principle (*anima*) is ontologically prior to the masculine (*animus*). That which, as the seed of 'grace' is mysteriously received into the inmost recesses of the soul, comes forth as an independent self-active entity having a life of its own.

146

We can now grasp more fully the difference between the two points of view which may be conditionally designated as Augustinianism and Pelagianism.[1] Each of them if taken as an exhaustive definition of the relation between God and man, or between grace and freedom, is, as we have seen, untenable and leads to hopeless contradictions. But if they be taken to express a relation which holds *upon two levels* of spiritual being, they both prove correct and easily reconcilable. 'Augustinianism' is perfectly right in contending that *ultimately* the only positive creative power is God, and that man conceived apart from his connection with God, or as severed from Him, is an utterly impotent creature. It does not, however, sufficiently recognize that man as an independent and active spiritual reality is not alien from God, but is the progeny and special expression of God's own creative energy and, as such, himself has creative power. 'Pelagianism' on the other hand is perfectly right in affirming the positive reality of man's creative free will and therefore the possibility and necessity of its free co-operation with the transcendent gracious power of God; but it loses sight of the fact that this independence of man as a bearer of a special creative will is merely a reflection in the external layer of reality of his indissoluble inner connection with God. It may be said that Augustinianism, concerned with the inmost depth of the human spirit, forgets that this depth gives rise to an external aspect of man's being, in which he as an independent entity confronts God and is outside Him— whereas Pelagianism, concentrating upon this external layer, ignores the divine basis of man's being. The synthesis of both those points of view—of the consciousness that ultimately God is all, and I am nothing or merely a passive recipient, and that in the external layer of my being I am a bearer of creative reality proceeding from God, and must therefore come into interaction with Him—can alone express the antinomic fulness of the actual relation between God and man. Thomas Aquinas has expressed this with the force of genius in the simple words 'we must pray as though everything depended upon God; we must act as though everything depended upon ourselves.'

[1] I have in mind not the exact historical content of Augustine's and Pelagius's teachings, but two general types of thought, one of which denies, and the other affirms the positive value of the independent being of man as a bearer of free creative will. 'Pelagianism' in this sense includes the perfectly orthodox theory of synergism between freedom and grace, as two independent forces.

It must not be imagined, however, that the duality in question implies a splitting of personality. It is a *super-rational bi-unity*—a duality wholly embraced and interpenetrated by the indivisible unity of personality or selfhood. The more thoroughly I am aware of it, the deeper and more secure is my personal self-consciousness; the mystical experience of the super-human, divinely-human basis of my being gives for the first time wholeness and stability to my own personality. This spiritual condition might be compared in music to a calm, prolonged, stable bass accompaniment of a tempestuous, changeable melody. Following Walt Whitman's formula I have called the surface layer of our being 'the self'—identifying it with that which we *are*, and the deeper layer—'the soul', identifying it with that which we *have*; but such designation, though natural for the normal, prevalent type of self-consciousness, has only a relative significance. The depth of my soul which I distinguish from my immediate self-consciousness or from my 'self' is the very root and ground, i.e. the inmost essence, of my 'self'. For in virtue of the general position established above (Chapter I, 3), in the domain of reality I *am* that which I have.

Insight into this ultimate ground of human nature leads to one very important conclusion. In the preceding pages man has been described as a 'created spirit'—a term generally accepted in prevalent religious thought. By createdness, as already explained, is meant the inherent groundlessness of an entity, its dependence upon something else, different from and external to it. After all that has just been said, can human spirit be regarded as wholly and entirely 'created' in this sense? It will be remembered that Meister Eckhart's doctrine of the divine spark in the depths of human soul has led to the accusation that he took a heretical view of man as uncreated. Whether this accusation is right or not with regard to Eckhart's own teaching, there can be no doubt as to the real point at issue. Mystical experience and insight into the inmost depths of the human soul in which it is akin to God and at one with Him means a break with pure createdness, and in this sense a recognition of the un-created principle in man. Whatever the traditional dogmatic doctrine may teach, the immediate experience of that deepest level testifies that there abides within me, as a part of my soul, something absolutely stable, eternal and therefore 'un-created'. In apprehending myself as indissolubly connected with those depths I cannot feel that the whole of me is groundless, unstable, dependent for its being upon a power alien from and external to me. That which forms the basis of my personality as such, that which I apprehend as 'myself' in contradistinction to my involuntary and groundless mental states that come and go, is directly experienced by me as un-created, as proceeding from God and rooted in Him, and not as 'made' by Him. Of course, my being is somehow 'bestowed' upon me; it is not a primary and absolutely initial reality, but consists in my connection with God; God is its ground. But precisely in virtue of this intimate connection, it derivatively participates in the eternity of God Himself. Direct awareness of the eternity and perfect stability of my innermost 'self' as existing in God is the ground of the ineradicable faith in my indestructibility and immortality. This does not at all mean deifying man or identifying him with God. No sane person would dream of simply identifying man with God; (deification of certain human beings, e.g. of kings in ancient Eastern monarchies, was based on quite a different and primitive conception of God, and even then was not understood in a literal sense). To begin with, this eternity and un-createdness only belongs to me as a personal spirit indissolubly connected with God through the inmost depths of my being; it does not belong to me as a carnal entity including all the concrete, empirical contents of my life. That aspect of my being forms part of the natural world and is recognized by me as groundless, unstable and purely 'subjective'; it has no secure basis in itself, and must therefore be regarded as purely created, wholly dependent upon a higher reality external to it. And, secondly—and this perhaps is even more important—the problem must not be rationalistically simplified and reduced to the dilemma, is man (or only the higher principle in him) 'a creature' or 'God'? For the prevalent religious consciousness, which takes this dilemma as its starting point, all that is not God—all that is finite, limited, particular, not absolutely perfect—is therefore 'creature'. But this broad definition of createdness omits one important distinction. There is something which, though 'created' in the sense of differing from God and being dependent upon Him, is 'un-created' in so far as it is not 'groundless', not utterly heterogeneous to God or separate from Him. In that sense all that is dependent upon God, but unseverable from and akin to Him is uncreated. It might accordingly be said that in its inmost depth human spirit is not God's 'creation' but His 'emanation' —something that is 'born' of Him or 'proceeds' from Him; it should be remembered in this connection that emanation is not merely a particular and derivative manifestation of the Deity, but (even in the Neo-Platonic doctrine) a manifestation qualitatively limited and modified. This aspect of the human spirit, not being identical with God and not forming part of Him, stands as it were midway between 'creature' and God: it is 'something divine' or, in the words of St. Francis de Sales 'superhuman' in man.[1] A ray from the central Sun of reality glows in me like 'a spark', and is the ultimate basis of my own being.

The gist of the matter is that the super-rational relation between human spirit and God cannot in any case be adequately explained in the simple logical categories of identity and difference. Man is clearly something quite other than God, but—as already pointed out with regard to reality in general—the 'otherness' in this instance is quite other than the usual logical category of difference. Making the necessary reservations, one might define human spirit in Hegel's terms as the *Anderssein* of God. God's own essence manifests itself in the human spirit in quite a *different ontological form*, as it were on a different, derivative level of being. The prevalent conception of man as 'God's image and likeness' implies that the same or similar form is imposed upon quite a different ontological material (like a portrait painted on canvas as compared with the person represented in it); but in truth the contrary is the case: to put it crudely, God and the human spirit are, so to speak, made of the same material and have the same nature, but exist in two categorially different forms—in the form of primary, actual and infinite being in God, and in the form of derivative, potential and limited being, as though in miniature, in man. Of course this way of putting it is also rationalistic, and therefore is but an approximate expression of the inexpressible, super-rational relation between God and man.

A ray issuing from the central Sun of reality and retaining something of Its nature forms the very essence of my personality; therefore, that essence is not simply 'created', but 'proceeds' from God and, as derived from Him, preserves its inner kinship and unity with Him.

Is this conception as 'heretical' and opposed to the recognized church doctrine as it at first sight appears? True, it is extremely difficult to explain on this view how a being akin to God and united to Him can break away from Him and 'fall into sin'; the Church obviously fears that the idea of man's divine kinship may diminish

[1] St. Maximus the Confessor uses the phrase 'man's spirit is not un-divine'.

the necessary sense of his sinfulness. But apart from this problem, which will be discussed later, the view in question can be expressed in a perfectly orthodox form. Man as such is a created entity. But God does more than merely create man and grant him special 'creaturely' existence outside Himself: He comes down and dwells within the depths of that created spirit, makes His 'abode' in it and thus hallows it, transforming it into a being akin to Himself, other and greater than a mere 'creature'. In virtue of this man becomes not merely a creation, but 'a son' or 'a child' of God 'by adoption'. These terms, sanctified by the Scriptures, express precisely the 'emanational' aspect of man's being—his 'procession' or 'birth' from God, 'from above' or 'from the spirit' in contradistinction to physical birth, as Christ Himself said to Nicodemus. It may be thought that there still remains a difference in the interpretation of the sequence of these two 'births': the traditional view is that 'at first,' and therefore primarily, man is simply a 'creature' and only afterwards and derivatively can he become 'a child of God', 'born from above'. But the temporal order of the soul's development must not be confused with the super-temporal relation itself: man could not *become* 'a child of God', if he had not been one from the first— if this were not God's *idea* of him. In the ontological order priority belongs to man's higher being, as the true final end of God's conception of him. The *recognition* of the 'birth from above' is an act of faith taking place in the temporal sequence of our life, and in that sense is a 'second birth' (which, by the way, is not, as some sectarians believe, a unique and final event, but generally is a lengthy process, admitting of interruption and repetition, increase and decline); in the ontological order, however, 'birth from above' is primary, all-determining and, in its metaphysical essence, eternal. It alone makes possible the everyday miracle of the emergence, in the naturally-born psycho-physical organism, of the mysterious supernatural being which we call human soul, potentially divine in its depths.

As already pointed out, the fact of man existing as an independent entity distinct and separate from God, i.e. the inevitable duality between God and man—is not a primary category under which their correlation is to be conceived. Man's existence as a derivatively-independent and free being is the expression of his kinship and intimate bond with God. Man has 'selfhood' and is conscious of himself as 'I', as an independent active centre of life, not because he is self-contained and self-sufficient, but on the contrary because his being reflects and expresses in a derivative way the intrinsic primariness of God from Whom he proceeds. The bond which unites man with God is inseverable; in physical birth the umbilical cord has to be cut so that the newborn child can begin its independent life—but in the super-temporal spiritual birth it unites man forever with his original ground; the life-blood that unceasingly pours through it is such that its nourishing power makes man a person, a derivatively independent centre of activity. Man as a 'self', as a conscious free agent is, as it were, a representative of his divinely-human inmost being in the objective world of nature alien from him. In that capacity he is a free servant of God with an independent position of his own in the realm of natural cosmic being. Just as an ambassador, while remaining a subject of his state, a member of his nation, a servant of his government, lives in a foreign country and freely, by the light of his own reason, defends in it the interests of his native land, so must man freely to realize the behests of God and to represent his divinely-human fatherland in the sphere of earthly life. Being such an ambassador, he must combine, in his mind and actions, humility in carrying out his duties with the sense of his dignity as a representative of his great divinely-human native land.

Thus, on the one hand the human spirit abides forever in the bosom of God (or, to use another metaphor, contains within its own bosom the seed of God), and, on the other, is a free personality and God's responsible and autonomous representative in the world; this is the basis of the inevitable duality between the sphere of man's inner, divinely-sanctified life, and of the sphere of independent human creativeness, including the whole domain of culture and history—of secular, as distinct from religious life. Man's 'secular', consciously organized existence is, on the one hand, autonomous— or, rather, is the expression of his autonomy—and on the other is wholly based upon that aspect of his being in which he is a passive recipient and not an agent, and which is not consciously created by him, but involuntarily lives and grows in him.

The true boundary between these two spheres lies in the invisible depths of the human spirit. It cannot be identified with any empirical distinction (such e.g. as that between the church and the secular life, between priesthood and laity etc.) but cuts across them all. The source of our constant tendency wrongly to identify this invisible bi-unity with external distinctions is to be found partly in the nature of rationalistic thought, which transforms indivisible bi-unity into definite duality, and in the last resort in human sinfulness; more will be said of this in a subsequent chapter.

I pass now to discuss the bi-unity of human nature as expressed in creativeness.

6. *The creative nature of man*

The bi-unity of human nature manifests itself in quite a different way in man's inherent power of creativeness.

According to the traditional religious view (shared both by Augustine, and Thomas Aquinas in spite of their differences in other respects) the conception of 'creator' is applicable to God alone, and no creature, including man, can create anything. Of course in the specific sense in which God is called the Creator, and the creation of the world is conceived as a miraculous emergence of the world 'out of nothing' at His will, creativeness is something absolutely unique and unrepeatable within the confines of an already existing world. This subject will be dealt with later. At present it is sufficient to point out that the very fact of human mind being able to conceive of God as Creator shows that creativeness is in some sense accessible to it too—else the word itself would have no meaning for it.

Apart from any theories, it is obvious that the element of creativeness is present in human life. In addition to purely rational conscious activities in which man purposively combines the already existing elements of the surrounding world, he is capable of another kind of activity, giving rise to something new and hitherto non-existent. In this sense he is a creator in the artistic, cognitive, moral and political spheres. But the element of creativeness enters even into purely rational activity, provided the purpose of it is not automatically forced upon man by the pressing needs of his natural being, but is something as yet unknown and not met with in the world of fact—some ideal born in his inmost heart.

The most typical instance of creativeness is art, and in that sense it may be said that all creativeness bears an 'artistic' stamp. How are we to define it?

Art is always *expressive*.[1] The word 'expression' is one of the most

[1] See Ch. II, 3.

153

mysterious words in human language, and as a rule we use it without dwelling upon its meaning. Taken literally it signifies both the 'impress' and 'the process of impressing' something upon an external object or material—somewhat similar to the process of putting a seal upon a surface that preserves the form of the seal. By analogy we use the term 'expression' when something hidden and invisible becomes evident to eyes or mind, leaving its mark upon something else. Something spiritual and invisible lies hidden in a man's heart; he craves to make it visible and manifest; he achieves this by means of words, sounds, combinations of colours and lines, images, or (in acting and dancing) by the movements of his body. In so far as he strives for it and achieves it, he is an artist. Art, being 'expression', is *embodiment*: in it something spiritual is clothed with flesh, is, so to speak, embedded in the material and appears in it as its 'form'. This is the essence of creativeness.

But what exactly does man want to express? The simplest and therefore a very usual answer is 'himself'. In a sense this is perfectly true and understandable: since man's inner being is spirit, in expressing something spiritual, he is inevitably expressing himself. On the other hand, however, as a 'self'—both as a pure self, a contentless bearer of life and consciousness, and as 'myself', i.e. an absolutely unique and unrepeatable entity—man is essentially *inexpressible*, for he is an innermost point of being which cannot be exteriorized. Only indirectly, by means of what he *has*, he can somehow make perceptible what he *is*. An artist (like any other 'creator') in his creative work thinks of himself least of all: he wants to express a certain hidden treasure, a spiritual 'something' in his heart. Even in pure lyrics a poet expresses his spiritual experiences not merely as subjective, but as containing something in a sense objective and universally human. What is that 'something'? As already pointed out (Chapter II, 3) this question cannot be answered for a very simple reason: to define that 'something' means to express it—i.e. to do precisely what the artist does, but as it were in a different form. Since, however, the expression must be adequate to the subject expressed, it can have one single form only—the very one which the creative artist gives it.[1] It may be asked, however, whence does this

[1] This is why every attempt to express or formulate 'the idea' of a work of art is fruitless and self-contradictory. When asked what was the idea of his novel *Anna Karenin*, Tolstoy answered 'I could express the idea of that novel in one way only—by writing it again.'

'something' arise, what kind of reality has it, in what way is it present in the artist's mind.

Since it does not as yet exist in any definite shape, it obviously does not form part of the objective world. It has characteristics that belong to reality as distinct from the world of fact—and in particular to that aspect of reality in which it is *pure potentiality*, i.e. 'being' in the form of ripening, of self-realization. In the process of artistic creativeness the content is given by 'inspiration', is 'born' and not deliberately constructed; some superhuman voice suggests it to the artist, some power—other than his own intention—compels him to nurture it, to give it form and express it. But this 'something' begins to exist in a definite form only from the moment when the artist has made the necessary effort to express it. It is precisely in this that creativeness consists. It is an activity in which the artist's own effort, his own 'doing' is indissolubly bound up with the involuntary development in him of a certain 'gift from above'.

The artist, of course, creates 'of himself'—mere repetition of other people's ideas is not creativeness—but the creative 'self' is not simply the individual in his subjectivity, and not an impersonal bearer of consciousness in general: it is an individually-human embodiment of the super-human spirit acting in man. The degree of interaction between the individually-human and the super-human, or between the actively-deliberate and the passively-involuntary aspects of creativeness, may differ. Sometimes a genius creates *almost* like a will-less medium of a higher power acting through him; in other instances an artist makes long and painful efforts and repeated attempts in order to express (or, what is the same thing, adequately to apprehend) that which is given him from above. But in any case his own activity and his passive attention to the voice speaking within him form an indivisible unity. And this implies that creativeness presupposes the bi-unity of the human being—its independence, freedom, purposiveness, and its inherence in and dependence upon a transcendent spiritual reality.

Is this bi-unity identical with the divinely-human nature of man, discussed in the preceding pages? Artistic or creative 'inspiration' in general is of course something other than 'grace', i.e. the presence and action of God in man, which constitutes the essence of religious experience. Artists, thinkers, men of moral and political genius may have no religious experience at all in the strict sense of the term. Creative activity differs from prayerful contemplation, from being in the presence of God or apprehending Him. The artists themselves speak not of God's action in them, but of a higher spiritual power that inspires them, of the 'muse' or 'the demon' (in the classical sense of a superhuman, divine being or spirit). The artist (or any other creator) does not seek or contemplate God, does not deliberately strive for spiritual enlightenment or nearness to the Divine; his task is different and consists in creativeness itself, in the production of new forms of being, new embodiments of ideal principles latent in his spirit.

At bottom, however, every reality and every spiritual force (in so far as it acts through the centre of human personality and therefore is merged with man's creative freedom) issues from that centre and primary source of reality which we call God. In trying to understand the meaning of human creativeness so to speak from without, i.e. in explaining its metaphysical significance, we can say that in the state of creative inspiration man experiences the action of God in only one of His aspects—namely, as a *creative principle* and thereby as the source of his own creativeness; all other 'attributes' of God revealed in religious experience remain outside his field of vision. What is particularly characteristic of the experience of artistic inspiration is the peculiar relationship that obtains in it between man and the creative power of God. In purely religious consciousness man is aware of himself primarily in his distinction from God—as 'creature' in contradistinction to the 'Creator,' or as a moral agent subordinated to God's supreme power; in mystical experience man is conscious of his nearness to God—of God's presence in him or of himself being rooted in God. But in the experience of creative inspiration, in which the superhuman creative principle directly passes into human creative effort and is merged with it, man is conscious of himself as a creator; that means that he is aware of his kinship with the creative primary source of life and of his participation in the mysterious metaphysical process of creation. It is as a creator that man is most conscious of himself as 'the image and likeness' of God. In the domain of reality experience is the ultimate criterion of truth, since experience is self-revelation of the reality present in it; there can therefore be no question of illusion or error here, as in the case of our knowledge of the world of fact. Hence we are entitled to express it in ontological terms and say that man as creator is a co-partner in God's creativeness.

The metaphysical implication of this is that God not merely

creates entities, including man, not merely is Himself present as the supreme transcendent principle in the human spirit, but that He also bestows on His creatures a measure of His own creative power, i.e., He *creates creators*. God creates derivatively-creative beings, and grants His creatures a share in His own creativeness. This is of course merely another aspect of the active presence of the Divine principle in the human spirit.

Such is the general correlation between God and His creatures manifested in the mysterious presence of creative processes in cosmic nature itself. It was recognized by Aristotle in his doctrine of purposive form or entelechy, but during the last three centuries the world has been regarded as a lifeless machine. In our own time, beginning, approximately, with Bergson's doctrine of 'creative evolution', the presence of creativeness has once more received recognition, at any rate with regard to organic nature; and the development of modern physics inclines scientists to admit that something similar may be found in the so-called inorganic nature as well.

Human creativeness in all its forms is obviously profoundly akin to this cosmic creativeness. The difference is that in nature creative power is impersonal or super-personal and has a generic character, so that individual entities are merely its passive instruments, whereas human creativeness is individual, and its active bearer is a personal self-conscious spirit. Man not merely creates, but is *conscious* of doing it: creativeness is the work of his own autonomous 'self'. Although in creative activity he feels that a certain higher, super-human power is acting in him, he is also conscious of himself as a co-worker with it and not merely its passive instrument or medium —which he feels himself to be in the case of purely natural processes such as child-bearing. Human spirit is a created entity to which God as it were partly *delegates* His own creative power, authorizing it to be an active partner in His own creativeness. The element of autonomy or self-determination which constitutes man as a person manifests itself at the same time as creativeness. Spontaneity in determining one's own life—the derivative primacy which is the essence of personality—is also spontaneity in building up new forms of being, i.e. conscious creativeness. This is another confirmation of the truth that man is something greater, and other than, merely a 'creature'.

To grasp the ontological significance of this fact it is essential to understand that—contrary to the usual idea—creativeness is by no means the privilege of a few chosen, exceptional natures. There is, of course, an important difference in this respect between different types of people: a poet, for instance, is inclined, and to a certain extent quite justly, to be conscious of himself as one of 'the elect', superior to the ordinary average man, and to despise the *profanum vulgus*. The spiritual world, like the world in general, is built hierarchically and contains God's true elect, and spiritual leaders who determine the paths of its development. But this hierarchical structure is combined in it with 'democratic' equality. In this sense the difference between a 'creator' and the average man is merely one of degree. Every human being is to some extent or potentially a creator. Wherever the purpose of activity springs from the depths of the human spirit, there is creativeness. Every craftsman who loves his work and puts his best into it is guided by the ideal he has before him, and in that sense creates by inspiration: the difference between a craftsman and an artist is only relative. That was obvious in the old days of handicrafts; our epoch of machine-production has made a clear line of demarcation between the mechanically prescribed, automatic work and free creativeness, but it has done so at the cost of lowering and suppressing the truly-human element in man, and unnaturally transforming him into a lifeless tool or a beast of burden. That, however, is only possible up to a certain point. Man cannot cease being a personality; therefore he always introduces creativeness in however small a measure into his work. Further, a creative element is present in all knowledge, since knowledge means bringing the light of truth into the world of existence, ontologically raising existence to the level of self-conscious being. Great new scientific and philosophical syntheses obviously mean the creation of something new, hitherto non-existent, and enrich the world; but the difference between a creative genius and a humble scientific worker—however striking in extreme cases—admits of imperceptible gradations and is therefore relative. Equally relative in the moral and political sphere is the distinction between an administrator and a political creative genius, or between the humblest person fulfilling the moral law and a moral genius whose conscience discovers and introduces into human relations a new moral consciousness. For in that realm the most ordinary average man not merely fulfils duties imposed upon him, but introduces into his work an element of intuition, improvization, conjecture, and deals with an individual situation in some new, hitherto untried way originating in his own mind, and in that sense is a creator. Every person who impresses his personality on his surroundings, every wife and mother who introduces a moral style of her own into the life of the family, and her own aesthetic taste into the home, every educator of children—is a creator.

Man as such is a creator. The element of creativeness is inherent in human life. In that sense man may be defined as a being that consciously takes part in God's creativeness. In no other respect, perhaps, does the divinely-human nature of man manifest itself so clearly. Man is not only the servant of God, obediently carrying out His will, but a free co-partner of God's creativeness. Or, to put it differently: since God's will is creative, it cannot be adequately expressed in any general, automatically applicable rules and commands; it consists in spontaneously imparting unique and individual form to the manifold variety of existence, and hence can only be truly carried out through free creativeness. All slavish, blind, mechanical fulfilment of the Divine will means failing to fulfil it in its real essence. A man who is merely 'God's servant' is a 'wicked and slothful servant'—just as a workman who carries out slavishly and mechanically the work entrusted to him, without taking interest in it or putting into it any voluntary effort, is a potential *saboteur.* God has called man to be not simply His servant, but His free, i.e. creative co-worker.

On the other hand it is essential to recognize that human creativeness cannot, from the nature of the case be the realization of God's will in all its fulness. God's will is not only the will to create new forms of being, but to *deify* creation and unite it to Himself, since God is more than simply the creative primary source of reality: He is also personified holiness, the ideal principle of the inner perfection and intrinsic value of creation. It is only in the moral and religious domain that man's creative effort to imbue his own being, both collective and individual, with the Divine holiness is a voluntary fulfilment of the Divine will in its entirety. But it is precisely in this domain that man is least of all a 'creator' and most of all a mere recipient of God's gracious reality.

The difference between man's creative power and the integral will of God may also be indicated by saying that man as creator always expresses only some one of the many aspects of God's creativeness, only some one of His many designs. For in virtue of His super-rational nature, God is not only a pure absolute unity, but also a unity of the manifold. His creativeness is realized in a multiplicity of designs, and man realizes some one of them, experienced by him as a power acting within him, as a kind of divine force. Human creativeness therefore manifests the action of forces which, though they proceed from God, are as it were intermediary between Him and man. The mysterious fact of human creativeness brings out the multiplicity and, so to speak, the derivatively polytheistic structure of reality. At this juncture the idea of *reality* as an intermediary connecting sphere between the Creator and the creature proves once again to be of value.

It follows from what has just been said that man's creativeness is inevitably limited. I am referring not merely to its external limits—not to the fact that, after all, God delegates only a part of His creative power to man (or to the super-human spirit possessing him), so that certain tasks remain beyond man's reach (thus e.g. man cannot himself, by his own design and effort create another living and creative being). I have in mind the immanent limits involved in the very nature of human creativeness as such. As a manifestation of only one of the innumerable metaphysical forces proceeding from God, and not of God's nature in all its depth and fulness, it is limited by a principle which lies beyond it. In its own domain it is autocratic—thus, artistic creativeness knows no criteria except artistic perfection, and in this sense is 'beyond good and evil'—but in spiritual life as a whole it is subordinated to the principles of *holiness*. This is clear from the fact that there can be no true creativeness apart from moral earnestness and responsibility; it requires the moral effort of truthfulness, it must be combined with humility and is achieved through the discipline of disinterested service. Else, creativeness not merely decreases, but even may, contrary to its real nature, degenerate into destructive titanism; the derivatively-divine spirit 'inspiring' the artist may, under certain conditions, transform itself into a 'demon' or a 'devil' by whom man is possessed.[1]

This introduces quite a new problem which so far has been only cursorily mentioned. The idea of man remains incomplete and therefore false in so far as no account is taken of the fact that human will may deflect from man's true ontological essence—in other words,

[1] It will be remembered that the same possibility—with regard to the experience of beauty—has been noted by Dostoevsky: 'There the devil struggles with God, and the battlefield is the human heart.'

in so far as no account is taken of the mysterious fact of sin and of arbitrary freedom. Much has been said about the divinely-human basis of human nature—about man as on the one hand indissolubly connected with God, and on the other as an autonomous personality, so to speak, a kind of ray projected outwards from the divine innermost core of his being; this seems to contradict the possibility of man falling away from God, or of having an arbitrary will which may be hostile to Him. How can this be possible if man's very essence consists in his being rooted in God, and if the bond between man and God is unseverable?

Obviously, the conception of man worked out in the preceding pages must be completed, and therefore corrected, by a new and apparently contradictory aspect of him. But, as has already been shown, metaphysical apprehension of reality is only possible through recognizing the antinomic unity of opposites.

CHAPTER V

Sin and Freedom

*

1. The problem of sin and freedom

The most obviously and strikingly real of all religious conceptions is that of *sin*. A man may deny or doubt the existence of God, but no one can, with his eyes open, fail to be aware of sin as a reality both in his own experience and in the social and historical experience of the world. It is obvious that dark, evil, destructive passions, deeply rooted in man's nature, play a part in human life. A considerable amount of good-natured optimism or indifference is required in order to believe that man is good by nature and that evil is merely the result of wrong education or of wrong social order. On that view it remains inexplicable how the element of 'wrong' could have appeared at all. The utopian idea of overcoming sin, and realizing a perfect human life by means of social or educational reforms is again and again proved fallacious by the fact that in spite of new ideas and new social forms, man obstinately manifests his old ineradicable sinfulness. According to a wise remark of Kant's, 'nothing quite straight can be fashioned out of the crooked piece of wood that man is made of'. Recognition of the reality of sin does not imply conscious religious convictions. An unbeliever may avoid the word 'sin' and replace it by the words 'moral evil', but this makes no difference to the point at issue.[1]

In contradistinction to the now prevalent type of thought, inclined, against all evidence, to ignore and deny sin as a metaphysical power or a reality, the Christian consciousness has always been keenly aware of it as part of the general relation between man and

[1] At present I am only concerned with moral evil ('sin'); the problem of the so called physical and metaphysical evil will be discussed in the next chapter.

God, i.e. part of man's essential nature. At times the Christian sense of sin has been so keen that it resulted, as in Augustinian theology, in a one-sided view of man's nature and of his relation to God.

Sin or moral evil manifests itself in two different spheres. In the first instance we are aware of sin as wrong action, wrong conduct, wrong attitude to other people. Both in the historical development of mankind and in the spiritual development of the individual, wrong or sin is always first of all detected in this external sphere. More subtle and penetrating moral insight shows, however, that sin lies deeper—that even if outwardly we behave rightly and abstain from morally reprehensible actions, we may be, and generally are, guilty of something else—of the wrong state of our inner spiritual life. Christ's teaching that not only to kill, but even to be angry with one's neighbour is a violation of the Divine commandment, that to lust after a woman is secret adultery, transfers moral emphasis from sinful conduct to the sinful state of the heart. Beside the commandment not to commit certain actions ('thou shalt not kill', 'thou shalt not steal' etc.) there arises a general commandment to preserve one's soul from sin, *not to be sinful*—which culminates in the final ideal 'be perfect even as your Father which is in heaven is perfect'.

These two species of sin may to a certain extent be unconnected with each other. A man may commit e.g. the sin of killing without being guilty of anger or hatred for his victim (in war or in defending others against criminal violence); and a man may lead an outwardly moral life and commit no sinful acts, while inwardly his heart may be full of sinful pride, selfishness, indifference or hatred for others. As a general rule, however, sinful actions are a result of the sinful state of the soul; this is why, according to Christ's teaching, moral condemnation is largely, if not entirely, transferred from the former to the latter and applied to it with special force. In any case, if abstention from sinful actions is due to a morally indifferent, or actually sinful state of the soul (fear of punishment or of public opinion, timidity, coldness, or a desire to appear righteous and obtain praise), it has no positive value and is condemned as hypocrisy. And on the contrary a repentant sinner shows by his very repentance that his sinfulness was not deeply rooted in his soul and is compatible with moral health; he is therefore less sinful than an outwardly righteous Pharisee. When repentance leads to inner purification, a man overcomes the sinful element in himself to a degree utterly inaccessible to one wholly engrossed with the righteousness of his behaviour; accordingly, 'joy shall be in heaven over one sinner that repenteth, more than over ninety and nine just persons, which need no repentance'.

Thus sin is, at bottom, a wrong state of the soul. But what does this mean? How are we to interpret sin and the possibility of it? The reality of sin is obvious and as it were strikes the eye, but every attempt to explain sin, to deduce it from something else, to understand it through logically defining its place in the scheme of things, involves serious and, indeed, unsurmountable difficulties. The idea of sin contains something essentially irrational and therefore, although it is clearly given in the 'experience of the heart' it is hardly susceptible of rational explanation. The divergence between the purely religious and the philosophical path is more pronounced with regard to this particular manifestation of spiritual reality than to any other. A philosophical explanation of sin in the sense of a rational 'deduction' of it from something else, more understandable and reasonable, would be altogether impossible, for it would be self-contradictory. If sin had a true ontological basis and followed with necessity from the structure of reality, or was connected with its ultimate depth and primary source, it would be 'normal' and ontologically justified, and therefore would no longer be sin. Such an explanation of it would be both logically impossible and morally inadmissible, for it would, in a sense, be a justification of sin. From what has been said above (Chapter II, 5) about moral value or the good coinciding with the supreme and ultimate reality—it follows that sin or wrong has, as it were, no true i.e. no ontologically grounded place in reality. But this idea often leads philosophical reflection to another kind of 'explanation' of sin, as untenable as the first. Theodicies of the usual and highly prevalent type, intended to show the essential harmony and rationality of the world's structure, tend to assert that sin, like all evil, is unreal and illusory. The element of truth contained in this assertion will be pointed out later; meanwhile, however, it is important to recognize quite clearly than an explanation which consists in denying the fact to be explained is logically untenable.

In dealing with the problem of sin, sound philosophical thought must be more than ever guided by the correlation expounded above (Chapter III, 1) between rational thinking and concrete religious experience. It must be clearly aware of its own limits; without seeking rationally to explain sin, i.e. reduce it to something intellectually self-evident—which is from the nature of the case impossible—it must confine itself merely to describing and stating in intellectual terms the actually given 'primary phenomena' (*Urphänomene*), irreducible to anything else.

To begin with, sin cannot be interpreted as an immanent element of the objective world. Although we come across it at every step in our earthly experience, it belongs to quite a different dimension of being and is inexplicable in the categories of the natural world. Nature as such knows no sin: in it everything simply is what it is, and everything is, in a general sense, necessary. But sin as a moral wrong presupposes the possibility of being or of not being—presupposes the element of primariness and freedom which transcends the limits of the world of fact. Just as it is meaningless to speak of the sinfulness of a stone that has killed someone, so it is meaningless to apply the category of sin to the actions and inner states of man conceived as simply a natural being, a psycho-physical organism. Sin presupposes valuation, contrasting the empirically existent with a certain ideal criterion—and that means, as we know, transcending the world of fact and entering the sphere of reality. This is self-evident. But although the valuation of sin, or the consciousness of sin, means entering the sphere of reality, *sin itself* has no definite place within reality in the sense of being univocally determined by its structure or of following from it of necessity.

And yet, as just pointed out, sin presupposes the element of freedom and primariness which transcend the world of fact. Sin obviously refers to man's inner self-conscious being—to the domain which is for us the nearest and most obvious manifestation of reality (Chapter I, 2–3). Thus, sin belongs to the sphere of reality, but at the same time it cannot be rooted in it. How is this to be understood?

It has always been believed, on the ground of direct religious experience, that sin is bound up with *free will*. Only a being endowed with freedom is capable of sin, and also, in some general sense, capable of abstaining from it; this correlation enters into the very conception of sin. But what precisely is meant by 'freedom' in this connection?

Both in the traditional theology of the church and in philosophical literature the most prevalent view is that freedom of will means freedom of choice. Man is endowed with the faculty of 'freely', i.e. in accordance with his own judgment, choosing between different possibilities in deciding upon his actions—hence, of choosing between good and evil. Consequently, in so far as sin and moral evil exist in the world, they are the result of man's free choice or of his free will, ontologically not determined by anything. God has granted man free will—the freedom to choose the ends and the paths of his life—as the only form of existence worthy of him; He wished man to follow the path of the good without compulsion, of his own free choice. Man abused this freedom by choosing the path of sin. Thus, on the one hand the existence of sin is accounted for, and on the other, sin proves to have no ground in the divinely determined world-structure, since it is simply the consequence of man's arbitrary decision.

This simple explanation, obviously convenient in elementary religious instruction, is seen on closer inspection to be beset with the greatest difficulties, both religious and philosophical. Painful and insoluble questions arise of themselves in a religious mind. Why did Almighty God, obviously foreseeing what would happen, provide man with the fatal gift of freedom of choice at all? Was not His action somewhat similar to that of foolish parents allowing their small children freely to play with fire or firearms? And does man really need the freedom of choice between 'that devilish good and evil' as Dostoevsky called it once in a moment of despair? And if such freedom is necessary for human dignity, why does not God give weak men at the same time that actual fulness of His grace which helps the saints to refrain from sin and overcome its temptations? In short, all the agonizing perplexities that had long ago been expressed in the Book of Job, arise in human heart once more.

There is no need to discuss these insoluble questions. The point is that their very formulation presupposes the idea of free choice to be significant and justified. But that idea, taken in its usual sense, does not bear philosophical criticism. Bergson has convincingly shown that the usual interpretation of that idea contains a crude intellectualistic distortion of the real, irrational nature of the process of willing. A clear, calm choice between two alternatives appearing before the human mind, so to speak, 'ready made' takes place only when it is a case of selecting on the strength of intellectual considerations between different means; the choice is made not between one desire and another, but between the most efficient ways of achieving the purpose. When, however, it is a case of the purpose or the desire itself, there is no conscious choice at all between

SIN AND FREEDOM

two definite possibilities, but only an utterly irrational hesitation, a certain indefiniteness of the dynamic process of attraction, creativeness, becoming. A purpose is not anything that precedes volition or determines it: it is itself first determined in the process of attraction or desiring. Freedom of will is something totally different from, and irreducible to the freedom of choice.

This true and subtle psychological description of the mysterious aspect of the human being which we call 'freedom of will' must be completed by a philosophical exposition of the idea of freedom. What do we mean by it? It is usual to define freedom by contrasting it with necessity: freedom is absence of necessity or of univocal determination. However prevalent such an interpretation of freedom is, it is obviously untenable. Thomas Aquinas argued against it, showing the fallacy of the sophisms to which it leads with regard to absolute freedom or to God's omnipotence. Those sophisms are well known: if God is absolutely free and can do anything, He can, for instance, become evil or destroy Himself, or give His place to the devil, or limit His omnipotence etc. Thomas Aquinas opposes to these absurdities the conception of God's absolute freedom or omnipotence as unhindered, unlimited by anything external, as self-realization or self-expression. But it is precisely in this that the idea of freedom consists. Freedom means action from within, self-realization, absence of external compulsion. Hegel aptly defined it as *bei-sich-selbst-Sein* (being at one's own self). Freedom certainly is not groundlessness, utter indeterminateness, a possibility of anything whatever: on the contrary, it is not merely combined with necessity, but *is* necessity—namely, inner necessity as self-determination; its opposite is slavery, external compulsion. Saints are not less, but more free than sinners, though precisely in virtue of their holiness they *cannot* sin. Augustine expressed this with his characteristic brevity: *magna est libertas posse non peccare, sed maxima libertas—non posse peccare* (great is the freedom of being able not to sin, but the greatest freedom is not being able to sin.[1]

On such interpretation it becomes obvious that freedom is incompatible with sin. Freedom, as just pointed out, is self-realization. But as we have seen, man's self-realization is the realization of his

[1] A modern German philosopher, Nicolaj Hartmann, arrives at an opposite conclusion: starting with the idea of freedom as freedom of choice he comes to affirm that holiness, i.e. inability to sin—is incompatible with morality. This is a classical instance of a *reductio ad absurdum* of an erroneous theory.

inmost depth in which he is akin to and unseverable from God; it cannot be sinful, but is the supreme and the only righteous purpose of human life; sin, on the contrary, far from being man's self-realization, is a betrayal both of God and of our true independent selfhood, which is the expression of our kinship with God as our ultimate ground. In this general sense the old dictum of Socrates that no one sins voluntarily is perfectly true: we seek freely only the good which corresponds to our divine essence and is that which we truly need, or, as Socrates put it, which is 'useful' to us. The sole mistake of Socrates's intellectualistic doctrine was that he regarded sin as merely the result of intellectual error and weakness of thought; St. Paul, and Augustine following him, had a deeper understanding of the matter. They saw that we can clearly distinguish good from evil and still fall into sin; man's weakness lies not in the weakness of his intellect, but of his will. And yet Socrates's general idea that we commit sin not freely, but involuntarily, holds good. We do not *will* sin, but are drawn to it, we fall into sin, it 'possesses' us. It is the expression not of our freedom, but of our lack of freedom, of our captivity. This is by no means disproved by the fact that man often does evil deliberately, i.e. desires it consciously (the fact which Kant regarded as a manifestation of the 'radical evil' as he called it—*das radical Böse*). Deliberateness of action or, what is the same thing, the conscious character of will, must not be confused with *freedom* of will. Law justly punishes deliberate crimes more severely than crimes committed under the influence of passion. But this certainly must not be interpreted as meaning that in the first case man commits a crime 'freely', and in the second, under the compelling and irresistible effect of passion. In both cases he acts under the influence of blind passion which enslaves him, i.e. deprives him of freedom. In the first case (that of deliberate crime) the enslavement is even greater than in the second, and for that very reason punishment imposed by the law is more severe. For in the case of affective crime, passion merely paralyses thought or excludes it, but in deliberate crime thought as a whole in its concrete living nature is, as it were, taken captive, deprived of inner independence and forced to act at the bidding of blind passion. When a man deliberately performs an evil action, that means that his very thought, his very mind is permeated through and through by the enslaving passion. His conscious desire—'free' only in the sense of being deliberate—is no longer under the control of his free will as the expression of his primary essence. His freedom has shown its weakness by submitting to the dark force which it is called to dominate. Deliberate willing of evil testifies to the absence of freedom as *self-determination* which, in a creature subject to elemental forces, can only express itself as *self-conquest*. This means not conquest of *selfhood* (which is both impossible and unnecessary), but of the inner forces hostile to man's selfhood.

The mistake of regarding freedom in the sense of self-determination as the source of sin lies at the basis of the popular version of the doctrine of 'original sin'. That doctrine contains a true and profound thought, as will be shown later. But the usual, prevalent version of it —quite apart from its mythological setting in the Biblical story— gives no real explanation of sin at all. It has already been pointed out that the very idea of the freedom of choice (*liberum arbitrium indifferentiae*) is false. Therefore there could have been no original 'choice' of sin, no primary abuse of the freedom of choice, and the doctrine of Fall in this form is no solution of the problem of sin, but merely its reduplication—the logical fallacy of *idem per idem*: both man's first 'fall', and his subsequent falls which are supposed to be its consequences prove to be of the same nature. To say that man 'fell' or 'abused his freedom' means, in truth, really to admit that man has not made use of his essential freedom, and 'fell' not freely, not in virtue of the freedom granted to him as a being akin to God, but in virtue of some other, dark force opposed to it.

If, however, sin is the result not of man's freedom but, on the contrary, of his lack of freedom, does this cancel his responsibility for sin and render meaningless the feeling that he *ought not* to have sinned and therefore *might* not have sinned? We have already seen that apart from a certain element of primariness—apart from the consciousness that sin springs from the depths of man's inner reality—the very idea of sin would be impossible, for it has no place within the categories of the world of fact. (This is why all naturalistic philosophy is logically bound to deny the idea of sin or moral evil.) We are thus faced with an antinomy: on the one hand, sin is not the result of true freedom, i.e. is not the self-realization of personality, and on the other, sin presupposes responsibility and therefore, in a sense, freedom. What is the answer?

2. Freedom as groundless spontaneity. The true nature of sin and the true meaning of original sin.

It is obvious that if the problem is to be solved, freedom must be recognized to have more than one meaning. In addition to *true* freedom which means man's self-realization as a being unseverable from and akin to God, there is another kind of freedom which is compatible with bondage or may degenerate into it. It cannot be the 'freedom of choice', the idea of which is, as we have seen, untenable, but perhaps it may be identified with the freedom of moral consciousness or spirit discussed in dealing with the Augustinian-Calvinistic view (Chapter IV, 4). After the Fall man lost the true freedom of active will, but he preserves the freedom of moral judgment about his own actions and states. Although he is actually incapable of refraining from sin, he is conscious of his responsibility for sin, since he still remains a free judge of his actions. On such a view freedom would be—contrary to the usual idea—not the actual condition of moral responsibility, but simply a constitutive element of the idea of responsibility, or rather, it would mean exactly the same thing as moral responsibility.[1] The consciousness of sin as a *wrong*, as something from which we ought to refrain, and in committing which we feel guilty, would be compatible with lack of freedom of action, i.e. with the inevitability of sin.

This view unquestionably contains some truth in so far as it recognizes man's unique character as a spirit and his distinction from purely natural entities as a being capable of judgment and evaluation. But it is obviously based upon the conception of an unsurmountable dualism between that which is and that which ought to be, and of total heterogeneity between the ideal and the real. Man's dignity as 'God's image' in so far as he is endowed with the faculty of passing judgment on himself (i.e. of ideally transcending himself) is recognized, but the consciousness of 'ought' is regarded as impotent, and any dynamic, active power is denied of it. Man, then, is utterly and irremediably insignificant and entirely subordinated to natural forces. The limitations and defects of this view have been already pointed out (Chapter IV, 4), and only

[1] This idea has been developed at the end of the nineteenth and the beginning of the twentieth century by a subtle German thinker Georg Simmel who transformed Kantian transcendentalism into universal relativism and scepticism. (Georg Simmel, *Ethik*, Band II.)

a few supplementary considerations need be added. However frequently the controlling ideal aspect of human nature may prove to be powerless in practice and do nothing but pass judgment on and condemn sin *post factum*, unprejudiced evidence of experience testifies that the consciousness of right and wrong at any rate *may* be an active determining force; the faculty of moral judgment may and actually does fulfil the functions of a guiding and ruling power. Hence the consciousness of freedom, inherent in the consciousness of sin, is not limited to moral judgment and a sense of responsibility. Inner experience tells us that although sin bears witness to our bondage, it is in some sense bound up with our freedom which is a real force. As already mentioned, it is an illusion to imagine that we do evil "of our own free will", in virtue of a decision or of an act of will proceeding from the primary inmost centre of our personality; but that illusion is only a wrong interpretation of a certain reality which does after all deserve, in a sense, the name of 'freedom'. In the last resort the view we are considering is false in so far as it fails to take account of the unity of the 'ought' and the 'is', the ideal and the real, in the ultimate depths of reality (cp. Chapter II, 5); consequently it also overlooks the indisputable fact that man's nature is creative (Chapter IV, 6). That leads to the rejection of the whole domain of active human life and culture, and of the historical world as distinct from the sphere of purely natural being.

The freedom presupposed by the idea of sin cannot be either the *true* freedom which is the self-realization of human personality, or the abstractly-ideal and practically impotent freedom which simply amounts to a sense of responsibility and moral valuation. It must be a freedom which, in a certain sense, is not free; or, speaking even more paradoxically we might say—contravening or, rather, overcoming the law of contradiction—that it is a freedom which both *is* and *is not*. This is in keeping with the fact that sin, and all that is presupposed by it, stands on the very boundary of the fathomable and the unfathomable. Therefore, the freedom presupposed by it can only be understood by means of cognition which Plato called, in reference to a kindred problem, 'illegitimate'.

Of what can we say that it 'both is and is not'? Of that which abides in the state of *pure potentiality*. Reality, as I have tried to show, is an indivisible unity of actuality and potentiality; it is being and becoming, self-creation (see Chapter I, 5). The ultimate basis and primary source of reality—God—is not only *actus purus*, (as Aristotle thought, and Thomas Aquinas after him), pure form, absolutely completed and in this sense stationary being. Rising above and embracing all determinations, the primary basis and therefore the inmost essence of reality is only thinkable as the unity and coincidence of actuality and potentiality, of finality and creative dynamism. In this sense God is freedom itself—not arbitrariness or groundless, indefinite possibility of all that is not yet and may only come into being, but as eternal self-realization and self-creation, as absolute creative dynamism, in which the categories of completed being and creative life coincide.

In so far as man is 'an image and likeness of God', i.e. in so far as his personality is grounded in the hidden depths of his being, which as it were receive and preserve the seed of Divinity, (Chapter IV, 5), he derivatively and in a limited form, as a created entity, possesses this higher freedom inherent in God. 'Where the spirit of the Lord is, there is liberty'. In philosophical language, inasmuch as man, too, is a reality or a unity of actuality and potentiality, he is something completed and definite, and at the same time has dynamic being, which manifests itself as self-creativeness or self-realization; he possesses primary spontaneity—the *true* freedom, which is the direct opposite of sin.

This freedom includes an element of *potentiality* or pure possibility, containing all that 'is not yet ready' but may be, all that is becoming and is being created. In so far as potentiality is merged with actuality and interpenetrated by it, it is not arbitrariness, not a possibility of anything whatever, but determination from within, the activity of self-realization or self-determination. In so far, however, as human personality loses or weakens its connection with its ultimate ground which is receptive of the divine principle, its potentiality is dissevered from actuality and manifests itself to a certain extent as pure potentiality, i.e. as formlessness, chaos, utter incompleteness, readiness for anything. This is the essence of the 'other' freedom—fictitious and illusory in one sense, and real in another—which has to be admitted as conditioning the possibility of sin.

This freedom essentially consists in *groundless spontaneity*. Let us try to make clear in what precise sense it is a fictitious freedom. True freedom is, as we know, self-realization or self-determination. Truly free will is a will issuing from the inmost core of personality, from the 'self' as an active guiding centre of spiritual life. This 'self' is so securely rooted in reality that except in extreme pathological cases it is constantly present in our mental life and as it were accompanies every volition. Mental life, however, contains more than its centre; it is not a point, but a sphere with a multifarious dynamic content. A great deal in it does not proceed from the actual 'self', and is not determined by it. For the most part our volitions and immediate involuntary strivings arise *in us* in virtue of the general dynamic potentiality of our mental life, but not *from us*, not from our personal centre. Since, however, this 'self' or personal guiding centre is always present in us and accompanies all our mental processes, we cannot help confusing it with the formless dynamic potentiality of our mental life as a whole. A voluntary process, the only adequate expression of which would be 'I feel a desire', i.e. something in me desires, is experienced as 'I (myself) desire'; the two phrases are usually regarded as synonymous, but 'I (myself) desire' is the formula of freedom. It is noteworthy that consciousness of freedom is often combined in mental life with its opposite, namely, with the consciousness that I am not the source or creator of my desire, but, on the contrary, am possessed by it. I may 'want' something so intensely that I feel *compelled* to want it, I am powerless to suppress the desire. The position is somewhat analogous to that of a weak government: it 'sanctions' the demands forced upon it by its rebellious subjects, i.e. it pretends that such was its own intention and command.

In so far as these involuntary, uncontrolled desires are merely manifestations of the elemental dynamism of our mental life, i.e. of potentiality as its general characteristic, they are spiritually and morally neutral. Such are the desires which, from the objective point of view, are expressions of man's being as a psycho-physical organism and are directed to the satisfaction of his natural needs as a creature. But man is also a spiritual being: he is a *person*, i.e. he has a controlling centre of consciousness. In virtue of this all his natural involuntary desires are subject to the control of that higher centre. He not simply 'wants' as an animal does—he also approves and sanctions, or disapproves and rejects his desires. Like the central power of the state which at times, in the interests of the nation as a whole, limits the natural needs of its subjects, this controlling centre—in the interests of man as a person, i.e. as a spiritual reality may sometimes reject, forbid or limit even our natural elementary desires. This is the meaning of the phrase that self-determination is only possible in the form of self-conquest, self-mastery. Asceticism in this broad sense of self-control is therefore a normal and necessary element in the life of man as a spiritual being. Self-limitation is the condition of true freedom. Freedom is directly opposed to self-will as an anarchic, disorderly state in which no limit is set to one's desires. This is the reason why all a-moralistic doctrines, from that of Callicles in Plato's *Gorgias* down to Nietzsche's, in sanctioning anarchic self-will lead in fact not to the expansion, but, on the contrary, to the destruction of the true freedom of personality. The contradiction inherent in this trend of thought shows itself in the fact that anarchic self-will is regarded as something which *ought* to be fulfilled, i.e. as a command of the supreme controlling centre of personality whose right to be obeyed is denied.

But man's spiritual nature, which distinguishes him from an animal or a merely natural being involves another and more important consequence. In a purely natural entity elementary vital dynamism is simply a psycho-physical factor confined to the task of preserving and reproducing life; in man it is also an element of his being-for-himself as a spiritual reality. This spiritual reality, as we know, is not limited from within, but potentially infinite. Hence, man's involuntary elemental strivings are also not limited to his normal needs as a natural entity, but are capable of increasing indefinitely and developing from simple physiologically justified impulses into boundless, destructive passions. In this respect an animal, strange to say, is more rational, or, rather, more reasonable than man. Man is the only living creature whose sad privilege it is that his instinct of self-preservation is liable to became insanely-proud egoism, the need for food—gluttony and *gourmandise*, the sexual instinct—a wild ravaging passion or perverse and insatiable debauchery, simple animal insensibility to the sufferings of others—a sadistic enjoyment of cruelty. In other words, the spontaneity of man's desires ceases then to be a manifestation of the natural dynamism of his mental life, but is transformed in his spiritual being into the dynamism of boundless potentiality as an independent sphere of its own.

In view of what has been said about the general nature of reality and of man's place in it (Chapter I) this correlation may be expressed as follows. Man's inner being comes into contact with the rest of reality and communicates with it not only in and through the inmost centre which constitutes man as a *person*—i.e. in which he is connected with God and contains a divine principle within himself; he is in touch with reality as a whole and subject to its impact on all sides, so to speak, along his whole periphery. As soon as the connection between the personal centre of mental life and the primary source of reality, God, is weakened—in other words, as soon as man's inmost personal being isolates itself, the pressure of inner spiritual dynamism breaks down the barriers which separate it from reality as a sphere of pure potentiality; boundless and formless forces inundate the soul and gain possession of it.

Reality connected with its primary source and naturally proceeding from it is, as it were, the divine ground of the created world, or a divine element permeating it; but as severed from that primary source, i.e. as mere formless dynamic potentiality, it is a dark, destructive, demonic element. It is, so to speak the principle of pure groundlessness, (*Ungrund*) and is deceptive pseudo-being (since all real being is constituted by its connection with the primary source and ground); and yet it is not a fiction or illusion, but a reality.[1] It is devoid of all creative activity, but is endowed with a certain inchoate, destructive dynamism; it is as it were, existent nothing, the abyss of non-being, chaos as a real and powerful force. That this chaos is somehow close to the ontological, i.e. to the divine depths of reality can be seen from the fact that a man possessed by sinful passions may sometimes *through them* turn to God. Religious consciousness expresses this in the idea that the devil, 'the prince of this world' is a fallen angel who rebelled against God. This idea, of course, also explains nothing, but merely describes the inexplicable. As already said, we find ourselves at this point on the dividing line between the intelligible and the unfathomable and must confine ourselves to merely stating the 'primary phenomenon' irreducible to anything else. All further attempts at explanation would be arbitrary and fictitious, 'science falsely so called' (I Tim. 6, 20) postulating in inaccessible depths imaginary correlations, as inexplicable as that which they are supposed to explain.

[1] The idea of groundlessness (*Ungrund*) finds expression in the mystical teaching of Jakob Boehme, and is used by Schelling in his doctrine of human freedom (*Das Wesen der menschlichen Freiheit*). My interpretation differs from Boehme's and Schelling's in that I do not include the principle of *Ungrund* in the nature of God, but find it only in the severance from God. The infinite depths of God's being are something utterly different from the groundlessness of pure formless potentiality.

The relation between human soul and this demonic element is itself super-rational and cannot be expressed in the rational categories of cause and effect. Who or what is the primary source of evil and sin—human soul or the demonic force that enslaves it? Unreflecting, immediate religious consciousness instinctively avoids this question, and this is perfectly legitimate. The demonic element is not—any more, than God is—a reality utterly heterogeneous to the human soul and definitely external to it. On the contrary, here too we have a certain indivisible and yet distinct bi-unity. The demonic force not only presses upon the soul from without, but is potentially present, as it were slumbering, within it. In the words of Tyutchev 'the ancient chaos' is 'native' to us, stirring in our very heart, and we 'eagerly listen' to its voice. This chaos stirring in the soul weakens its bond with the primary source of the personal principle in it, and the weakening of that bond in its turn increases the pressure of the demonic element upon the soul. The struggle between God and the devil takes place in the depths of the soul, which is not merely a passive battlefield, but takes part in the struggle. The antinomy of this correlation may also be expressed as follows: man's true, higher freedom as the realization of his personality (including its function of controlling his desires) and the lower, fictitious freedom as groundless spontaneity are not two heterogeneous, mutually independent principles; they co-exist in the indivisible unity of the human soul as a spontaneous dynamic entity. In virtue of participating (in a limited and derivative way) in the creative unity of actuality and potentiality, man is exposed to the danger—as soon as the element of actuality is weakened—of falling under the sway of the chaotic force of sheer anarchic potentiality. Precisely because man's chaotic spontaneity is a perversion of his creative freedom of self-realization, he is responsible for the sin into which he falls. As Jakob Boehme puts it, the light of divine love perpetually burning in the human soul becomes, inasmuch as the soul shuts itself off from God, the devouring flame of hell.

As true freedom degenerates into the fictitious, man falls into a curious illusion. It has already been mentioned that desires involuntary arising 'in me' appear to have been generated by my own self; the impersonal experience of being 'drawn to' or 'attracted by' assumes the character of 'I myself freely want'; but the illusion goes further. In losing the consciousness of its ultimate ground, in and through which it is securely rooted in reality, the self *loses* its own reality and as it were helplessly hangs in the air, becoming a plaything of impersonal strivings—and as it does so, it acquires an increasingly deceptive sense of freedom, independence, self-groundedness. I then have the illusion that in my self-contained detachment I become for the first time an autocratic master of my own life. This illusion is connected with the very structure of the human spirit, namely, with the duality between its ground and its autonomous personal consciousness (Chapter IV, 5). That which I usually apprehend as my 'self' is not the whole fulness of my spirit, but only its 'upper layer'; as issuing from my inmost depths inseverable from God, it functions, so to speak, as a plenipotentiary ambassador from those depths in the world of objective earthly reality. It is this that constitutes its 'extra-territorial' character, its independence from external forces and its inner freedom; that freedom is determined by the self's loyalty to its native land. But the situation easily leads to the illusion that through renouncing and forgetting his origin man will free himself from the duties laid upon him by his rank as ambassador, and become for the first time fully master of his life. To a certain extent this illusion is a permanent feature of our usual superficial self-consciousness; man regards his 'self' as a primary, absolutely independent and self-sufficient starting-point of life as activity; indeed this is precisely what we usually mean by the self. Therefore it is quite a natural illusion to imagine that the more self-willed and arbitrary I am, able to wish anything I like, the more free I am, the more I am *myself*, the autocratic source and master of my fate. In truth, however, in severing myself from the depths which connect me with the true primary source of my reality, I become utterly impotent, an empty point, possessed by overwhelming external forces. An ambassador who has renounced his own country does not acquire independence; he becomes, on the contrary, a rightless and defenceless refugee in an alien land. Groundless self-will is not freedom, but slavery. As already said, when the depth that unites the soul with the primary source of reality is locked out, chaotic forces of reality burst the dam of personality, invade it, and man becomes the plaything of his lusts and passions—the slave of demonic forces. Autocratic self-will proves to be impotence. Generally, it is only by degrees that man awakes to this truth as he approaches the end of the fatal path, and is on the verge of completely losing himself. Fortunately, he does not as a rule wholly renounce his native land, i.e. his own essential being, and his connection with it goes on invisibly functioning in his inner life; he therefore retains his balance and can stop at the brink of the abyss into which he was ready to fall. This alone accounts for the fact that sinfulness may be man's usual, permanent condition, i.e. may be compatible with the inner stability of his being. But how often innumerable and invisible conflicts due to man's weakness and his enslavement by sin end in sudden tragedy!

We can now define the true and profound meaning of the doctrine of Fall which in its popular form fails to give a satisfactory explanation of sin. All man's sins, and his subjection to sin in general, have their source in the degeneration of his autonomous personality into a groundless, pseudo-existent, arbitrary self; it is this degeneration that is the fundamental, 'original' sin from which all man's sinfulness and subjection to manifold particular sins follows. Original sin is the severance of personality from its divine root and its transformation into a fictitiously self-subsistent 'I'. *Original sin is the pride of self-assertion*. This is the profound meaning of Kierkegaard's formula 'the condition of sin is sin'. The tragic awareness of 'original sin' as separateness of the self from God, as isolated existence of the self-sufficient 'I', is expressed with great wisdom in the paradoxical saying of the Persian mystic Al-Halladje:

'Between Thee and me there stands "this is I" which torments me. Remove with Thy "this is I" my "this is I"—the barrier between Thee and me.'

The same ontological meaning attaches of course, to the words of the Gospel 'whosoever will save his life shall lose it: and whosoever will lose his life for My sake shall find it'. In virtue of the presence of this arbitrary self-sufficient 'self' man is not himself—not the being conceived and created by God. We cannot help thinking of this disharmony as due to a kind of break or laceration—as the result of 'Fall', although philosophical reflection makes it clear that this 'event' did not happen at any particular moment of time, but is supertemporal. But once it has 'happened' and forms part of our actual existence, the consciousness of our true godlike nature —and therefore religious consciousness in general—is only possible in connection with, and as it were through the prism of, the sense of sin. To deny man's sinfulness is equivalent to godlessness, and, vice versa, the sense of our sinfulness is a reminder of our divine origin, and a necessary condition of spiritual recovery. Simple

178

psychological observation of man's actual condition clearly testifies that this 'damage' is not something acquired and is not individual, but refers to some fundamental aspect of human nature in general. To convince ourselves of this it is sufficient to observe attacks of rage and anger in a new-born baby, or manifestations of greed, love of power, hatred, sadistic cruelty in children. All this abundantly shows that human nature as it actually is contains, beside its true spiritual and personal essence, the fictitious, arbitrary 'self' which delivers man into the power of demonic passions. In so far as we are aware in metaphysical and religious experience of our true being as a reality rooted in God, the presence of such an arbitrary, unstable self, a plaything of blind passions, is inevitably apprehended as a distortion of our real nature.

But how is the possibility of original sin to be explained? Does not its reality contradict the truth that in the spiritual birth 'the umbilical cord' which connects man with God out of Whom he is born is not severed, but is preserved forever and is the condition of the very being of man as such? This is another instance of a 'primary phenomenon' which cannot be explained by reducing it to something more primary and intelligible; we must confine ourselves to a mere statement and description of it.

A symbolical description may be of some assistance: we may picture the tie which unites man to God as so elastic that it allows man unlimited freedom of movement; consequently, he can withdraw from God indefinitely, but as he does so, the tie shrinks in width and the flow of sustaining power grows less and less.

The meaning of this symbolic description is that original sin is not some supplementary reality with a positive content of its own; it can only be interpreted as a certain diminution or weakening of being. Since the positive content of man's nature and existence is his connection with God, original sin of self-asserting being can only consist in the weakening or attenuation of this connection. It is preserved in some hidden metaphysical depths, but grows more and more potential so that its effect upon man's empirical nature is reduced to a minimum; in consequence a kind of vacuum is formed in man which constitutes his fictitious self-subsistent being. And this vacuum is filled by the inrush of formless, chaotic, demonic forces of pure potentiality severed from the primary source of being.

Original sin—the condition of all concrete manifestations of sinfulness—is a certain deficiency, defectiveness, lack of spiritual intensity. We must not, however, succumb to the temptation of simply identifying this deficiency, as is often done in theology, with man's finitude, and concluding that since everything except God is inevitably in some sense limited, God could not have created other than potentially sinful entities. Finitude as such is not opposed to positive power and fulness, and can contain infinity in a derivative sense. Every creature, being finite, contains infinity: as we know, positive reality is from its very nature present in every one of its parts. Human spirit especially, being a certain derivative emanation of God and more than a mere creature, is, in its positive content, fulness and power; its actual weakness is an aspect contrary to that positive content. Accordingly, original sin is not predetermined by God, but is an unnatural and illegitimate distortion of the positive reality proceeding from God.

Although, primarily, sin is merely a decrease in the depth, fulness and active power of reality, it is a terrible and powerful force in its effects and manifestation. Weakness and insufficient intensity of spiritual energy lead to weakness of self-control and let loose the forces of chaos; it is analogous to the weakness of a rider of a wild unmanageable young horse. Once sin or moral evil has manifested itself in all its unbridled nature, it is not mere negation or simple absence of something, any more than pain is a mere absence of pleasure. Disregard of this fact is a fatal illusion of good-natured optimism. Denial of sin is itself a sign of sinfulness. As Franz Baader used to say, the devil's most cunning trick is to convince men that he does not exist at all.

3. Two spheres of human existence. The task of protecting life from evil, and the task of overcoming evil

The duality of human spirit leads, as has been shown (Chapter IV) to the duality in man's life—to the distinction between the purely-human sphere in which man is an active agent, building life by his own conscious and autonomous will and the divinely-human sphere sanctified from within, in which man is as it were merely the soil receiving and reflecting God's activity, and, apart from his own will, growing the seeds of grace. It has been pointed out that the boundary between these two spheres lies in the invisible depths of human spirit, and that to transform this unseen bi-unity into an empirically obvious duality between the secular and the sacred spheres of human life is a rationalistic simplification and, indeed, a downright distortion, due to man's sinfulness, of the divinely-human bi-unity.

Autonomous human will and its realization in deliberate human activity is essentially the expression of man's free fulfilment of God's will, i.e. the expression of man's connection with God or of God's activity in and through him. As the realization of absolute values (or the fulfilment of man's creative vocation) it is no less sacred than the intimate, and as it were involuntary, action of gracious forces in the depths of the human spirit. This duality is simply the expression of the two aspects of the relation between God and man, both transcendent and immanent at the same time—the transcendent having the immanent for its basis. If man were sinless, i.e. if his actual state corresponded to his true nature, all human life would be hallowed and form a harmonious divinely-human unity, expressed in a twofold form: God would act *in* man, and He would act *through* the free and independent human will springing from the depths wherein man is united with God. We find something similar to this even now in the life of prayer, in man's concrete communion with God: its inner side is absorption in God and mystical union with Him, in which man is passively-receptive; its external side is man's activity, in which through discipline, ascetic achievement, deliberate concentration of attention—in short, through his own free will— he realizes the life of prayer; and this voluntary striving of human soul towards God is itself apprehended as 'a Divine gift'.

But in fact man is a sinful being. Besides his autonomous will expressive of his connection with and striving towards God, he also possesses an arbitrary will which conditions sin and draws him to sinful actions, destroying, or at any rate damaging the normal, harmonious basis of his being. This arbitrary will forms an aspect of his life in which he is separated from God and antagonistically opposed to Him. It is ontologically groundless, but real in fact. This arbitrary will is inseparable from the true ontological core of human freedom—of man's God-given autonomous will. The whole of man's nature is damaged by sin and therefore his actual will is always twofold: its ontological essence is the God-given autonomy, directed towards God, but it is inseparably mixed with sinful arbitrariness. It is this actually indivisible unity of legitimate autonomy and illegitimate self-will that determines man's empirical existence. Its expression is the so-called 'secular life'. Secular life is precisely the indivisible combination of voluntary striving for goodness with involuntary ('arbitrary') falling into sin; it reflects both man's groundless, subjective, sinful will, and the perpetual striving of the autonomous God-given will to suppress and banish the chaotic play of sinful impulses and its fatal consequences. It is in this sense that secular life clearly stands out as a special purely-human sphere in contradistinction to man's hidden, inner life in communion with God—the sacred sphere, divinely hallowed and theonomous.

As already said, the true boundary between these two spheres lies in the invisible depth of the human spirit; hence, the division between them embraces both man's personal and collective life—human culture and history. In his personal life man (if he has not altogether lost his true nature) devotes one part of his time and energy to the pursuit of his secular, earthly interests, while controlling his actions by his conscience, and another part to prayerful or, more generally, spiritual life—to moral introspection, development of his mind and his spiritual nature. In man's collective historical life there corresponds to this, in Gospel terms, the division between things which are Caesar's and things which are God's: between the sphere of external and technical organization of life (the state, legal justice, economic relations), in which the realization of secular interests is combined with morally-juridical control of anarchic strivings, and the sphere of spiritual culture as a collective expression of man's spiritual being. This finds expression both in creativeness (artistic, scientific, philosophical and religious) and in collectively guarding the sacred divinely-human basis of human existence—which is the special task of the church. In personal life, where man's true nature is, so to speak, directly perceptible, the problem of the relation between these two spheres is, in theory, solved easily, as it were of itself, however painful it may sometimes be in practice; in the collective life, on the contrary, the problem tends to be obscured and distorted, and the two spheres are apt to be confused. As already pointed out the division between them is the result of man's sinfulness, of his fictitious, arbitrary freedom; only if man becomes sinless and the principle of sin is wholly and finally destroyed in him, can God really be 'all in all', and human life become harmoniously and entirely divinely-human. On the other hand, the attempt to confuse or merge the two spheres, or to deny their separateness while the sinful principle in man is not yet overcome, means falling into a new and worse sin. We know that the consciousness of one's sinfulness, and therefore a practical recognition of the reality of sin proves the presence and action in us of the good principle which overcomes sin; to ignore and deny sin means, on the contrary, that the mind is possessed and enslaved by it. Whenever man imagines that he can by his own efforts and deliberate action completely hallow his life and make it perfect, rejecting or ignoring the difference and the division between the secular and the sacred sphere, he falls into the illusion of ignoring the reality of sin and regarding himself as sinless.

This illusion may take two forms, similar in practice, though based upon different theories. The first, frequently met with in the past, characterized all the attempts to organize life theocratically, i.e. to introduce a social order in which life would be automatically and compulsorily subordinated to the sacred principle in man. Some person or some group of men was regarded as God's elect, as an adequate embodiment of God-manhood, as an irreproachably holy and therefore absolutely authoritative instrument and expression of the Divine will, and in that capacity strove to rule the world in order to sanctify it completely and finally. In the Middle Ages this faith found expression both in the idea of Papal theocracy and in many heretical sects of 'pure' or 'spiritual' people; it flared up with new force in the extreme tendencies of the Reformation— Thomas Münzer's preaching, anabaptism and puritanism.

Another form of the same illusion possessing human mind in recent centuries and down to the present day is belief in man's absolute value and power (optimistic humanism and titanic antitheism, discussed in Chapter IV, 2). This spiritual movement strives to attain righteousness and perfection by purely worldly means, and thus do away with the division between the 'secular' and the 'sacred' spheres of life.

In order to see clearly why this is impossible it is essential to understand the conditions and nature of man's conscious, active struggle with life's imperfections. That struggle is itself inevitably affected by the principle of sin, and in two respects at once.

To begin with, as already pointed out, autonomous will—the striving for goodness and righteousness—is in practice inseparable in mental life from the arbitrary sinful will, and is always tainted by an element of subjectivity, caprice, self-interest, pride and partiality. Righteous indignation is indissolubly mixed with resentment, hatred and vindictiveness, and easily degenerates into them;

disinterested struggle against evil imperceptibly changes into love of power, pernicious despotism, etc. The imperfect man's dream to make his life perfect by his own efforts is as unrealizable and self-contradictory as Baron von Münchhausen's attempt to pull himself out of the bog by his hair. The historical experience of all social movements directed to this purpose confirms this: after an early period of enthusiasm, when on the whole they are beneficial, they invariably degenerate. Captured by the evil forces of greed and love of power, they enter a stage when the idealistic slogans become merely a cloak for sinful human appetites, and life, instead of growing more perfect, suffers from evil more than ever.

This is particularly characteristic of the prevalent revolutionary-utopian schemes in which man as a purely secular being tries to realize by his own resources the ideal of social justice and righteousness. But the same criticism applies to the idea of compulsory theocratic organization of life. Although in principle it implies the subordination of human will to God as absolute Holiness, in practice it, too, manifests itself as sinful human pride and self-glorification. There is pride in the very idea that a definite human institution is an adequate expression of the Divine will, an embodiment of the Holy as such. Divine will acts only in the invisible depths of the human spirit, affecting it not by external compulsion, but partly by constituting the very essence of true freedom, and partly by attracting man's will by its inherent excellence and gracious influence. But whenever man takes upon himself the function of being an adequate representative of the Divine will, he invariably adulterates it with his own arbitrary sinful self-will. Neither the church, nor monasticism, nor any sect of 'spiritual Christians' is free from this sinful element; they are all equally subject to the danger of degeneration.

Another relevant consideration in this connection is that in any attempt to overcome sin and evil from without, by man's own efforts —*even if subjectively it is morally right*—no account is taken of the fact that sin and evil have a certain inner, spiritual nature impervious to external impact. Since this inner nature of evil follows from man's freedom and is ineradicable, external struggle with evil inevitably has the character of compulsion. In the first instance it is moral compulsion through instilling shame, or fear of public opinion, but it finally leads to physical compulsion, which may—as for instance in police action or in defensive war—end in killing the bearer of evil will. But compulsion as such is itself an objectively sinful action, even if it proceeds from a subjectively righteous motive, for it is a violation of the God-given freedom expressive of human personality as akin to God. Thus, because of the power of sin, man finds himself in a tragic position: in his external, consciously-human struggle against sin he is *morally* compelled to use sinful means. This is the essence of the fatal inadequacy of law, expounded by St. Paul: being a corrective of sin, law is its correlate, is itself affected by the principle of sin, and therefore cannot really overcome it. Law, authority, the state, and even stern moral discipline if imposed upon man from without and expressed in general norms— are all expressions of a compulsory organization of life, of compulsory, external struggle against sin and evil, and in that sense are themselves sinful and therefore powerless to overcome and destroy sin as such.

Both the legitimacy of such externally-compulsory struggle against moral evil, and its natural limits (beyond which it becomes illegitimate) become intelligible if we bear in mind the twofold way in which sin manifests itself (see Chapter V, 1). Sin which essentially refers to human will and the inner structure of the soul expresses itself in human actions and relations. In this latter aspect it is not only the moral evil of unrighteousness, but a calamity, inasmuch as it destroys or spoils life and is a source of unhappiness for other people. Greed, malice, hatred, selfishness, cruelty, love of power—all these poison and ruin people's lives. It is therefore man's moral duty to counteract these manifestations of evil and to safeguard life from their deleterious consequences. This cannot be done without using compulsion. To arrest a thief or a dangerous hooligan, to put a limit to selfish actions which make other people suffer, in short to use all legitimate measures for rendering criminal will harmless—is a moral duty; and it is in this that deliberate forcible struggle against evil consists.[1]

The purpose of this struggle must, however, be carefully distinguished from the completely different purpose of overcoming

---

[1] The necessity in some extreme cases of actually killing the criminal cannot, however, justify capital punishment as a legal institution. Capital punishment means killing a criminal *who has already been deprived of freedom of action and made harmless*, and is therefore a terrible and absolutely inadmissible sin against the sacredness of human personality. It is a *greater* sin than simple killing, which may be a 'pardonable' sin, if it is inspired by the altruistic motive of preserving another person's life.

sin as such. External struggle against the expressions of evil may do away with or diminish the troubles and sufferings brought about by evil will, but it does not in the slightest degree overcome evil will as such. To render a criminal harmless or to bridle his evil will by intimidation is the business of the law-courts and police; to re-educate him and develop a good will in him is the business of the priest or the teacher, or, more exactly, the business of the sinner's own free, divinely-human inner being, to which a priest or a teacher can only act as a helper. Compulsion does not destroy a single atom of evil; even the physical destruction of the criminal cannot achieve this, for in generating resentment and vindictiveness in other people it perpetuates evil: the flame of sin, extinguished in one place, may break out in another. This is the meaning of Christ's teaching of not resisting evil by force. For sin is, so to speak, existent non-being and can only be overcome if the ontological root of personality—holiness—puts forth shoots in the heart of man. Sin disappears of itself in the face of love and goodness, as darkness is dispelled by light.

Confusion between these two different purposes is one of the constant pitfalls that beset man in his striving to improve the collective life and implant goodness in it. The task of externally and deliberately protecting life from evil by compulsory organization is so urgent and imperative that in pursuing it man is apt to forget his other and more fundamental task of truly overcoming the actual source of the trouble—sin. He often either confuses these two different tasks, or goes even further, and in concentrating all his energies upon relieving pain and suffering, completely forgets that their source is human sinfulness or evil will. In that case the striving for perfection loses its moral and therefore its religious basis, and is understood simply as a secular, empirical and, one may say, technical task of saving man from pain and suffering. Of course in one of its aspects human suffering has nothing to do with sinfulness, but is simply a consequence of man's being a natural entity, subject to the forces of nature, and it certainly is perfectly right to help him to escape such suffering. But the purpose of organizing society and establishing right relations between men is not limited to the purely technical side of the matter. Social order must be not merely efficient in the sense of satisfying in the best possible way man's earthly needs, but must also be *righteous*, and right organization of the moral and voluntary structure of society is the basis and necessary condition of its practical efficiency. Law and the state are subordinate not only to the idea of order, but first and foremost to the idea of moral justice.

It is precisely at this point that the limitations of the compulsory organization of life become apparent. Such organization cannot directly affect man's inner spiritual life or include it within its scope. For, as we know, that life essentially consists in the activity of God in the human heart, and the direct expression of it is the autonomy of man's personality. And since in practice the autonomous will is inseparable from the arbitrary will (they can and must be distinguished only in man's inner, spiritual life as such), freedom of personality *including the freedom of sinful will is* inviolable and admits of no external compulsion. The law and the state must protect life from harmful consequences of sinful will, and limit its freedom of action, but cannot aim at man's spiritual re-education, which is the business of his own autonomous will—and God. The only thing that the law and the state can and may do is to create the most favourable *external conditions* for man's free striving after moral improvement and the development of the divine aspect of his being. Inner spiritual life is the concern, first, of that life itself as expressed in man's individual self-consciousness, and secondly of the collective spiritual life in holiness, which is called the church (including its prophetic and teaching function in the widest sense of spiritual leadership).[1]

The state is outwardly sovereign as the highest seat of human authority; inwardly, however, it is not autocratic, but is limited by the sacred and inviolable sphere of personal freedom—the freedom of personal initiative, within which alone the struggle between man's moral will (created and inspired by God) and his sinful, arbitrary, pseudo-free will can be successfully carried on. Mankind is always falling into the temptation of confusing the external supremacy of the state with its inner unlimited autocracy. But it behoves us to remember St. Augustine's immortal words 'apart

---

[1] Of course the division is not as simple as suggested here. The church—even in the broad sense just indicated—has its own purely 'secular' side, in so far as it includes the element of organization, law and administration. This, however, does not affect the essential point of difference between it and the state: subordination to the church is voluntary and based upon the free recognition of its inner authoritativeness. This implies that all compulsory theocracy is a radical perversion of the very conception of the church.

SIN AND FREEDOM

from justice, what are states but big bands of robbers?' (*remota justitia, quid sunt regna, si non latrocinia magna*). The state that regards itself as the supreme master of man's life is one of the most terrible and dangerous manifestations of pride and demonism in human existence. It then becomes, in Nietzsche's words, 'the coldest of all cold monsters'. The living embodiment of such demonism is the idea and the practice of a totalitarian state. It must not be imagined that any purely external measures, i.e. any definite forms of state administration, however useful they may be, can as such automatically overcome this demonism. Those measures are carried out by concrete individuals, on whose faith and moral spirit their beneficence ultimately depends. The only thing that is of decisive significance is the absolutely firm and clear awareness of the difference between the task of externally protecting life from evil and the task of overcoming sin as such—and therefore the recognition of the freedom and inviolability of man's inner, divinely-human being. The state and all other secular unions can create the relatively best external forms of life, but must never set themselves the task of *saving* man. Salvation exceeds human powers and is God's work (with the humble participation of man's inner, divinely-determined spiritual activity). This is the meaning of the Christian doctrine of redemption.

It follows from this that there is one domain of human creativeness which stands by its very nature in dangerous proximity to demonism—in spite of all that has been said about the essential difference between creativeness and sinful arbitrary will. It is the domain of statecraft and politics. Politics as such is a necessary and legitimate sphere of human creativeness, and there are real geniuses in it. The creation of new and better forms of social life is the natural purpose of man's creative will. But the material of that creativeness are living people, and the means is *power* over men, compulsion, which, as we have seen, contains as such an element of sin. Thus on both sides—both with regard to the material and the means—political creativeness must limit itself if it is to be truly legitimate. It is constantly in danger of falling either into the sin of unrestrainedly ordering human destinies (even if it does so with the good intention of improving them) or into even worse sin of identifying the ruler's lawless arbitrary will with his autonomous moral will. Power demoralizes and inclines man to self-deification and to the belief that all things are lawful for him. This is why even

188

really great statesmen are often tyrants and criminals, and on the other hand, why criminals who attain power often *seem* great and inspired men of creative political genius. True and profound religious humility is needed for carrying on creative political work without falling into sin and wrecking people's lives.

CHAPTER VI

Man Between the World and God

*

In the two preceding chapters we have been considering man's being in its inner aspect—in relation to its basis, God; little has been said of man in his other aspect, as a natural entity forming part of the world of fact. In addition to the bi-unity of the divine and the human principles in man, his being contains another duality, pointed out at the beginning of the present essay—namely, the difference between man as a part of nature and related to the objective world, and man as a subject or a spirit, participating in self-conscious *reality*. In summing up the argument of the book as a whole we must connect the conception of man with that of the relation between the world of fact and reality, pointed out in the early chapters. Reality has its absolute centre and its primary source in God. Therefore, in order to understand man's ultimate nature and the conditions of his existence, it is essential to grasp his relation both to the world of fact and to God, and to interpret him as standing midway between them as a kind of connecting link. The general meaning of the idea of God has already been made clear; it behoves us now to elucidate the idea of the world, in so far as this is necessary for understanding man's relation to it.

1. The character and degree of the world's natural perfection

The mechanistic view which almost entirely dominated scientific thought from the XVIIth century till nearly our own day, regarded the world as an aggregate of lifeless material particles and blind forces. Contrary to deceptive appearances which man had trusted for thousands of years, his native abode, the earth, proved to be not the centre of the universe, but a mere speck, a part of a planetary system which itself was only an insignificant appanage of one of the innumerable stars lost in boundless space. Kant and Laplace provided a mechanistic explanation of the way planetary systems originated.

The origin of organic beings with their marvellous purposive structure was, apparently, finally accounted for on Darwin's theory as an unconscious result of natural selection of accidental variations and of the extermination of numberless other beings unfit for survival. The very structure and functioning of organisms, apparently so different from the blind mechanical interaction of physical and chemical forces was explained simply by a more complex combination of those forces; an organism was taken to be merely a particularly complex machine. Consciousness, mental and spiritual life, differing so profoundly from the world of mechanical forces and dead matter by their purposiveness, spontaneity and rationality, were regarded as an 'epiphenomenon', a practically useless and passive accompaniment of the material world. Man himself was not exempt from this all-embracing realm of soulless being. An accidental descendant of ape-like ancestors, a member of the organic world with no ontological privileges of his own, he was considered as simply a part of the universal cosmic machine. This view has found its final expression in Freud's theory which reduces human soul or spirit to the activity of the blind cosmic force of sex.

At the same time it was supposed to be man's vocation to rule cosmic forces and to organize life in accordance with reason and justice; the contradiction between this idea and the mechanistic view of the world was not perceived (see Chapter IV, 3).

This cosmology was directly opposed to that of the mediaeval and ancient thought (apart from the theories of Democritus and Epicurus, not typical of classical philosophy and anticipating the modern mechanistic view). The thought of antiquity was permeated by the conviction of the rational purposiveness and harmony of the world's structure and existence. The greatest representatives of ancient thought—Heraclitus, Anaxagoras, Socrates, Plato, Aristotle, Zeno, Plotinus—however much they differ in other respects—agree in recognizing supreme cosmic reason as the world's architect or as the principle which interpenetrates it. Aristotle, a sober and dispassionate observer of the empirical world, has a passage of unwonted eloquence in one of his extant writings: he says that if the whole picture of the universe were suddenly revealed to a man for the first time and he saw the regular, orderly movement of the heavenly bodies, the harmonious adaptation of the different parts of the world for a common life, the purposive structure of living beings, he would at once perceive with perfect clearness that there was a supreme rational power imparting order and system to the world.

Mediaeval thought wholly adopted this conviction, confirmed and strengthened by the religious anthropocentric cosmology of the Old Testament. The world was created not only by an omnipotent and omniscient, but also by an all-merciful God, who having willed to create man, created and organized the world as an environment suitable and necessary for man's existence. All cosmic being as the creation of an all-wise and all-merciful God is perfect. True, by arbitrarily falling into sin through his own fault and contrary to God's will, man introduced an element of disharmony into the world. But as sin has no substantival existence and is merely a wrong direction of human will, it cannot destroy the perfection of cosmic being as created by God. Hence, a keen sense of man's sinfulness did not in the least interfere with the recognition of the world-structure and cosmic life as ontologically perfect.

The teleological character of the Jewish and Christian cosmology had a purely religious source and was in no way connected with intellectual knowledge about the world; in mediaeval thought, e.g. in the system of Thomas Aquinas, it was combined with the cosmology of the Greek thinkers. The latter, as represented by Plato (in the *Timeus*) and especially by Aristotle, accomplished a task unique in the history of human thought: they arrived at monotheism by a reverse process—in a purely intellectual way, through the contemplation of the world.

It is a remarkable fact, insufficiently recognized as yet, that after some two and a half centuries of wandering along the by-ways of a mechanistic interpretation of the world, the mind of man has for the last fifty years been tending towards a new version of the classical world-conception (enriched by all the latest discoveries of science), and even to a scientific confirmation of certain elements in the Judeo-Christian cosmology.

This fact escapes recognition because of another and utterly new tendency in the development of science. In its attempt to understand the world as a whole and conceive it as an all-embracing system, scientific thought has reached a point at which any concrete idea of the world seems altogether impossible. That which has usually been called 'the world' and taken to be a real objectively existing system becomes a disconnected conglomeration of separate presentations, determined by the observer's point of view (this is the philosophical conclusion drawn from the theory of relativity); or (as in the theory of the ultimate constituents of matter) it is conceived as a combination of mutually contradictory ideas, a kind of undifferentiated mixture of mathematical symbols of thought and objective contents of nature. This tendency is strikingly akin to the process of general spiritual anarchy and dissolution that has been affecting mankind of recent years, and can scarcely be regarded as the final philosophical result of modern scientific development. Rather, it reflects the bewilderment of philosophical thought that has not yet fully grasped or spiritually digested the recent achievements of science. Most modern physicists are very poor philosophers and the conceptions they use are vague and contradictory.[1] Philosophical thought is still waiting for a new Descartes or Leibniz to grasp the full implications of modern scientific developments and to sum them up.[2]

It is all the more striking that in spite of the confusion that reigns in scientific cosmology, and its tendency to scepticism and relativism, a number of recent discoveries, opening out totally new vistas to science, not merely undermine the mechanistic view of the world, but actually lead to a revival of the ancient conception of the harmonious and teleological structure of the universe—a conception that had but a short time ago seemed finally discredited. The universe, which from the times of Giordano Bruno, Galileo and Newton was pictured as infinite in space in the sense of being indefinite and boundless beyond the reach of thought—like Hegel's 'bad infinity'—is now once more conceived as finite, although unlimited. The discovery of inter-atomic processes, the Quantum

---

[1] A devastating critique of the philosophical helplessness of modern physicists is to be found in Jacques Maritain's *Réflexions sur l'intelligence et sa vie propre*, 4 ed. 1938; see also Susan Stebbing's *Philosophy and the Physicists*, 1944.

[2] The only thinker who has suggested a really philosophical interpretation of the most recent achievements of science is A. Whitehead. It is significant that he conceives cosmology as the 'philosophy of the organism' and combines it with Platonism.

theory, the principle of indeterminism, present riddles as yet unsolved by human thought, but at any rate they indubitably prove that the view of matter as a passive and lifeless substratum, mechanically determined throughout, it utterly untenable. Matter has been reduced to immaterial bearers of energy or activity, resembling Leibniz's monads, and natural processes appear more and more to be similar in character to conative activities. The proud claim of Darwinism to explain the purposive structure of organisms as a chance result of the cosmic process, and to conceive of the organism as a physio-chemical machine has been dashed to the ground; only scientifically backward minds, hidebound by tradition still believe in it. In the domain of organic nature a number of facts have been brought to light, incontrovertibly proving, as against the principle of universal struggle for existence, the presence of mutual adaptation and harmonious co-operation between different kinds of organisms;[1] it has also been found that in the general economy of nature certain physio-chemical properties of matter manifest a purposive and harmonious adaptation for supporting life.[2]

But perhaps the most striking philosophical outcome of modern science is the fact that it has undermined the perennial and, it would seem, natural idea (prevalent in ancient thought as well) of the essential stability of the universe—the idea which implied that it was unrational and unscientific to conceive of the world as beginning and ending. It is precisely with regard to this point that modern thought, going beyond the ancient cosmology, suggests a rational justification of certain trends in the Old Testament and Christian cosmology. Under the influence of classical thought and of the direct impression of the world's absolute stability, so orthodox a mediaeval thinker as Thomas Aquinas decidedly maintained that there were no rational grounds for denying the world's eternity (so that faith in its absolute beginning, i.e. creation, and its end could only be based upon positive revelation, unverifiable by reason); but the modern theory of entropy, of dispersion of matter through radio-activity, in short, of the continual process of the disintegration and extinction of cosmic life completely shatters the idea of the world's inherent permanence and stability. Scientific thought has a dilemma forced upon it, and has to admit, either, that the world

[1] See e.g. E. Becher, *Die fremddienliche Zweckmässigkeit.*
[2] Henderson, *The Fitness of the Environment.*

had an absolute beginning, separated from us by a definite temporal interval (so that it has not *yet had time* to fall to pieces and die down), or that it contains an element which maintains its harmonious and orderly functioning, i.e. which counteracts its inherent tendency to disruption and death. It is utterly incredible that the world as a unified multiplicity, as an integrated system with unequally distributed active energy (a necessary condition of all physical processes) could be a product of blind forces. A world which has any order in it, and is able to function at all, appears to be the most improbable of all conceivable states of being.

The final attempt to vindicate the idea that the forces active in the world are blind and meaningless consists in supposing that in the course of infinite time the most improbable things may have happened accidentally. This is illustrated by the hackneyed comparison: a monkey striking at random the letters of a typewriter for an infinite time may accidentally type the letters in such sequence that they will form the text of Homer's *Iliad*. But even this last desperate expedient is disproved by the law of probability. The degree of dissymmetry necessary for the emergence of a molecule of living matter is so unlikely to originate accidentally that the probability of this happening is almost innumerably greater than the probability allowed for by the dimensions of an Einsteinian universe.[1] One of the founders of the modern theory of probability, the French philosopher-mathematician Cournot, has demonstrated by a simple argument, which even the uninitiated can follow, that for a billiard ball to find itself in the exact mathematical centre of the table as the result of accidental strokes, a simple infinity of strokes, possible in a linear infinity of time, is insufficient, but an infinity of such infinities is required.[2] Considering the enormous number and complexity or purposive cosmic processes, it can be said with mathematical certainty that their existence infinitely exceeds chance expectation as determined by the law of probability.

Unprejudiced scientific thought is thus once more envisaging the world as the result and expression of purposively acting constituents subordinated to a higher teleological unity. It is no longer possible to deny that a certain relative perfection is to be found in the world-order, and this can only be explained teleologically.

[1] Lecomte de Nouy. *L'homme et sa destinée*.

[2] Because that centre is determined by the intersection of two co-ordinates, each of which contains an infinite number of points.

MAN BETWEEN THE WORLD AND GOD

The ancient sense of wonder at the harmonious co-ordination throughout the universe in spite of the unimaginable complexity of its structure is confirmed by the general results of modern science.

The perfection is of course only relative: it is combined with imperfection, disharmony, chaotic and blind conflict between forces. The thought of ancient Greece (in contradistinction to the Jewish and Christian cosmology) knew this well, and openly affirmed that cosmic architectonic reason meets with opposition from the material out of which it builds the world. This, roughly, should be the attitude of modern scientific thought as such, apart from all relation to religious consciousness. As Kant justly pointed out, the presence of design in nature may prove the existence of a cosmic architect, but not of an omnipotent creator. The same idea, suggested by the facts of biological evolution in particular, is expressed by the view that the purposively-creative power present in nature works as it were at random, trying different ways, sometimes going into blind alleys, making mistakes and then discovering new paths.[1] The element of disorder, disharmony and blindness in the cosmic system manifests itself in destructive antagonism and accidental conflicts between particular entities. It lies at the basis of the struggle for existence, in virtue of which an organism lives by destroying other organisms, of disease and perhaps of death itself, as well as of all irrational catastrophes and cataclysms in the inorganic world—ranging from the fall of a stone hitting a person's head to explosions of vast heavenly bodies.

This combination of rational and purposive order with blind and anarchic necessity was well known to the thought of antiquity; but the problem of the world's perfection has another and quite a different aspect which lies altogether beyond the Greek thinkers' field of vision. For them the actual purpose realized by the forces of nature (leaving aside the fact of its incomplete realization) simply coincided with the highest purpose and value sought by the human spirit. World's perfection in the sense of order and harmony was for the thought of antiquity the one and only expression of absolute perfection. Hence man and the world were in complete accord; their common end was to attain the perfect actuality and pure form predicable of God Himself; the moving power in this process of attaining perfection was the striving of all that is towards God. It

[1] This idea, it will be remembered, was brilliantly demonstrated by Bergson in his *Creative Evolution*.

is precisely in this respect that our spiritual standpoint underwent a radical change, due not to the development of scientific thought, but to a purely religious motive—namely, to the fact that for the Christian consciousness human personality is in principle distinct from the rest of the world. Henceforth we are bound carefully to distinguish between the end realized by the forces of nature, and the supreme final end which alone can satisfy human spirit, and is recognized by it as ultimate and absolute. That final end is not rational order and aesthetic harmony of the world, but moral goodness or *holiness*. This coincides with the Old Testament prophets' conception of God as the Holy, the bearer of absolute holiness. Accordingly, the 'deification' of being in which God is to be 'all in all' is in Christian consciousness something utterly different from the Greek idea of the world's striving towards Divine perfection. Perfection as holiness, as the ideal which satisfies the deepest spiritual needs of human personality is alien from the teleology of the natural world; nature is indifferent to good and evil. Even in so far as it is perfect, or even in so far as it contains a striving for perfection, that perfection is merely a formal aesthetic or mathematical harmony, or coordination of parts necessary for the balance and preservation of life, and not inner perfection, meaning the presence of supreme absolute value. We can no longer be content as the ancient thinkers were with identifying, in a kind of religiously-aesthetic contemplation, these two absolutely different perfections. On the contrary, nature's utter indifference to good and evil—its inherent amorality so to speak—even in its harmonious and purposively-rational aspect, is now felt by us to be the equivalent of what in human existence is called sinfulness. Of course the very duality between man and nature, resulting from the Christian discovery of human personality, does not allow us to transfer the idea of sin to natural being. As already shown, that idea, correlative to the ideas of responsibility, guilt and freedom is altogether inapplicable to the objective world: it has meaning only in the world of reality or of spiritual being, i.e. of self-consciousness aware of its inner relation to God. Accordingly, calamities that result from man's subjection to the natural world, and are a consequence of the anarchical element in nature and of its indifference to good and evil, must be distinguished from sin. The so-called physical and metaphysical evil is something quite different from the moral evil, unknown to nature as such.

Awareness of the difference between perfection as holiness and perfection as aesthetically-mathematical harmony is born from insight into the radical difference between human spirit and nature, and it leads metaphysical thought, guided by religous experience, to an essential dualism. At the earliest stages of Christian philosophising, that dualism found reflection in *Gnosticism*. Christian thought inspired by the idea of God as the Holy and therefore as the Saviour was bound to face, in painful perplexity, the question how was that idea to be reconciled with the moral and spiritual imperfection or, rather, a-moralism of the cosmic life. Gnosticism, it will be remembered, gave a simple and decisive answer to that question: the creator of the world is not the supreme true God of the Christian revelation—God the Saviour—but a deity of lower order, with which God the Saviour is perpetually at war.[1]

It must be candidly admitted that from a purely empirical point of view this standpoint seems perfectly natural. It forces itself upon us in proportion as we recognize all the immensity of the difference between man as a *person*, i.e. as an entity the very root of whose existence is his relation to the Holy, and the general character of the natural world. The blindness of natural forces, their destructiveness, their indifference to human personality—all this is directly opposed to our conception of God as the all-merciful and all-wise Providence, as the Holy and the Saviour. From this point of view, the creation of the world by an all-merciful God, the Heavenly Father, is an utterly improbable surmise. It is not surprising therefore that a view somewhat analogous to that of ancient Gnosticism has once again gained ground in modern thought in so far as it has broken away from the traditional church doctrine, but still recognizes the Holy as the essential basis of human life. In the XIXth century John Stuart Mill seems to have been the first to take up this standpoint, admitting that he believed in an all-merciful, but not in an almighty God. In our own day many of the most sensitive and honest religious minds are drawn to the same view.

On the other hand, however, this idea, natural as it is, fails to

[1] Little as we know for certain about the exact teachings of the various schools of Gnosticism, it may now be regarded as proved that the dualism in the theories of Marcion, Valentine and Basilides consists precisely in the duality between the moral and spiritual ideal of holiness and the moral imperfection of earthly, carnal life, and therefore differs from the religiously-metaphysical dualism of the Manichean type. See the conclusive investigation by E. de Faye *Gnostiques et Gnosticisme*.

satisfy the dearest, the deepest hope of the human heart—the hope that the power which brings salvation and refuge to man and is the true home of his soul, is at the same time the supreme power in the universe—or, reversely, that the supreme Creator and Lord of the world is the loving heavenly Father. This faith alone can overcome the bitter sense of the irremediable tragedy of human existence; it alone can justify the conviction that the disharmony between man and the world is not an ultimate and unalterable fact, but only an abnormal, derivative and superficial state of cosmic being.

The problem, thus, involves matters of first importance. It is concerned with the idea of God as the truly supreme reality combining the attributes of holiness or absolute value with the attribute of being the ultimate ground of all existence, and therefore all-powerful.

After a long and bitter struggle the Christian church overcame the dualism of the Gnostic position and established faith in the identity between the God of love, God the Saviour and God the Creator. A similar problem faces the religious and metaphysical thought of our own time. Philosophically it is the problem of reconciling the nature of the world and that of human personality. Before attempting to solve it we must make clear what exactly it involves.

2. The discord between man and the world

The formal cosmological perfection of the world is not, then, the perfection which human spirit needs and seeks. In so far as man is conscious of himself as a person in the full meaning of that term, he is doomed to feel homeless, lonely and forsaken in the world.

In the spiritual history of mankind this attitude took many different forms. Ancient Greeks were keenly aware of man's weakness and insignificance in the world and therefore of the tragic character of his existence, but since their religion deified the world, they bowed down in resignation before the divinely-cosmic order of being. And yet such an attitude was felt to be unsatisfactory, and an opposite tendency found expression in the philosophy of Plato and Plotinus, and in the religion of 'saving the soul' in the Mysteries. Even the Stoic philosophy which in its ontology was the most uncompromising expression of classical pantheism became, at the beginning of the Christian era, a religion of saving the solitary human soul from the world. This line of thought was in direct

contradiction to the original motive of worshipping the world as divine
and led to an opposite extreme, reminiscent of the Hindu attitude:
salvation of the soul proved to be possible only as an escape from
the world—'the flight of the lonely to the Lonely' in the words of
Plotinus. But however keenly the ancient thinkers felt the discord
between the human soul and the world, the idea of man as a *personality*, or of the absolute value of the individual human being remained foreign to them; hence the discord between man and the
world was alleviated by a pantheistic attitude—either, as with the
Stoics, by the consciousness that man himself was a part of the
universal Reason, or by the comfort of contemplating the divine
harmony and the divine meaning of the cosmos (as with Plato and
Plotinus)

The idea of personality in all its depth and significance could
only have arisen on Christian soil; it was fully grasped for the first
time by the genius of Augustine—the 'first of the moderns' as
Harnack calls him. That discovery coincided with the downfall of
the ancient world as represented by the Roman Empire—a period
when man, perishing in the whirlpool of universal anarchy, had
the actual experience of his loneliness. Social anarchy became an
irrefutably convincing proof of the imperfection of the world as
such—of the abyss dividing the blind irrationality of cosmic being
from God's holiness and perfection. It was then that Augustine,
in a flash of sudden revelation discovered the presence of God in the
depths of his own self, and therewith discovered personality as a
non-cosmic reality—a reality belonging to quite a different dimension of being. This awareness of man's kinship to God was not a
pantheistic mergence but, on the contrary, an affirmation of human
personality as such, in its antinomic bi-unity of finitude and infinity,
createdness and affinity to God. It was through this interpretation
of personality that Augustine succeeded in avoiding the simplified
religiously-metaphysical dualism both of the Gnostic and the
Manichean type, and in combining a keen sense of the heterogeneity
between the 'heavenly' and the 'earthly'—between the Holy revealed
to the human soul and the world as it actually is—with a firm faith
in the holiness and perfection of God the Creator. That synthesis
was one of the greatest achievements in the history of spiritual
knowledge, although the full significance of it was obscured by
Augustine's exaggerated sense of man's impotence and insignificance
due to the distortion of human nature by sin. The Old Testament

conception of man's slavery and insignificance as a creature inter-
fered with the Christian revelation of his divine sonship, and consequently the fundamental problem of religious philosophy—
the relation between God, man, and the world could receive no
complete and clear solution. Augustine's discovery of the special
nature and meaning of the human spirit as standing, so to speak,
midway between God and the world had to wait for more than
a thousand years before it bore its natural fruit in religious humanism. In the present connection, however, particular interest attaches
to the fact that in this discovery of man as a personality the difference between man and the world, and therefore the tragic discord
between them, was for the first time recognized in all its depth and
significance. True, it was the fundamental idea of Plato's philosophy
that man is a citizen of two worlds and, while taking part in the
empirical life, belongs to a totally different realm; but Augustine
was the first to grasp that this duality implied a basic difference
between man's inner life and the rest of the created world. He may
be said to have been the first 'existentialist' and to have discovered a
special tragic aspect of human existence as poised on the dividing
line between the world and God.

The consciousness of the duality, however, gradually became
less acute as a new stable order arose on the ruins of the Greco-
Roman civilization, and the Christian church gained power over
European nations. Without forgetting that he belonged to two
different worlds (mediaeval ascetic monasticism and mysticism
bear witness to this) man began to feel at home in the earthly realm.
The dualism between the two worlds came to be conceived as a
harmonious bi-unity of universal being, transcendentally-spiritual
or heavenly, and immanently earthly at the same time. The fact
that man belonged to both these worlds was no longer felt as a
discord, but was regarded as expressing his participation in the
universal harmony between heaven and earth. The increasing metaphysical sense of the security and stability of man's earthly existence
was, in the last resort, responsible for the acceptance of Aristotelianism—the highest rationalistic expression in the world of antiquity
of the belief in the order and meaning of cosmic being and of man's
part in the universal harmony. This conception of life found its
classical expression in the marvellous synthesis of Thomas Aquinas's
philosophy. Spiritual peace which permeates it is far deeper than
the peace known to the thought of ancient Greece, never able

finally to overcome the melancholy sense of resignation before man's inevitable helplessness in the world. Christianized Aristotelianism rested on the recognition that the Creator is man's loving Father, and that therefore both parts of creation—the world and man—are ultimately harmonized in a system of universal being. Moral evil or sin obviously could not be excluded from Christian consciousness but, as already pointed out, it did not radically disturb the harmony of the universe, in which cosmic evil—world's imperfections and calamities—was also finally submerged; no trace of metaphysical uneasiness, of the sense of the tragedy of human existence is to be found in this synthesis.

In the domain of philosophical and theological thought it was comparatively easy to establish a harmony between the world and the human spirit, but it was not so easy in practical life. *'Dicht bei einander wohnen die Gedanken, doch hart im Raume stossen sich die Dinge'*.[1]

The theocratical system, a practical correlate of the Tomistic synthesis, began to break down as early as the XIVth century; the movement of thought parallel to this process led in the XVIth century to the revolt of the Reformation and revived once more the idea of human personality as a non-cosmic principle, directly related to God and therefore transcending any kind of world order. Thus the sense of man's tragic destiny in the world, indicated by Augustine, came to the fore with even greater emphasis. The thinker who expressed it most profoundly was no rebellious reformer, but a believing member of the Catholic church—Pascal. However unsatisfactory the Jansenist theology which influenced him might be, the greatness and the universally-historical significance of Pascal's spiritual struggle lies in the fact that it was a spontaneous expression of a new attitude to life, deeper and more primary than any theological doctrine. It is sufficient to compare the spiritual world of Pascal with that of Thomas Aquinas to see what a profound change had taken place. A new historical epoch of religious unrest had begun—and it is lasting to our own day. In Thomas Aquinas's thought everything is rationally explained and put in its right place in the system of cosmic harmony; with Pascal man is conscious of himself as hanging over an abyss—although as a scientific genius, Pascal was aware of the mathematically

[1] Thoughts can be closely placed together, but facts cruelly conflict in space (Schiller).

harmonious structure of the universe, and as a religious genius discovered anew the intimate bond between human soul and God. He was awed by the eternal and mysterious silence of infinite space into which man has been hurled, and he dreaded equally the abyss of sin, irrationality, and meaningless chaos raging in the human heart. Man's soul, whose very being is constituted by its longing for God, is surrounded and penetrated by the irrational forces of the world. It is in this that the tragedy of human existence consists, insoluble rationally, and overcome only by the heroic effort of the believing heart and the influx of transcendent grace.

I do not propose to trace the further evolution of man's self-consciousness in its relation to the world.[1] Pascal's attitude coincides on the whole with that of the modern man. The superficial and metaphysically ungrounded optimism of the non-religious humanism, with its blind belief that man and the world can be brought into harmony by man's own good and rational will, appears to us now as a comparatively short and insignificant moment in that evolution. Man's awareness of life as inherently tragic lies at the root of the *Weltschmerz* of the early XIXth century, sounds in the music of Beethoven, and finds a striking expression in Kierkegaard's solitary struggle against Hegel's metaphysical optimism. But perhaps no one has expressed it so convincingly as one of the greatest XIXth century representatives of the traditional Catholic faith, Cardinal Newman. The fact that in his case, as in that of Augustine and Pascal, the sense of life's tragedy was combined with a profound, invincible faith in the truth of the Christian doctrine, makes his words particularly significant. I quote the relevant passage. After saying that the existence of God is as evident to him as his own existence, Newman goes on to say:

'The world seems simply to give the lie to that great truth of which my whole being is so full; and the effect upon me is, in consequence, as confusing as if it denied that I am in existence myself. If I looked into a mirror and did not see my face, I should have the sort of feeling which actually comes upon me when I look into this living busy world, and see no reflection of its Creator. . . . The sight of the world is nothing else than the prophet's scroll full of 'lamentations, and mourning, and woe'.

[1] The historical changes in man's attitude to the world are discussed with great depth and subtlety in Martin Buber's excellent essay *What is man?* in the book *Between man and man*, 1947.

MAN BETWEEN THE WORLD AND GOD

'To consider the world in its length and breath, its various history, the many races of man, their starts, their fortunes, their mutual alienation, their conflicts; and then their ways, that is, governments, forms of worship; their enterprises, their aimless courses, their random achievements and acquirements, the impotent conclusion of long-standing facts, the tokens so faint and broken of a superintending design, the blind evolution of what turn out to be great power or truths, the progress of things, as if from unreasoning elements, not toward final causes, the greatness and littleness of man, his far-reaching aims, his short duration, the curtain hung over his futurity, the disappointments of life, the defeat of good, the success of evil, physical pain, the pervading idolatries, the corruptions, the dreary, hopeless irreligion, that condition of the whole race, so fearfully yet exactly described in the Apostle's words 'having no hope and without God in the world'—all this is a vision so dizzy and appalling that it inflicts upon the mind the sense of a profound mystery, which is absolutely beyond human solution.

'What shall be said to this heart-piercing, reason-bewildering fact? I can only answer that either there is no Creator, or this living society of men is in a true sense discarded from His presence. . . . And so I argue about the world: *if* there be a God, *since* there is a God, the human race is implicated in some terrible aboriginal calamity. It is out of joint with the purposes of its Creator. This is a fact, as true as the fact of its existence. . . .'[1]

Perhaps only at the present age when man's sense of the tragedy of his existence has permanently affected the whole of his thought, can the convincing power of this remarkable profession of world-woe be appreciated to the full.

Newman says in conclusion that the view he takes of the world coincides for him with the theological doctrine of original sin. It is significant, however, that in the passage quoted he instinctively uses the words 'aboriginal calamity'; the identification of this calamity with original sin is a supplementary, carefully formulated inference, almost suggesting a doubt. In enumerating the distressing characteristics of cosmic life Newman mentions along with moral evil instances of so-called physical and metaphysical evil which lie outside man's sinful will. In dealing with this aspect of human existence he bewails the fact that the evidence of design and order is so faint and fragmentary.

[1] Henry Newman. *Apologia pro vita sua.* 1870, pp. 241–3.

MAN BETWEEN THE WORLD AND GOD

Two basic ideas can be detected in Newman's masterly exposition
of the tragic aspect of life. In the first place, man suffers not only
from the consequences of his sinful will, but also from the discord
between his aspirations and the blind course of nature. The disharmony between personal or spiritual, and impersonally-natural
principles of being is a primary and absolute fact. Man suffers from
being fettered to the soulless, blind and morally indifferent world-
process.

Secondly, moral evil—sin and its consequences—is not only
man's fault, but also his *misfortune*. True, even in recognizing his
actual impotence, man has no right to deny his reponsibility for
moral evil reigning in the world, or even to seek such explanations
of it as would remove that responsibility. This is the only spiritual
attitude that is morally justified, and our conscience demands it;
but nevertheless in contemplating sin and evil objectively, i.e. not in
ourselves but in others, as facts and forces acting in the world, we
can and ought to regard them as expressions of the impotence and
irrationality of human will—that is, of man's unhappy condition.
His conflict with blind forces raging in the human world is no less
tragic than his sufferings from the soulless and morally indifferent
forces of nature. Invasion by the savage hordes of Genghis-Khan
and Tamerlane—or in our own day, by equally savage hordes of
Hitler and Stalin—are calamities in no way differing from an earthquake, a flood or a hurricane—except in being incomparably more
destructive. But even in purely personal life considered from outside, i.e. in other people, passions that rage in human hearts, men's
inability to master them, and, even more, stupidity and unreason-
ableness are analogous to elemental forces of nature. They all may
be regarded as a kind of mental illness, and the latter is almost
always hereditary. And even if heredity is determined by the sins
of previous generations, moral consciousness cannot resign itself
to the fact of the fathers' sins being visited on the children. One of
the most insoluble riddles for a theodicy is man's suffering from
diseases conditioned by heredity, especially from mental diseases
(including mere impotence of moral will and abnormal elementary
force of lusts and passions) which destroy the spirit's creative
ability to deal with calamities and to triumph over them through its
contact with the powers of grace.

The consciousness of this tragic dividedness in human existence
has become particularly keen at the present time, in spite of the

revolutionary change in science that has largely confirmed the ancient conception of cosmic harmony. The explanation is that our epoch is dominated by man's intense, though vague, awareness of himself as a person, as a dweller in an inner world of reality. Cosmic harmony as such, even apart from its limitations, is, as already indicated, impersonal and has nothing in common with the principle of holiness; it cannot therefore truly reconcile man to the world.

3. *Kinship between man and the world as two manifestations of one and the same reality*

However great the discord between man and the world may be, it would be utterly one-sided and erroneous to overlook the opposite aspect of their correlation—their kinship. Although good-natured religious optimism which ignores the tragic solitude of the human soul in the world is inadmissible—and indeed, after Pascal, impossible for us—it would be superficial and conceited to pride ourselves on this new spiritual discovery and disregard the element of truth contained both in the ancients' perception of the divine harmony in the universe, and in the traditional Judeo-Christian idea of the bond between man and the world as together created by God.

Unprejudiced metaphysical thought discovers the kinship between man and the world first of all in their both being rooted in *reality*. This brings us once more to the idea with which the argument of this essay began and which provides the key to a philosophic interpretation of being. In Chapter I it has been shown that reality is the medium that connects the knowing subject with the object known and thus forms an ideal bond between the 'self' or man's inner conscious being and the objective world. In the last resort it is reality that makes possible the conception of objective being as being-in-itself, independent of the cognizing gaze directed upon it. Reality is thus a further unanalysable primary attribute in virtue of which anything *is* at all—not for somebody, or in relation to something else, but *is* primarily, is-in-itself. That 'is' in its inner nature is identical with the 'I am' revealed to us with immediate self-evidence in our own inner being. Of course man differs from inanimate things by being *conscious* of the 'is' in himself (in the form of 'I am'). But in so far as he *is*, at any rate in his immediate elementary mental life in general, he does not differ from any other animate being. Whether that primary element, 'is' be grasped by consciousness fully, or little or not at all—a stone, or an electron, and the greatest saint and genius are united by the fact that they *are*, i.e. that they are in the last resort rooted in reality. This is so obvious that as a rule it is not noticed at all; to minds untrained in philosophy this common feature seems so meaningless and insignificant that it is unnecessary to point it out—and only eccentric pedants called philosophers are absurd enough to do so.

But such is the fate of philosophic thought: it discovers that the apparently obvious is significant and enigmatic. In truth, the fact that we all *are* involves something more than a purely formal or ideal generality: it bears witness to a decisive and fundamental relation in virtue of which all that is—both the inner being-for-itself of the personal human spirit, and the totality of natural being—is inter-united by being rooted in the same ground—the ground of *reality*.

To see the force of this, we must recall the early stages of the present argument (Chapter I, 1). Midway between me as a knowing subject and the external world as the totality of all that is empirically given to me from without, there stands ideal, super-temporal being, discovered by Plato. It belongs on the one hand to the element of thought and is in this sense akin to my 'self' and, on the other, has objective significance. Neither the conception of an external world of objects, nor the knowledge of it is thinkable apart from the relation to this ideal, supertemporal realm. Hence, that which we call 'the world,' and are apt to imagine as an all-embracing reality, cannot, in truth, be all-embracing and self-sufficient; it is merely an aspect or part of something greater, which embraces and interpenetrates it and is the unity of thought and of the content of thought. All that *is* not merely exists as a fact, but also has an ideal significance. Existence would not be existence if it were not both real and ideal; all temporal being is also super-temporal, and in that ideal aspect it is inseparable from the reality which we call 'consciousness'. That is why both forms of being—being as 'is' and as 'am' constitute an indissoluble and mutually interpenetrating unity.

Hence it follows that the difference between reality and the world of fact is not a difference between two separate and totally heterogeneous spheres. True, reality transcends the world of fact, has depths which lie beyond it, and in that sense is 'super-cosmic'.

But it permeates the world and forms its basis, or, as it were, its substance. This is why super-cosmic reality, as manifested in man's inner conscious being and in superhuman forces which interpenetrate it, enters the world of fact and is active in it, i.e. has an aspect which forms part of it. That which is revealed in the inner and the metaphysical experience as reality is for external objective knowledge an active factor in the empirical world. Man's moral and creative activities, as well as his elemental desires, lusts and passions including possession by demonic forces, are in their external manifestations, or as perceived from without, either beneficent and constructive or baleful and destructive agencies in the world. And, reversely, natural elements appear to have an inner life. It has been pointed out (Chapter II, 3) that in the apprehension of beauty we detect the presence of a certain super-cosmic reality in physical nature. Watching the storm-tossed ocean or listening to the howling wind we are conscious, as it were, of animate forces in nature, of something analogous to human passions; this is not an illusion, but a vague apprehension of a real similarity. In reducing matter to non-material bearers of energy, dynamism, activity, modern physics has confirmed this direct awareness of the kinship between elemental forces of nature and elemental forces in the human soul. It is significant in this connection that physical science has detected a close analogy between the actual structure of natural and spiritual being. In nature there appears to be a certain unity—not yet logically expounded and therefore seemingly contradictory—of point-like bearers of reality (particles) and of continuous wave-like rays which fill up the field of activity.[1] This is completely analogous to the structure of spiritual being, self-evident and evoking no perplexity or sense of contradiction: it is, on the one hand, divided into certain centres or 'points'—subjective bearers of life who refer everything to themselves, and on the other hand it resembles rays that endlessly spread in all directions and are all-embracing. Spiritual being harmoniously combines discreteness with continuity, individuality with universal unity.

There is a close resemblance between this view and Leibniz's monadology, which also unites the spiritual and the material world in one all-embracing system—but the essential difference is that, in contradiction to Leibniz, monads not only 'have windows' but

[1] To designate this unity of 'particle' and 'wave' English physicists have coined a special word, *wavicle*.

in a sense *are* 'windows', i.e. centres that both absorb everything from without and give it out again. In spite of this difference, however, modern science entitles us to conceive of the difference between man and natural entities somewhat after the fashion of Leibniz's distinction between 'waking' and 'sleeping' monads.

It has been pointed out at the beginning of the present essay that there is only one idea by which the all-embracing unity of reality may be described. Reality in all the multiplicity of its manifestations is *life* in the widest sense of that term—a kind of immanent dynamism. Man's highest spiritual activity, the intensity of his intellectual, moral, artistic and religious strivings, the dark forces of passion that possess him, the unconscious elemental dynamism that interpenetrates the organic world, the physical energy throughout the universe, the terrible concentration of it that constitutes the nature of an atom—all these are manifestations of universal dynamism, or, as Bergson called it, speaking of the organic life, *élan vital*. One and the same life pulsates in all that is, life distinct in every separate bearer of it and yet merged in one continuous and harmonious unity. Leaving aside the aspect in which it is permeated by ideality and is *a content of thought*, life may be said to be *potentiality* in the twofold meaning of the term: both as passivity or material upon which form is superimposed (matter in Aristotle's sense) and as active *potency* striving for self-expression or realization of its latent possibilities and, at the highest stage, as the energy of self-formation. The same inexpressible principle which is the hidden transcendent essence of our inner being, and which we apprehend in the depths of our self as reality in contradistinction to the visible objective world, is at the same time the hidden basis of universal being as a whole.

Reality in this respect is that which Plato and his followers called the world-soul. In this sense it is the derivative and potentially-divine basis of cosmic being. The fact that this divine element can break away from its ultimate ground and, as groundless potentiality, degenerate into a blind, destructive and demonic force does not disprove its true derivatively-divine nature. God as absolute Holiness and absolute Spirit, apprehended by us as personal, transcends all created and derivative being; when He enters the world through the Incarnation, or through theophany, or through the gracious presence of the Holy Spirit (or His 'gifts') in the depths of the human soul, He descends, as it were, from His far-off transcendent abode. But in another aspect of His being He is the immanent ground of universal life. That aspect is creative dynamism and 'omnipotence'.[1] Reality is the derivatively-divine substratum of existence.

Whatever interpretation be given to the idea of the 'creation' of the world by God, accepting that idea provisionally we may, in any case, say this: the first act of creation (not of course in the chronological, but in the ontological order) obviously consists in God's positing *reality* outside Himself, radiating forth, so to speak, the primary element of 'being' inherent in His own nature. By an act as it were of self-division He posits a realm external to Him and bestows upon it, in a derivative form, His own primariness. This element of 'being' is not an inert substratum or a lifelessly-passive state—it is an active, dynamic principle of *life*.

This interpretation is compatible even with the literal sense of the Biblical account of the creation of the world. V. Solovyov has rightly pointed out that in the first sentence of the book of Genesis 'In the beginning God created the heaven and the earth', the Jewish word *bereshith* (and its Greek translation αρχη) should be understood not as an adverb meaning 'at first' or 'to begin with', but quite concretely: God created the world in the *beginning*, i.e. in a primary substratum of being.[2] The creation of the world in the strict sense is ontologically preceded by positing the 'beginning' as a kind of foundation or a general element of being. This 'beginning' or, in my terminology, this *reality* is the primary ground or substratum of universal being: in it the world and the human soul form a unity and are related by an inner bond of kinship.

The empirical confirmation of this is the fact that the spiritual depth of human personality is in direct ratio to its breadth and solidarity with the world around it. Saints and men of genius understand life in all its fulness, and respond to it, for their individuality in its incomparable uniqueness is rich in general ontological content. In virtue if the super-rational conicidence, in

---

[1] This distinction presents a certain analogy to the teaching of the Greek mystical theologian of the fourteenth century, Gregory Palamas, who distinguished in God His 'energy' that penetrates created being, from His unfathomable and inaccessible 'essence'.

[2] *Bereshith* is derived from the word *reshith* (feminine form of the word *rosh*—'principle' or 'ground'. Its meaning (as that of the Greek ἀρχή) can be best expressed by the conception of 'substratum' or 'primary element'. Obviously the same interpretation applies to the first words of the prologue to St. John's Gospel: 'In the beginning was the Word . . .'

the spiritual realm, between discreteness and continuity, human spirit may be compared to a cone whose base extends to infinity; its summit is a point—one of innumerable individual points constituting the multiplicity of being—but its base is an all-embracing infinity. The greater the depth, the greater the width. Spiritually deep and broad natures, responsive to all that surrounds them, are conscious of their inner kinship not only with the human world but, ultimately, with nature as well. Christ pointed to the lilies of the fields and the birds of heaven as a witness to God's love for all creation. St. Paul speaks of 'all creation' 'groaning' in the hope of the coming fulness of redemption. Francis of Assisi regarded all living creatures, all natural forces and entities as his brothers and sisters. Poets—Goethe, Wordsworth, Tyutchev—have a direct apprehension of the soul of nature. Men of rich and profound individuality, in whom the *personal* principle finds its fullest embodiment, are particularly conscious of the harmonious unity of all that is, and perceive in all things the reflection of one God.

The point of view of radical and irreconcilable dualism is, thus, both religiously and philosophically intenable. Philosophical thought discovers, behind the duality between human spirit and the natural world, one all-embracing and all-pervading reality which must have a single centre and primary basis. Religious consciousness, if sufficiently deep and comprehensive, perceives and feels the presence of the Deity in all that is.

But then how are we to reconcile this ontological kinship between all world-entities with the clear and irrefutable fact of the profound heterogeneity between human personality and the world? In order to answer this question a philosophical interpretation must be given to the idea of creation of the world by God, meaning by God a loving Father. The Christian church, in spite of all the inevitable doubts, upholds its steadfast faith in 'One God, the Father Almighty, Maker of heaven and earth and of all things visible and invisible'. Can a philosophical basis be found for that faith, and can it be reconciled with the duality between the world and man?

4. The world and man as God's creation

Let us, first, be clear as to what is meant by the doctrine of the creation of the world by God.

In the traditional formulation, its religious meaning must be distinguished both from the mythological setting of the Biblical story (as of course is recognized by theologians) and from its dogmatic formulation, asserting that God created the world 'out of nothing'.[1] In a purely religious sense this statement is concerned not with the origination of the world, but expresses the direct awareness, common both to the Old Testament religion and to Christianity, of the absolute dependence of the world upon its only primary ground—God. The world and man have no immanent basis in themselves and are in no way self-subsistent; their being has a transcendent ground, it wholly rests upon God and is due to the Divine will which bestows existence upon them. It is in this that their 'createdness' consists; and from the religious point of view the doctrine of the creation of the world means that all being, except God Himself, is 'a creature'.

In this general sense the doctrine in question is absolutely true from the point of view of free metaphysical thought—with the reservation which was discussed in Chapter IV. The ultimate ground of the universe transcends it; the world (including man) is not, as naturalism takes it to be, self-subsistent and irreducible to anything else, i.e. is not a ready-made eternal fact. On the contrary, the world contains living depths in which its being is seen to spring from something that lies beyond it—in the first instance, from a super-cosmic 'reality' which in its turn presupposes a primary ground, an absolute centre or first source by whose creative power it *is*. Metaphysical thought discovers in this first source features that bear affinity to the inmost being of man; hence it can be designated by the traditional ancient term originating in religious consciousness—'God'.

But the usual dogmatic formulation of this truth—'God created the world out of nothing'—does not express it adequately and, at any rate if interpreted literally, meets with insuperable difficulties. In popular thought the idea of creation out of nothing, in connection with the mythological Biblical story, results in picturing

---

[1] This formula is not found in any of the canonical books either of the Old or the New Testament. It is only used in a casual way in a later, non-canonical second book of Maccabees (7, 28). As an expression of a dogma it first occurs in Irinaeus in his arguments against Gnostic dualism.

The word *bara* (created) in the first verse of the book of Genesis literally means 'moulded' or 'formed'. In the second verse the Spirit of God is said 'to hatch'—i.e. to form by means of some organic process—the world out of chaos which, evidently, is assumed to be pre-existent.

God as a kind of magician who actually does what a conjurer pretends to do, and makes the non-existent come into being at his command. This childish idea had long ceased to satisfy serious religious thought even of the strictly orthodox type. It is untenable because it identifies creation with *coming to be*, i.e. presupposes the existence of time; but time is an attribute and form of created being and cannot be conceived as preceding it. It was already pointed out by Augustine that God created the world not *in* time, but *together with* time (*non in tempore, sed cum tempore*). Besides, as a temporal process, 'coming to be' inevitably implies origination of something out of something else, replacement of one state of being by another—which constitutes the immediately apparent nature of the temporal process. Hence, 'origination out of nothing' is unthinkable even as a miraculous supernatural event—it is simply unmeaning, a *contradictio in adjecto*.

If this popular conception be set aside, the formula that 'God created the world out of nothing' can only mean that He created it *not* out of some pre-existent raw material or substratum of cosmic being. As Thomas Aquinas says 'created out of nothing' simply means 'did not create out of something'. This sober and reasonable interpretation is perfectly true *negatively*, that is, as a denial of the dualistic conception of two independent primary principles—God and cosmic 'matter' existing before the creation. But a negative judgment has meaning only when the denial of a false assertion is based upon the presence of a positive correlation, opposed to it ('whales are not fishes—*because* they are mammals'). Consequently, we cannot rest content with this negative interpretation. If God 'did not create the world out of something', *how* are we to conceive creation positively?

It is no answer to say that God's creation of the world is a unique act, ontologically preceding all existence, so that all our comparisons and ideas are inapplicable to it; hence it admits of no explanation, but must simply be accepted as something miraculous and unfathomable. This plain dismissal of the problem must be dismissed in its turn on the strength of methodological arguments set forth in Chapter III. In it I have endeavoured to show that although the nature of God, and indeed of all concrete contents of religious experience, is unfathomable, some light may be indirectly thrown on it by means of 'docta ignorantia' and transcendental thought. We could not use the term 'creation' at all if its meaning were absolutely inaccessible to us.

The idea of the creation of the world 'out of nothing,' and refusal to seek for its positive implications involves the danger of affirming God's infinite, unlimited and absolute omnipotence. Following the basic religious tendency of the Old Testament—and in direct opposition to Greek thought—everything 'created' is conceived as a kind of existent non-being, as an inert, impotent and passive product of God's creative will. On such an interpretation the problem of theodicy, i.e. of reconciling evil with the existence of God— proves to be insoluble (or leads to denying the reality of evil); the idea of God as all-merciful and omniscient makes the imperfection of the creature utterly incomprehensible. Thomas Aquinas has many deep and subtle considerations intended to give a rational meaning, and therefore to set logical limits, to the idea of Divine omnipotence, but they are all annulled by his saying that God could have created a better world than the existing one had He wished it. In the last resort Aquinas's God proves to be the same kind of ontological arbitrary tyrant and autocratic despot as Mahomet's Allah.[1] Such a conception of God is the result of slavish psychology —of mystical worship of fearful unlimitedly-autocratic power. A despotic autocrat has only to utter a word or to indicate his will by a frown, and his slaves' fate is sealed; in the same way, God has only to wish, and His wish is miraculously realized. Such slavish obeisance to God, conceived as a cosmic despot, is unworthy of man, however true our sense of the vanity and transitoriness of created existence may be, and however valuable is the attitude of submission to God's will and reverent worship of His greatness. To extol God's unlimited omnipotence is a very doubtful compliment to Him, and indeed is more like blasphemy than true praise.[2] At bottom, it is in contradiction with the main content of Christian faith. Why should God incarnate, come down into the world and bestow upon it the saving power of love and holiness by His death on the cross, if He could, by simply expressing His sovereign will, as it were by merely moving a finger, save or improve the world? No theological artifice can

[1] This is justly remarked by a competent modern interpreter of Tomistic philosophy, R. L. Patterson, *The Conception of God in the philosophy of Aquinas*, 1933, p. 285.

[2] Among modern thinkers A. Whitehead emphasises this; he opposes to the conception of boundless omnipotence the Platonic idea that God acts upon the blind power of necessity through 'persuasion' or 'appeal', the force of which is naturally limited.

reconcile the idea of God's boundless omnipotence with the Christian idea of a suffering God—of God who, out of love for the world, voluntarily took part in the world's tragedy.

If this anthropopathic idea of God's unlimited tyrannical omnipotence be given up, how are we to conceive of the 'creation of the world'? We must recognize that it is a super-rational mystery and can only be understood analogically, by way of *docta ignorantia*; in attempting to grasp it, we must start with the data of our own spiritual experience. The only spiritual experience relevant here is that of human creativeness. Divine creativeness must either remain for us devoid of meaning, a mere *flatus vocis*, or, in spite of its uniqueness, be conceived on the analogy of human creativeness (much as the notion of it may have to be modified.)

The first difficulty which this analogy involves is that human creativeness, like all processes in the world of existence, takes place *in time* while the relation between God the Creator and His creation must be conceived as eternal or supertemporal. In prevalent religious and metaphysical thought this distinction finds expression in the idea that the creation of the world by God takes place *at once*, and is an instantaneous birth of the existent from non-being. That instant of creation is naturally, and for human consciousness inevitably, conceived as an instant of *time*, its *first* moment, after which there begins the abiding time of the created world; this further existence of the world in time and all the changes taking place in it are no longer related to the act of creation.

This naive, popular idea is both religiously and philosophically untenable. With regard to the religious interpretation it is sufficient to observe that even the Biblical narrative describes creation as a lengthy process (six days) and that the creation of man in particular is conceived as a special act, distinct from the creation of the world. For Christian thought the Incarnation is a new creation—the appearance of a 'new Adam'; the action of the Holy Spirit, whether in the general course of the cosmic process or in separate acts of grace, must obviously also be understood as a series of acts of Divine creativeness; finally, the book of Revelation speaks of new creation in the future ('behold, I make all things new'). Accordingly, from the purely religious standpoint creation of the world must be conceived not as a momentary act, but as somehow extending to the whole existence of the world in time. The naively-anthropological idea that having created the world God 'rested from all his work' must obviously be somehow combined with the consciousness that Divine creativeness is continuous and unremitting.

Purely philosophically the creation of the world must be conceived as super-temporal on the part of God, and, on the part of the creature, as reflected in a temporal process. If time be symbolized by a horizontal line, the creation of the world is not in that dimension but is, as it were, perpendicular to it, in a vertical line going from above downwards—i.e. is supertemporal. But this vertical dimension is in touch with the horizontal time-line and present at every point of it, throughout its length. Therefore, from the standpoint of the creature, i.e. in time, creation has the character of a lengthy process unfolding in time. The *existence* of the world is simply its continuous creation—this is the only possible interpretation both of human and of cosmic history. Modern physics has accustomed us to the idea that there are not eternal laws of nature, and that its familiar features are merely an expression of a certain state of it, of a certain stage in cosmic history; and the same idea is even more pronounced in evolutionary biology. As to human history, it is obvious that, in spite of all its irrationality, it contains a creative element.

Pursuing this line of thought we may say with Bergson that the very character of temporality inherent in cosmic being, i.e. time itself as the dynamism of transition and duration, is an expression of creativeness, of creative striving, lying at the root of existence. From that point of view the world is not so much the result or the fruit of Divine creativeness as its immanent expression.

Does not this, however, mean confusing the mysterious primary relation between the Creator and the creature with derivative creativeness present in the creature and manifested in its evolution? Theoretically, of course, the two must be distinguished. But it has already been pointed out (Chapter IV, 6) that human and natural creativeness is only explicable as a derivative manifestation of the Divine creativeness in the creature. Divine creativeness, in contradistinction to the human, consists in *creating creators*. God creates beings that are creative agents carrying out His design (one might use the simile of a composer or playwright requiring creative performers of his work).

Strictly speaking, the fact that God creates the world with the participation, and through the instrumentality, of the created creators who carry out His will, is only another expression of the truth that the Creator is inseparable from His creation and that His nature is revealed only in the indivisible, though distinct, biunity of Creator and creature; or, in other words, that the nature of the absolute primary source of being is only revealed to us when we apprehend Him both as the transcendent primary source and the immanent basis of creation.

But however legitimate an analogy between the creation of the world by God and creative processes within that world may be, it does not dispose of the fundamental difference between primary and derivative creativeness, and it is precisely this difference that constitutes the main difficulty of the idea of creation. Both the formula of 'creation out of nothing' in its popular interpretation, and the dualistic conception of creation as imposition of form upon pre-existing material are untenable; how, then, are we to conceive of the creation of the world by God?

The answer to this question is predetermined by the general methodological consideration that categories constitutive of our knowledge of the world of fact are altogether inapplicable to God (or to 'reality'). To ask whether God uses something external to Himself as material for creation, or whether His creativeness and its result are wholly determined by His own inner power is misleading, because the categories of 'within' and 'outside', both in the spatial and the general logical sense, are essential to all particular contents of thought and their inter-relations, and cannot be applied to God. God is not a particular content, but an all-embracing and all-determining unity. The ideas of 'within' and 'outside' do not determine Him, but are determined by Him. Therefore *outside* of God there can be, in the absolute sense, nothing at all: every 'outside', as well as every 'within', is posited by God Himself and is an element in His all-determining infinite fulness. Everything 'other than God' is 'other within God's own being'—it is 'God's other,' or an element of 'otherness' arising out of God's self-unfolding; for, as we know, God is the unity of 'this and the other'.

With reference to the subject we are discussing, this means that in creating the world, God is not using any material foreign to Himself and existing independently of Him; nor does He 'create out of nothing'. His creativeness, like all creativeness, consists in imposing form upon material, but the difference is that He posits the material Himself. That material is 'God's *other*'—a principle which He counter-opposes to Himself *as* 'other'. This 'other' is not an empty abstraction. Its general content can be determined, or, to speak more exactly, apprehended as potentiality, pure elemental dynamism, or reality in its distinction from the unity of the actual and the potential which constitutes God's being. Reality conceived in its fulness, i.e. in its primary connection with God, is also, in virtue of that very connection, a unity of the actual and the potential (Chapter II, 5). But reality regarded as an element or principle counter-opposed to God is pure potentiality, formless dynamism and plasticity. Creation of the world is the formation, distribution and integration of this material, through instilling into it the actuality and perfection of God.

This really is the answer to the basic difficulty of reconciling the world's imperfection with the omnipotence of an all-merciful God (omnipotence should be understood not as unlimited despotic power, but as the all-conquering force of the creative ultimate ground of being). We have a right to conceive of Divine creativeness on the analogy of the human. True, human creativeness works derivatively, by the power of 'inspiration', which is a Divine gift or suggestion, while God creates by His own power. But this difference implies at the same time a close affinity. Human creativeness, typified most clearly by artistic creation, is a difficult process of straining the will, overcoming obstacles, meeting with alternating failures and successes, and finding that the end achieved is always inevitably imperfect. This dramatic nature of creativeness is due— apart from the weakness of man's powers—to the resistance of the material. The greater a man's creative genius, the more easily he overcomes that resistance, but in any case the element of struggle is inherent in human creativeness as such. The same thing is applic-able to God's creativeness. The material He deals with is His own progeny, the principle of 'otherness', as it were, brought out of His own being by Him. Yet this material *is*, and it is not pure passivity, indefiniteness and general receptivity, but living formless dynam-ism that needs curbing, if it is to receive form and fit into the Creator's plan. We are entitled to conceive God after the manner of the highest type of creative genius, whose creativeness is a spon-taneously free outpouring of his very being, unhampered by any inner weakness. Nevertheless this cosmic genius must reckon with the anarchic, disorderly forces of the material to which he imparts form, and can only realize his creativeness gradually, through a series of successive acts intended to make the material more and more perfect (all this of course holds good in a certain perspective only, namely from the point of view of the creature). Omnipotent, i.e. all-conquering power of the Creator is thus compatible with creative effort and *with comparative imperfection of the result*. From the point of view of the creature the process of creation is still going on; the very being of the world consists in its continuing creation. The Creator of the world cannot, any more than a human artist can, fully embody his creative design at once. He expresses his general design either through a consecutive series of particular creations, or through continually re-making, correcting and varying the details of creation; and since all multiplicity is subordinated to unity, both these possibilities are in the last resort merely two interchangeable variants of increase in perfection, taking place through unceasing creative effort. The history of the world and of man with all its disasters is the expression of the struggle between God's creative power and the chaotic disorder and elemental obduracy of his material, i.e. of the sheer dynamic potentiality of being.

At this point we can see at last the purpose of our laboured argument about 'the creation of the world'. We are now in a position to understand the nature and the source of the heterogeneity between human spirit and the world, and to reconcile it with the kinship between them as God's creatures.

In Chapter IV I have attempted to show that human spirit stands in a different relation to God than does the rest of creation. Although it is created, it is 'an image and likeness of God'—and this means that in its ultimate depths it participates in God's spirit and is a creature in which God himself potentially and invisibly abides. Creation in this case is therefore a kind of partial or potential Divine incarnation. I have described this aspect of human spirit as 'man's uncreated essence', since 'creature' and 'creaturely' is generally taken to mean something utterly heterogeneous to the Divine nature. The same idea can now be expressed in a form perhaps more acceptable to orthodox thought. As already pointed out, man is in one respect a creature in exactly the same sense as the rest of the world: as a purely natural being, he is a part of the cosmos, a part of organic nature; in man's inner life this fact finds expression in the domain of involuntary mental processes, strivings and appetites, and in the blind interplay of elemental forces. But as a personality, as a spiritual being and 'an image of God' man differs from all other creatures. While all other creatures are expressions and embodiments of God's particular creative ideas, man is a creature in and through which God seeks to express *His own nature as spirit, personality and holiness.* An analogy with human artistic creativeness will make the point clearer.

In poetry (and to some extent, by analogy with it, in other arts) we distinguish between epic and lyric works, between the artist's intention to embody some idea referring to the objective content of being, and his intention to express his own self, to tell of his own inner world, and as it were to make his confession. The difference, of course, is merely relative. The poet's creative personality involuntarily makes itself felt in the style of an 'objective' epic; on the other hand, a lyric outpouring is not simply a revelation of the poet's inner life as it actually is, but an artistic transfiguration of it, and therefore inevitably contains an element of 'objectivization'. With this proviso however, the difference between the two kinds of poetry holds good.

Using this analogy we may say that man is, as it were, God's 'lyric' creation in which He wants 'to express' Himself, while the rest of creation, though involuntarily bearing the impress of its Creator, is the expression of God's special 'objective' ideas, of His creative will to produce entities other than Himself. The fundamental point of difference is the presence or absence in the creature of the *personal* principle with all that it involves, i.e. self-consciousness, autonomy, and the power of controlling and directing one's actions in accordance with the supreme principle of the Good or Holiness.

I repeat, however essential and profound the difference is, it still remains relative; it therefore admits of transitional forms and is compatible with inner affinity between these two forms of creation. This is why, on the one hand, man is conscious of his kinship as a creature with all other created entities which together constitute the world, and on the other, his aesthetic and religious insight enables him to detect a soul-like element in the impersonal natural entities and see them as akin to his own spiritual being. To put it imaginatively, the world of nature as an 'epic' work is, as it were, God's preliminary sketch of creation, a kind or preparatory material in which He must subsequently embody His 'lyric' self-expression; created nature has to become a free spirit and thus realize its kinship with man.

Being a natural creature and at the same time an image of God, a created embodiment of the Divine spirit, man stands midway between God and the world, and participates in both. Accordingly there is a sharp opposition between man as a spirit and a personality, and the world in its actual condition. And yet man is at one with the world both in his deficiency as a natural being, and in his awareness of the world's potential humanity and divinity. Man is so to speak an elder, grown up brother of infantile creatures of which the natural world consists. He alone has risen (though far from completely) to understanding the purpose of his life, and responsibly directing his actions; he naturally suffers from the irrationality and unruliness of his younger brothers, but at the same time is aware of his blood-relationship with them. Thus the tragic character of human existence is compatible with a secure and happy sense that all being is harmoniously rooted in God.

5. *The tragedy and the harmony of being*

As already pointed out, the difference between creation as production of something heterogeneous to the Creator, and creation as self-revelation or self-incarnation of the Creator, is after all merely relative. Using the comparison with poetry once more and conceiving the relation in the form of temporal sequence, one might say that having created the world as an 'epic' work, God strives to interpenetrate it more and more with His inner being as Personality and personified holiness, and to make it a 'lyric'. Man is thus the expression, as it were, of the highest stage in the creation of the world. In man as a spiritual being, creation attains maturity which the rest of the world is lacking. The world's growth in perfection consists not merely in its having fuller and richer content, and in its life becoming more complex and harmonious, but also in spiritual enlightenment, in the development of the Divine principle in it through, so to speak, the ever-increasing 'humanization' of the world. The process of 'creation' (continuing in the order of time) and the process of 'salvation' or 'deification' of the world are two aspects of one general creative act in which God's being and His creative activity coincide. We have seen (Chapter V, 3) that human activity has two aspects, inner and outer, and is, on the one hand, organization and external arrangement of life's structure and, on the other, spiritual self-education and enlightenment—both individual and collective. The two forms of divinely-cosmic creativeness must be conceived in accordance with this analogy. No enrich-ment, no increase in complexity or even in the harmony of the world's structure can, as such, 'save' the world and establish its inner harmony, while its constituent elements, the bearers of life, remain blind 'sleeping' monads. Increase in outer perfection must be accompanied by an inner creative process of spiritualization, trans-figuration and deification of the world, culminating in the promised ideal state when 'God shall be all in all'. The whole world shall then be His Kingdom, as it were merged in Him, and forming simply the outer, embodied sphere of God's own being.

This might be understood as a metaphysical justification of the idea of continuous pre-established progress. But such an interpre-tation would be a mistake. As we have seen, all creativeness involves an element of conflict. The creation of the world in the primary sense of the word is achieved through a strenuous effort of creative will doomed to many failures and set-backs, through cancelling unsuccessful results and seeking new ways; the case is the same with the world's spiritual enlightenment and growth in perfection. Here, too, continuous progress is not guaranteed, and there are failures, interruptions, catastrophes, periods of stagnation and regress. To bring Divine holiness into the world, to make creation at one with God, is an arduous task, requiring much struggle. We are only entitled to believe in Divine omnipotence in the sense of the all-conquering power of the creative source of all being, and the only thing of which we can be unquestionably certain is God's *final victory*. But that final victory will come after a long and painful struggle full of dramatic developments.[1]

We have no guarantee whatever that the level of moral and spiritual culture attained during the last centuries of historical development will be preserved in the future; it may be and indeed probably is doomed to go through the catastrophe of temporal break-down and decay; this has happened more than once in the past. We even have no grounds for the certainty that our small planet is the fore-ordained centre of the world's spiritual history, that is,

---

[1] We are witnessing one of these developments now—the breakdown of the external concordance of life and the decay in the inner power of holiness. Over a hundred years ago it was forseen with remarkable keenness of insight by Goethe, who shortly before his death said to Eckermann: 'I foresee a time when God, once more dissatisfied with His creation, will mix everything again, so as to begin creation anew.'

222

of the gradual process of the universe attaining harmony and deification. It is conceivable that this process, begun on the earth, as God's first essay in creation may continue and end in another place in the universe. The uncertainty about the order and character of the dramatic process of the world's creation and spiritualization— coinciding with the mysterious metaphysical process of God's self- unfolding—in no way conflicts with faith in its final success, guaranteed, as already pointed out, simply by the fact that God is the only primary source of all being.

Christian consciousness rightly supposes that this final victory is likely to be sudden and unexpected, following the apparent defeat of the Divine powers by the unbridled forces of evil and chaos. Not only the created world and man in it, but the Creator Himself must follow the arduous path of suffering that leads to the final triumph. God Himself takes part in the ascent of cosmic being to perfection through tragic conflict and struggle. But it is precisely His participation in it that guarantees the final victory.

Moreover, although on the plane of temporal being this victory can only be thought of in some indefinite future, infinitely remote according to our usual measurements of time, on the metaphysical plane it must be conceived as supertemporarily *real*; in human language, subject to the categories of time, this can only be expressed by saying that in the metaphysical depths of being the victory *has already taken place* and has only to bear fruit or be revealed on the empirical plane. 'In the world ye shall have tribulation; but be of good cheer: I have overcome the world'.

Cosmic life, including man as its highest representative, is all of a piece; and consequently the duality between the tragedy of the continuing creative struggle and the blessed peace of the victory already attained on the metaphysical plane (or, rather, the inviolable primordial eternity of this inner victory as the expression of God's omnipotence) is present in every human soul. Man's life is tragic because his spirit is solitary in the natural world, hostile and alien to him (including the world of his own passions); he is compelled to waste his powers on the arduous and never wholly realizable task of preserving and perfecting his life, and to take part in the work of outer and inner creativeness, imparting form and light to the world around him. But however great his sorrows and disappointments and the blows of fate he has to endure, however hopeless the torments of his own conscience, in the ultimate depths of his spirit he is securely rooted in God, and through this is in inner harmony and joyfully-loving unity with all that is. The pain of discord and the peace of harmony dwell in his heart side by side; indeed the discord and tragedy of his existence have their source in his privileged, aristocratic position as a being superior to the world, a child of God (Pascal justly says that man's misery is *misère d'un grand seigneur, d'un roi dépossédé*), and bears witness to his inviolable security in the bosom of Divine holiness and omnipotence.

Modern man has long lost the consciousness of the essentially unbreakable ontological bond with God which forms his very being, and is inclined both to feel despair and unnaturally to relish the tragic character of his existence. But this renders the idea of 'tragedy' altogether meaningless. Tragedy is intended *to be overcome* and contains a dynamic aspect leading to its solution. Every tragedy has an issue, even if it be the death of the hero—which also is a way out of the impass. A tragic situation to which man gets passively accustomed, regarding it as his normal state beyond which he knows nothing, is a travesty of all that is meant by 'tragedy'. Tragedy implies a loss of balance, an unstable situation demanding a solution, and has only meaning as contrasted with peace and harmony. The very possibility of tragedy presupposes spiritual depths in which man finds a secure basis of his being in the blessed peace of harmony. Hence the modern tendency to regard tragedy as the sole and exhaustive content of life is an absurd contradiction, testifying to man's spiritual blindness and despair in the face of the incomprehensible temporal process of creativeness with its continual failures. There are no grounds for thinking that the world's history is meaningless and is merely 'the devil's vaudeville', to use Dostoevsky's phrase, or for resting our only hope upon the final transfiguration of the world at the infinitely remote end of its history. Each human soul conscious of being rooted in God bears within it supertemporally, and therefore at every moment of its life, *its own* apocalypse, *its own* transfiguration and final completion in the absolute harmony of ultimate fulness and bliss. Tragedy and harmonious peace coexist in the human spirit, and the connection between the two is so intimate, that the experience of tragedy is *the path* to the perfection in which the spirit first clearly discerns its own nature as determined by its bond with God, and therein finds peace. This is a great and mysterious manifestation of the transcendental omnipotence of Divine holiness, in virtue of which the sorrows and calamities of human life become a gracious gift of God, showing to us that we too have a part in the bliss of harmonious fulness of being. In actual life, man's primary divine-like essence is indissolubly bound up with his sinful arbitrary will, his slavish bondage to earthly goods and demonic passions, and his true image is, as it were, unrecognizably concealed by those extraneous elements; by bringing to light the difference and opposition between the truly human, i.e. the spiritual principle in man, and the blindness of cosmic forces, tragedy and suffering reveal to him for the first time his true being, and point the way of return to his fatherland. There is no purification and salvation apart from suffering. As Meister Eckhart says 'the fastest steed that will bring you to perfection is suffering'. For the most part it is only through suffering that man first learns to see the great world of spiritual reality hidden in him and forming his inner being. 'Blessed are they that mourn for they shall be comforted.' The transfiguration, enlightenment and deification of the world as a whole and of each human soul is achieved through suffering. Suffering both bears witness to the world's imperfection and is the necessary accompaniment and instrument of the process of overcoming this imperfection: the victory of universal Meaning and Goodness over chaos is won through it alone. This entitles us to detect a mysterious positive meaning in the universal fact of death. Death in its concretely visible form is the most striking sign of the inherent imperfection of existence, and therefore of its tragic character; but at the same time death in its inner significance is an overwhelming mystery of transition from the sphere of disharmony, of the troubles and longings of earthly existence, to the sphere of eternal life. The path of the soul to God, to the blessedness of final harmony, inevitably leads through death; this is well-known to mystics who even in this life experience a state similar to death. Thus, following the words of the Easter hymn 'overcoming death by death', we may say that 'the last enemy, death' is overcome by death as the path to resurrection.

But since man is the image of God, this necessary and indivisible coexistence in him of conflict and harmony, of strenuous creative activity and inviolable blessed peace in the inmost depths of his spirit, must be understood as manifesting the compresence of those two principles in the nature of God Himself. God is not only the creator and saviour of the world; the Divine life is not only the creative activity of forming the world and hallowing it from within: God is also the completed fulness of all, the peace of perfect holiness and perfect bliss. From all eternity there is achieved and realized in Him all for which, in another aspect of His being, He is creatively striving. God the Creator, God who comes down into the world to take part, through suffering, in man's painful ascent to salvation, and God Who enters the world from within as the Holy Spirit— the spirit of holiness, drawing the world back to His own bosom— these three aspects of God expressed by the Trinitarian dogma are, as it were, only external manifestations or expressions of the inaccessible being of God, or of His 'essence'. That essence is the peace and beatitude of all-embracing completed fulness, the Alpha and Omega of universal being. Christian consciousness has rightly condemned 'sabellianism', i.e. the doctrine that God in the fulness of His being came down to earth and suffered on the cross; the same condemnation should be extended to the pernicious error contained in the now prevalent religious and philosophic doctrine that God in all His fulness and perfection is not from all eternity, but merely 'becomes', is born and develops in the painful course of cosmic evolution, and that therefore time or temporal process is an adequate expression of the absolute primary essence of being. In this connection, as in others, *docta ignorantia* must, on the contrary, affirm that God is the unity of 'this and the other', the indivisible unity of completeness, all-embracing fulness, and creative process and striving. God's absolute unity is both out of time, and includes time within itself, embracing and interpentrating it. It is the unity of super-temporality and temporality, of completed fulness and creative striving; creativeness, and therefore the whole process of cosmic life, is only one of the aspects of God's being ànd essence. In another aspect, He is eternal rest of the already realized—or, more correctly, of the eternally present—fulness and harmony.

Only the elect, at moments of the highest mystical contemplation and union with God, are vouchsafed full and real apprehension of this ultimate secret depth of God's being. But it is granted to every human soul to feel vaguely, though with unmistakable self-evidence, this inmost essence of Divine fulness, sanctity and harmony, and to know that the final and deepest ground of all being is the peace of perfect holiness—that the temple of cosmic being has this 'holy of holies' which is from the first and forever present in the human heart. Amidst all our strivings and sorrows, trials and solitude in the world, we not only must, but actually can, feel our primary indissoluble bond with the Kingdom of bliss and holiness. Whatever course our life may take, we are 'in God's hands' and are not only guided through the network of dark and blind forces, pushing us hither and thither, by the all-merciful and almighty Providence, which converts every evil into a means to the good, but we actually are in the bosom of God, and only through spiritual carelessness and shortsightedness fail to see it.

> Und alles Drängen, alles Ringen
> Ist ewige Ruh' im Gott dem Herrn.[1]

[1] Goethe: 'And all our days of strife, all earthly toil
Are yet a part of God's eternal peace.'

Selective Index

*

Note: *where alphabetical sub-classification is of no real value, order of mention in the developing argument has been preferred.*

INDEX

Being—*cont.*
space, 8, 8 n.; objective world seen as true being, 7; reality as basis of our, 23–8, *and see* Reality; an error of naturalism concerning, 137–9; and sense-data, 5; 'subjective' (a prevalent ambiguity), 21–2, 77; Plato on temporal and imperfect, 77; Tomist, Pelagian views on man's 'independent', 138, 138 n.; true self-subsistent, 16

Berdyaev, Nicolas, vii, viii

Bergson, Henri: philosophy of 'becoming' of, 76, 77; on the élan vital (universal dynamism), 209; doctrine of creative evolution' of, 157; on free choice, 166; *Creative Evolution*, 196 n.; *Les deux sources de la morale et de la religion*, 91 n.; on temporality inherent in cosmic being, 216

Bi-unity, *see* Man; antinomies involved in God-man relation, 133–41; expressed in creativeness, 153–61

Boehme, Jakob, on 'groundlessness', 175 n., 176

Borgia, Cesare, 130

Bossuet, J. B., in dispute with Fénelon, 100 n.

Bradley, F. H., *Appearance and Reality* 75 n., 83

Brémond, Henri de, *Histoire littéraire du sentiment religieux en France*, 124 n., 142 n., 143 n.

Bruno, Giordano: as disciple of Nicolas of Cusa, 125; concept of the universe, 193

Buber, Martin: on fundamental difference between monotheism and paganism, 96; *Between man and man*, 203 n.

Bulgakov, Sergius, vii

Calvin, Calvinism, stern Old Testament views of, 120, 121, 170; and human freedom, 136; in work of R. Niebuhr, 135 n.

Capital punishment, 185 n.

Cartesian, and English, empiricism, 87 n.

Catullus, quoted, 139

Claudel, Paul, on duality within human soul, 143

Communion, 59–69, 96–7, 113–14

Communism, compulsory socialization under, 67 n., *see* Marx

Compulsion, ineffectiveness of, against evil, 184–9

Comte, Auguste, 'religion of humanity' of, 128

Concrete: description, knowledge of reality as, 36–44; unity of multiplicity, reality as, 44–54

Conscience, the Old Testament concept of, 117

Conscious creativeness, definition of, 157

Consciousness: and reality, 14, 15, 22; religious, as compared with abstract conception of the 'ought', 115; nature of, 30, 31; nature of religious, 115–18, 122; analysis of Christian, 119 seqq.; and manhood, 115; *see also* Self-consciousness

Cournot, M., as opponent of Cartesianism, 87 n.; as a founder of theory of probability, 195

Createdness, broad definition of, 149; primary and derivative, 217

Creativeness: element inherent in human life, 159; 171; essence of, 154; man's, defined, 153–5; and inspiration, 155; man's and cosmic, Kinship and differences, 157, 216–219; Creator of creators, 157, 216–217; in degeneration, 160; 'creation out of nothing', 212–13; *see* Conscious creativeness

Creator, God as sole, 153, 157, 211 seqq.

Croce, B., *Estetica come scienza del espressione et linguistico generale*, 55 n.

Dante Alighieri, 7

Darwin, Charles, 126, 194

INDEX

Death, the overcoming of, 225
De Faye, E., *Gnostiques et Gnosticisme*, 198 n.
Democrites, as forerunner of modern mechanistic views, 191
Descartes (and Cartesianism), 13, 14, 15, 30, 86, 87 n., 193; as discoverer of reality transcending world of objects ('Cogito ergo sum'), 12, 18, 25, 28; on soul's non-confinement by spatial determinations, 23; defines 'first matter', 50; on dualism of mind and body, 85 (*and see above*); anthropological proof of God's existence by, 105
Determinateness, 44–5; nature of, 45 n.
Dilthey, Wilhelm, distinguishes between two types of knowing (knowing subject, known object), 17
Dionysius the Areopagite, 38, 142
Docetism, 141
Docta ignorantia, *see* Wise ignorance
Dogmatic metaphysics (Kant), 6, 14, 46–7; *see* Kant
Dostoevsky, Fyodor, 127 n., 160 n.; on meaningless of the world's history, 224; *The Possessed*, 130 n.
Divinity: as a characteristic of man, *see* God-manhood; and man as creator, 153 seqq.
Dreams as events, 21; and detachment from universal reality, 23
Dualism between God and man, *see* Pelagianism, Saint Augustine: *see also* Bi-unity, Old Testament; *duality* of human spirit, 141 seqq., 180, 211; basis of, 152; and creativeness, 153 seqq.; nature of, between God and man, 151–2; and the final victory, 222–4; the Christian view of duality between world and man, 211 seqq.

Eckermann, J. P., 222 n.
Einfühlung, theory of, 57–8, 60
Einstein, Albert, 195

Empiricism, English, compared with Cartesianism, 87 n.
Entelechy, *see* Aristotle
Entropy, modern theory of, 194
Epicurus, as forerunner of modern mechanistic views, 191
Erasmus of Rotterdam, 124
'Essence' and 'energy' of God (Gregory Palamas), 210 n.
Evil, protection from, 180–5; the overcoming of, 185–90
Existence: of world, as continuous creation, 216; of God, the proof of, 104; essential duality of human (a summary), 34; *Existenz* (Heidegger), 33; finite nature of, 24; (Kierkegaard), and mental life, compared, 17, 19; Thomas Aquinas's doctrine of meaning of, 93 n.
Existentialism, 49 n.–50 n.; and spiritual blindness, 49 n.–50 n.; as modern pessimism, 132, 133
Experience: God as reality of inner, 92–7; 'subjective' element of, 3–4 n.; of the heart, *see* Pascal; as wider than thought, 2 seqq., 41; as act or as knowledge, 15–17; mental (subjective), 21–2; unique nature of moral, 70; *see also* Mental life, Religious experience
Expression, as mysterious word, 153–4

Fact, and ideal being, 1–12; reality as basis of world of, 28–35
Faith: as supra-rational domain, 86; reason as, 83–92
'Fall' of man: and man's nothingness, 121; doctrine of, as no solution of sin, 169; meaning of doctrine, 178–180
Fénelon-Bossuet dispute (on the love of God), 100 n.
Fichte, J. G., 14
Frank, S. L., *La connssaiance et l'être*, xiii 32 n., 37 n., 45 n.; *The Human Soul*, xiii; *A Solovyov Anthology*, x *The Unfathomable*, 37 n., 55 n.
Freedom: and sin, 162–9; nature of

231

INDEX

INDEX

INDEX

INDEX

Saint Francis de Sales, *Traité de l'amour de Dieu*, 143; Christian humanism in teaching of, 124; on the 'superhuman' in man, 150

Saint Irinaeus, 212 n.

Saint Maximus the Confessor, x, 150 n.

Saint Paul; on the self, 66; on soul's duality, 142; as mystic, 140; on man's will to sin, 168; on inadequacy of law, 185, seeing harmonious unity of all that is, 211

Saint Teresa of Avila, distinguishes between soul and spirit, 142, 143

Saint Thomas Aquinas, and Tomism, 6; and doctrine of degrees of reality, 75; as perennial philosopher, 76; finds proofs of existence of God, 92, 93 n.; on essence of created reality, 120-2; on fulness of relation between God and man, 147; on God as sole creator, 153; on primary source of reality, 172; influences on thought of, 192; on God's absolute freedom, 167; on world's eternity, 194; on spiritual world, 201, 202; on creation out of nothing, 213

Scheler, Max, *Wesen und Formen der Sympathie*, 60

Schelling, F., as critic of Kant, 102; uses *Ungrund* idea in his doctrine of human freedom, 175

Schiller, Friedrich, quoted, 202

Science and philosophy, 193 n.

Self: the self-given reality, 18, 19, 22, 101-2; and universal being, 26-7; alleged immanence of, 28-30, 103 seqq.; as 'singular number,' 61; inmost and other, 142-3; and soul, 143 seqq.; rooted in reality, 104; and the apprehension of God, 113-16; an erroneous concept of, 177; expressed through art, 154-5

Self-assertion, pride of, as original sin, 178-9

Self-consciousness: and God-man bi-unity, 148, 199 seqq.; and transcendence of the world of fact, 112, 143 seqq.

Self-limitation, *see* Freedom

Simmel, Georg, *Ethik*, 170 n.

Sin: and freedom, problem of, 162-9; abstention from, as moral indifference, 163; and freedom of will, 165 seqq.; expressed in human relations, 185; illusory nature of, asserted, 164, 169, 183; as metaphysical evil, 197 seqq.; as moral evil, 162-89, 202, 205; original, *see that entry*; primary source of, 176; as in, but not rooted in, reality, 165; inner nature of, 184-5; two types of, 162, 163, 176, 185; *see* Socrates

Sinlessness: as modern error, 122

Socrates: on sin as 'involuntary', 168; recognizing supreme cosmic reason, 191

Solipsism, 59

Solovyov, Vladimir, x, xi, xiii; on 'optimistic' non-religious humanism, 126; on divine-humanity of man, 141; on meaning of *bereshith* in Genesis, 210

'Sorrowful unbelief', 131-3

Soul, the, 23-9, 151; duality in, 142 seqq.; transcendence constituting, 28-30; and the beautiful, 57; and the spirit, 143; uncircumscribed from within, 67; consciousness of, 97-8; birth of idea of its salvation from world, 199-200; and sin, 164

Spinoza, Baruch, 48, 50, 51; on man's freedom, 136; distinguishes between *natura naturans* and *natura naturata*, 84 n.

Spirit: as boundary between the two aspects of man's nature, 152; distinct from mental reality of self, 17-22; 148-9; and natural being, analogy of structure, 208; the spiritual life, in its collective aspect, as reality, 17-22, 36, 63, 82; as emanation, not creation, 149-51, 219-20; spiritual blindness of existentialism, 49 n.- 50 n.; 'spiritual Christians', 184; spiritual world as hierarchy, 158

237